# DIVIDEND POLICY
# THEORY AND PRACTICE

# DIVIDEND POLICY THEORY AND PRACTICE

**George M. Frankfurter**
Emeritus, Louisiana State University
Network Professor, Graduate School of Management,
Sabanci University

and

**Bob G. Wood, Jr.**
Tennessee Technological University

Chapter 13 Contributed by
**James Wansley**
University of Tennessee

## ACADEMIC
## PRESS

An imprint of Elsevier Science
Amsterdam  Boston  London  New York  Oxford  Paris
San Diego  San Francisco  Singapore  Sydney  Tokyo

This book is printed on acid-free paper.

ACADEMIC PRESS
*An imprint of Elsevier Science*
525 B Street, Suite 1900, San Diego, CA 92101-4495, USA
http://www.academicpress.com

Academic Press
84 Theobald's Road, London WC1X 8RR, UK
http://www.academicpress.com

Library of Congress number 2003100452

International Standard Book Number: 0-12-266051-X

PRINTED IN THE UNITED STATES OF AMERICA
03  04  05  06  07  08    9  8  7  6  5  4  3  2  1

# CONTENTS

**CHAPTER 4**
## 200 Years of Dividend Practices

**CHAPTER 5**
## Dividend Reinvestment Plans: A Puzzle within the Puzzle

**CHAPTER 6**
## Preferred Stock and Dividends: A Revealing Divergence

# PART II
# THE EVOLUTION OF ACADEMIC RESEARCH ON DIVIDEND POLICY

**CHAPTER 7**
## Early Academic Thinking and Research          71

# PART III
# WHAT ACADEMIC RESEARCH PROVES AND WHAT IT DOES NOT PROVE

## CHAPTER 11
## The "Balance Sheet" of Academic Research: What It Does/Does Not Prove

# PART IV
# NEW WAYS OF THINKING ABOUT DIVIDENDS AND DIVIDEND POLICY

## CHAPTER 12
## Unconventional Explanations

## CHAPTER 13
## Dividend Policy of Regulated Industries

## CHAPTER 14
# What if We Do Not Pay Dividends? 187

## CHAPTER 15
# Other Methods of Distribution

## CHAPTER 16
# Conclusions: Future Research and Thinking 229

# PREFACE

This book has three purposes. The first is to provide an historical perspective of dividends from the emergence of the modern corporation in Great Britain, The Netherlands, and America to its growth in the 19th and 20th centuries. This material and a digression on preferred stocks and preferred stock dividends are presented in Part I. Part I includes these chapters:

- Chapter 1 offers introductory remarks and background on the subject of dividend policy.
- Chapter 2 discusses the evolution of the modern corporation in The Netherlands and United Kingdom.
- Chapter 3 traces the development of the modern corporation in the United States.
- Chapter 4 examines three distinct phases of dividend patterns over a 200-year period in America.
- Chapter 5 is about dividend reinvestment/purchase plans, a puzzle, wrapped in a mystery, inside an enigma (to paraphrase Winston Churchill).
- Chapter 6 presents a revealing digression on preferred dividends and their relation to stock dividends.

The second purpose of the book is to trace the evolution of academic models on dividend policy. This subject is presented in Parts II and III. Part II is about the evolution of academic research on dividend policy containing the following chapters:

- Chapter 7 discusses the early academic models on dividend policy.
- Chapter 8 presents other models of symmetric information.
- Chapter 9 focuses on models of asymmetric information.
- Chapter 10 covers academic models that explore the determinants of the dividend issue.

Part III discusses what academic research proves and what it can not prove:

- Chapter 11 is a quasi "academic" income statement and balance sheet of sorts. This chapter is devoted to a careful, meta-scientific analysis of what academic thinking has accomplished on the intriguing subject of dividends and dividend policy.

The third purpose of this book is to explore new ways of thinking about the dividend puzzle and other special subjects we could not put in the frame of the two previous sections, even though these subjects are as important, and perhaps more enlightening, than any other we have covered up to this point. Thus, Part III includes these chapters:

- Chapter 12 deals with unconventional, not wealth–maximizing explanations of the dividend phenomenon.
- Chapter 13 describes the dividend issue as it relates to regulated industries.
- Chapter 14 is about firms that do not pay a dividend, yet there are no start-up firms anymore. The puzzling question there is what are the factors that determine these firms' value?
- Chapter 15 discusses and surveys other methods of wealth distribution.
- Chapter 16 presents concluding remarks and suggests logical avenues for additional research on this topic.

This book is the condensed result of many years of thinking and empirical work by its authors on what we enthusiastically consider one of the most intriguing topics of financial economics. Because of that, it would be both ungrateful and somehow dishonest if we claimed exclusive originality to our writings. The book would never have been written without the help of many of our colleagues and, perhaps more important, our students who were unselfish enough to discuss with us the issues we raise and assist with the original, first published research we also present in this book.

There are many who deserve credit, but we must mention by name Myron Gordon, Bill Lane, Chris Lamoureaux, Elton "Skip" McGoun, Arman Kosedag, Mihail Topalov, Jasik Gong, and Vern Thibadeaux. May others, whom we do not mention by name, forgive us for our insensitivity. However, and because we alone are responsible for both our fairly strong opinions and possible errors, they might be just happy they are not considered guilty by association. But let the readers decide!

George M. Frankfurter
Bob G. Wood, Jr.

# PART I

# The Historical Evolution of Dividends

# CHAPTER 1

# Introduction

*The harder we look at the dividend picture, the more it seems like a puzzle with pieces that just don't fit together.*

Black, 1976

Dividends are commonly defined as the distribution of earnings (past or present) in real assets among the shareholders of the firm in proportion to their ownership. There are three parts of this definition, all equally important.

The first is that dividends can be distributed only from earnings and not from any another source of equity, say, paid-in surplus.

The second is that dividends must be in the form of a real asset. It is common practice to pay dividends in cash (sent as a piece of paper) because of the convenience of the matter. It is hard to imagine that Boeing, for example, would send the right wing of a 747 as a dividend to one of its major stockholders. Regardless, evidence shows (from abroad) that some firms during high levels of inflation have paid dividends in the form of the product they were producing.

The third part of the definition states that all stockholders share in dividends relative to their holdings in the corporation. This part of the definition, although egalitarian, accounts for what (under certain circumstances) are the least desirable characteristics of dividends.

Dividends are paid from the firm's after-tax income. For the recipient, dividends are considered regular income and are therefore fully taxable.[1] This tax treatment results *de facto* in the double taxation of dividends in America (but not in several other countries, e.g., Canada and Germany), the only source of income that is subject to such treatment.

Given all these considerations, the economic consequence of dividends is an involuntary tax liability to the owners of the firm imposed on a marginal liquidation of their ownership. The incongruity is that dividend announcements and payment are considered good news, held and hailed as such by investors and

---

[1] In this instance, we are not going into small details of dividend exclusions of up to a certain amount during some periods for a certain segment of the personal tax base.

most analysts, whereas dividend cuts and reductions are considered bad news, suggesting impending financial doom.

This incongruity is now commonly referred to as "the dividend puzzle," from Black (1976), who gave this name to the positive relation between dividend announcements and/or payments and the value of shares. Black was referring to five decades of academic research on the subject of dividends and to dividend policy that for 50 years never failed to empirically show the positive effects of dividends and dividend announcements on the price of stocks.

Black (1990) later amended his views on dividends and on whether dividends are indeed a puzzle. In an editorial viewpoint column in the *Financial Analysts Journal* titled, "Why Firms Pay Dividends," Black offers a "sort-of" solution to the riddle.

This editorial piece, which is just four paragraphs, offers, in closing, a short prediction. The prediction, sadly, is just as false as most financial analysts' forecasts, as we will see later, with the burst of the stock market bubble in the new millennium. The reader should note, however, that, in 1990, Black was writing as a senior partner of Goldman Sachs Asset Management, rather than as the academic he was in 1976. In his new role, he was expected to be "realistic" rather than arcane, to focus on the practicalities rather than some obscure mathematical construct. On the surface, the change in roles may seem a minor point; this point, however, may explain what the puzzle is in the dividend puzzle. In essence, the puzzle is academe's obsession with the explanation of the dividend phenomenon as another means of share value maximization.

Let us go through all four paragraphs of Black's editorial,[2] because each is important to the point we are trying to make in this monograph. We take the liberty of discussing them in the order that is more conducive for the purpose of making our case. In the first paragraph of his editorial, Black asserts that firms pay dividends because "investors simply like dividends" and then explains why this is so. Whether one agrees with Black's reasoning is purely a subjective conclusion. The fact is, however, that *all* his reasons are not economically rational. This does not mean, of course, that investors are irrational, or that there are no perceptions other than those Black cares to mention.

Black's disclosure makes it clear that the rationality of the economic person does not apply. Yet, for 40 years, this rationality has been the overwhelming framework within which academia tried to solve the dividend puzzle. This

---

[2]The editorial is actually five paragraphs, but the last one is just one sentence and it is a prediction. It says that dividends that are ". . . taxable will gradually vanish." So far they have not and we do not think they will. In fact, we do not think that taxes, a favorite ratiocination in academia of dividend payment patterns, have anything to do with firms' dividend policies. This little empirical fact, indeed, was a real killer of the tax rationality explanation of dividends.

approach is like fishing for sharks in freshwater lakes.[3] The proponents of this methodology (underlying logic and methods of analysis) argue, and rightly so, that just because the puzzle has not yet been solved using this logic does not mean that it will not be solved someday, using this logic. Most Bayesian shark hunters, however, would assign a prior probability of zero to finding a single shark in fresh waters, although in fact there are sharks in fresh waters. Putting it a bit differently, the great lakes and rivers of America are not crowded with vessels full of shark hunters.

As academics ourselves, we take the most delight in Black's fourth paragraph. It says, in words we cannot interpret any other way, that the dividend-signaling hypothesis, with all its variants of equilibria, simply does not hold. In two sentences, Black argues, in essence, that the 15-year bonanza of academic publishing on dividend signaling is no more than hokum. For some, the hokum was a career-making effort; and, for others, just one of many attempts to jump on the dividend bandwagon. This is so, Black argues, because "[p]ublic statements can better detail the firm's prospects and have more impact. . . ." Though "public statements" here is a reference to accounting statements and annual reports, the term reasonably can include any means of communication in the public domain.

This declaration from one of the leading financial economists of all time should have distressed enough of his peers to discourage any of them from offering new variants of dividend and other signaling scenarios. In fact, just the opposite happened. And to top that, a corporation finance textbook aimed at the MBA market—first published in the early 1990s—elevated signaling to one of the *principles* of finance.

From an academic standpoint, what Black *does not* say in his editorial is more significant than what he does say. He does not, for example, mention the free-cash-flow hypothesis of Jensen (1986). His "omission" is in contrast to Bernstein's (1996) lavish quotation of Jensen's conjecture for seemingly no purpose other than etiquette.

Black, who must have been thoroughly familiar with Jensen's hypothesis, knows full well that firms do not pay out all their free cash as dividends, nor should they. Siphoning cash from the firm implies that shareholders totally distrust their hired agents, who otherwise would squander "free" cash on projects with negative net present values. In this scenario (Reiter, 1994), shareholders are the "damsel in distress," imperiled by a dastardly villain (the manager or CEO), and saved, ultimately, by the knight in shining armor (the market). This fairy-tale explanation of the dividend puzzle would not, of course, jibe with the expecta-

---

[3]We use the shark metaphor because the many arpies (affluent, recreating professionals) probably fancy the sport of diving, and they know well that sharks cannot survive in fresh waters. Still, as a shark maven advises us, bull sharks were found (albeit not too happy) in some rivers, including the Ohio. Because nothing is impossible, we stick with the metaphor. As semi-Bayesians, we still assign a zero prior to meeting one in our favorite body of fresh water.

tion of most of the clients of Goldman Sachs, and would certainly place the firm among an insignificant minority of firms managed by a ruthlessly greedy CEO. We wonder how many flesh-and-blood Gordon Gekkos are out there or Enron's Kenneth "Kenny boy" Lay.

The third paragraph of Black's editorial is about what would happen if investors were "neutral toward dividends." The result, Black asserts, would be that not only would investors not demand dividends, but also, "A firm would apologize to its taxable investors when forced by an accumulated earnings tax to pay dividends." Makes sense, does it not? The fact is, however, that individuals are *not* neutral toward dividends, and firms not only fail to apologize for paying dividends, but to the contrary, also bluster about increasing dividends or paying an extra dividend, or so it seems.

Black's second paragraph explains how all this came about. We are in this quandary, he says, because professionals (e.g., investment advisers, financial analysts, and economists) are concerned about dividends. They treat high-yield stocks, he states, as "both attractive and safe" value stocks by "predicting and discounting dividends," and "study[ing] the relation between stock prices and actual dividends." This practice, he asserts, leads investors to believe that dividends are important and to "complain about dividend cuts."

Now, the last thing that CEOs and CFOs want is investors complaining. Hence, they pay dividends, which in turn makes them look good, which in turn makes them pay even more dividends, and *moto perpetuo*. This is exactly the behavioral model Frankfurter and Lane (1992) suggested. Although this model explains the puzzle, it is neither mathematical nor based on the logic of the economic person. It professes that the dividend issue belongs in the domain of Herbert Simon's bounded rationality, or perhaps an even more complex multifaceted rationality. That is, individuals may make decisions on a purely economic subject applying a rationale that is not in the least economic.

In the past, we had a term for such a phenomenon: irrational behavior. We vehemently denied the possibility that mass irrationality could exist, even for a very short period, and could thus be observed. That denial gave us impetus to search in the dustbin of "rational" models[4] for yet another "solution" that, as it turns out, could not be verified as consistent with the facts of observed behavior. In the words of T. H. Huxley: "The great tragedy of science—the slaying of a beautiful hypothesis by an ugly fact."

From social psychology, we know that individuals are very poor processors of information, especially information that contradicts what family, schools, youth groups, churches, political parties, employers, etc., taught them either to hold dear, or to reject. This very human predilection may come as a shock to many finan-

---

[4]Here we are referring to models that are consistent with the notion of the economic person and with neoclassical economics.

cial economists, but it is, nonetheless, well documented in scores of sociopsychological studies. When so-called professionals reinforce behavior that is not economically rational, instead of educating the public to correct their perceptions, it is not difficult to guess what will happen.

There is yet another dimension to academe's failure to solve the puzzle. Academic thinking about dividends—and whatever this thinking produced—has completely ignored the evolution of dividend payment in the modern corporation. Dividend payment behavior, which we also call "dividend policy," did not simply appear out of nowhere. It evolved with the modern corporation over a period of four centuries. The details of this evolution are chronicled in a number of publications, among them an article by Frankfurter and Wood (1997). Putting corporate dividend policy in a historical perspective makes one wonder how and why scholarly models of dividend policy could disregard such evolution.

In the 20th century, emphasis on the importance of dividends emanated from the publication of a major investment text, which, in a short time, turned out to be the bible of financial analysts. The text, written by Graham and Dodd (1934), was later updated (Graham et al., 1962). In this text, the authors proclaim dividends to be the only purpose of the firm's existence. They also contend that if two firms are operating in the same environment and are identical in every respect, the one that pays regular dividends would sell for a higher P/E multiple than the one that does not meaning that the former is less risky than the latter.

Serious academic thinking and concomitant research into the dividend decision and practice began in the early 1950s. Consistent with the Graham–Dodd thesis, early models (often referred to as *bird-in-the-hand* models[5]) intended to show that dividends are valued for the discounted cash stream they provide to the shareholder. These models advocated a dividend policy that amounted to a 100, 0, and anything-in-between payout ratio of earnings; that is, not much of a policy at all, even if one accepted the value-creating logic of *the bird-in-the-hand* models.[6]

A contradictory view of dividend policy theory was set forth in the seminal paper by Miller and Modigliani (1961), comprising the second part of their irrelevance theory. [The first part was the irrelevance of capital structure, set forth in their earlier work on cost of capital, capital structure, and value (Modigliani and Miller, 1958).] Miller and Modigliani (1961) showed that, in a no-tax world, the investor should be indifferent between dividends and retained earnings. With corporate and personal income tax liabilities, of course, the payout of dividends would be wealth dissipative and, for this reason, an economically rational investor

---

[5]The allegory is that cash today is preferred to cash in the future, as one bird in the hand is preferred to two in the bush. Of course, it would depend on what the two birds are doing in the bush and on whether we are one of the birds.

[6]Something many (ourselves included) criticize in the following chapters of this book.

would not be any more indifferent, but would prefer the retention of earning over dividend payouts.

During the last several decades, the best academic minds have grappled with the dividend puzzle. Financial economists posited—and still do—a variety of theories that tried, almost exclusively, to justify the payment of dividends using the principles of wealth maximization and the logic of the *homo economicus* (the economic man—should be economic person to be politically correct). All these models suffer from either logical inconsistencies or lack of correspondence with observable facts—the ultimate demise of models within the methodology of orthodox finance in which predictive ability is both a means and an end. A substantial portion of this book is devoted to the discussion of these models, their accomplishments, and their ultimate failure to explain the dividend puzzle and to lay down the foundation of an optimal dividend policy.

But how do practitioners view dividends? One insight into their thinking (although we do not argue universal concurrence of the view) can be obtained from a passage in his 1995 "Letter from the Chairman," an annual missive from Disney, Co., CEO Michael Eisner, to the firm's shareholders. Mr. Eisner had this to say:

> Eleven years ago I took, and since then I have taken and retaken again, a crash course in financial management from Gary Wilson and Sid Bass . . . I learned and reviewed every year the following: A company's management (meaning me and our senior executives) must use excess cash flow in at least one of four different ways. We can invest that cash in extensions of our current business. We can repurchase our own shares from time to time when market conditions seem appropriate. Disney has done that effectively over the years. We can distribute excess cash by paying out a large one-time-only dividend to our shareholders in addition to our regularly scheduled dividends that has grown 20% per year. This we have not done because our shareholders have expressed the desire that we use the company and its assets to gain higher return on cash than individuals can ordinarily achieve. Or we can make an acquisition.

Hmm. The crash course Mr. Eisner took in financial management was obviously not directed to a basic understanding of the difference between shoveling out cash at a clip of 20% growth per year and meeting the shareholders' desire to reinvest in the company because of the *spectacular* returns of Disney. And, if Mr. Eisner and his tutors had difficulty understanding the relation between dividends and share repurchases, and the difference between investing in profitable opportunities and partial liquidation of the firm, then what can one expect from ordinary shareholders?

In our discussions with CFOs and CEOs regarding alternatives to cash dividends, they expressed an unshakable belief in the necessity of dividends, if for no other reason than to pacify shareholders (i.e., "hush money" to shareholders in the parlance of Harvard's MBA handbook, following the teachings of Adam Smith). One CEO of a fairly large financial services corporation told us that his mother-in-law loves dividends; therefore, he cannot eliminate, or even reduce, quarterly dividends. This is, of course, one maxim, although not entirely economically rational, which is irrefutable by all means and standards, and we know not a single person who would take issue with that.

The confusion about, and misunderstanding of, the "dividend puzzle" is highlighted in an article in the November 20, 1999, issue of *The Economist*, one of the most respected nonacademic political economics journals. The article is titled "Shares without the Other Bit." *The Economist*, which laments the disappearance of dividends in corporate America, calls *this* phenomenon, paradoxically, the "dividend puzzle," for which it is hard-pressed to find a rational explanation. Although the author covers most of the ruling academic theories in laymen's terms, the journal appears flummoxed at the evanescence of dividends.

The article points out that—in contrast to the 1970s and 1980s, when shoveling out dividends was the rule not the exception—investment bankers today "tell their clients that paying dividends is like an admission that you have nothing better to do" (*The Economist*, 1999, p. 93). This wisdom has been gleaned from none other than Kenneth French of MIT, of Fama and French fame. At the end, *The Economist* conjectures that the disappearance of dividends might be "fashion." Later in the book we will revisit this and some other conjectures (relating to the dividend phenomenon) of the financial mavens.

This simple, short quotation is a remarkable epitome of the dividend misunderstanding. In fact, there is nothing new in it. For four decades, we have been teaching our students that increasing dividends is a sign that the firm can do nothing better with the money. Unfortunately, this "lesson" does not explain why shareholders like dividends, as Black points out, and why they reward managers who pay regularly increasing dividends [see Eisner, earlier, who usually earns more in an hour (albeit not just for Walt Disney's dividend policy) than the president of the United States is paid for the entire year of his services].

It appears that managers may indeed be wealth maximizers, not necessarily for their shareholders, but for themselves. In the past, they strove to quench the thirst of their shareholders for dividends. Now, however, capital appreciation of the share price—and their own compensation—is more important than a token increase in share price and the concomitant financing issue that arises when cash is shoveled out the front door instead of being reinvested. There is no doubt that the dividend issue, as both a policy and an act, is one of the most intriguing topics of financial economics.

# REFERENCES

Bernstein, Peter L. 1996. "Dividends: the puzzle." *Journal of Applied Corporate Finance* 9:16–22.

Black, Fisher. 1976. "The dividend puzzle." *The Journal of Portfolio Management* 2:5–8.

Black, Fisher. 1990. "Why firms pay dividends." *The Financial Analysts Journal* 46:5.

*The Economist.* 1999. "Shares without the other bit." November 20:93.

Frankfurter, George M., and William R. Lane. 1992. "The rationality of dividends." *The International Review of Financial Analysis* 1:115–130.

Frankfurter, George M., and Bob Wood, Jr. 1997. "The evolution of corporate dividend policy." *Journal of Financial Education* 23:16–33.

Graham, Benjamin, and David L. Dodd. 1934. *Security Analysis.* New York: Whittlesey House.

Graham, Benjamin, David L. Dodd, and Sidney Cottle. 1962. *Security Analysis 4th ed.* New York: McGraw Hill.

Jensen, Michael C. 1986. "Agency costs of free cash flows, corporate finance and takeovers." *American Economic Review* 76:323–329.

Miller, Merton H., and Franco Modigliani. 1961. "Dividend policy, growth, and the valuation of shares." *The Journal of Business* 34:411–433.

Modigliani, Franco, and Merton H. Miller. 1958. "The cost of capital, corporate finance, and the theory of investment." *The American Economic Review* 48:261–297.

Reiter, Sara A. 1994. "Storytellers, stories, and 'free cash flow.'" *The International Review of Financial Analysis* 3:209–224.

# CHAPTER 2

# The Evolution of the Modern Corporation in The Netherlands and the United Kingdom

Dividend payments to shareholders began over 300 years ago and have continued as an acceptable or even required corporate practice despite their apparent contradictory economic nature. The original payments to joint stock company shareholders in Holland and Great Britain were liquidating distributions of capital and profit that terminated the joint stock enterprise's existence. Later, payments were limited to the net profits of the venture, a procedure that permitted a more efficient use of investment capital, the better exploitation of the nexus of contracts, and a more productive use of managerial know-how and gave the firm perpetual existence.

More recently, the payments have become symbolic liquidations solely determined by managers. Although largely symbolic, a consistent and significant dividend payment to maintain shareholder contentment remains a managerial priority.

The purpose of this chapter is to trace the historical evolution of corporate dividend policy from its origins in The Netherlands and the United Kingdom.

## 2.1 EARLY JOINT STOCK COMPANIES: ORIGINS TO 1720

The embryonic origin of the corporation—groups united for a common purpose—can be traced to Greek and Roman times (Williston, 1888a). Precursors of the modern corporation occurred in 14th-century Italy, where

11

merchants formed loose federations for limited purposes (Scott, 1912). According to Kindleberger (1984), cooperatives of merchants and traders appeared in Denmark at approximately the same time. These coalitions became more specialized during the next two centuries (Scott, 1912).

In the first half of the 16th century, successful sailing captains began selling to investors "ventures on parts" in their voyages. As Masselman (1963) writes, parts were bought and sold in the open market; by the end of the 16th century, fixed denomination shares replaced these parts. The most common denomination of shares was 1/32 of the ship's property; but interests of 1/8, 1/16, 1/48, and 1/56 were also common. Investors regularly purchased shares from more than one captain to diversify their risk (perhaps the precursor of modern portfolio theory) of loss from the misfortunes that beset all sailing ventures of the period (Barbour, 1929).

Joint stock companies evolved from these merchant associations as a result of the high capital requirements of foreign trade (Kindleberger, 1984). Investors (the forerunners of modern shareholders) provided capital for these corporations, and sailing captains (managers) applied their special skills to the profitable use of the assets and paid dividends to the shareholders (Warren, 1923). The first joint stock company organized in Great Britain was the Eastland Trading Company, originally chartered in the 15th century and granted monopoly trading rights to the Baltic countries. This enterprise was followed in the 16th century by the Muscovy Company and the Levant Company, chartered for trade with Russia and with Turkey, respectively (Scott, 1912). The charters granted to joint stock companies were not perpetual; they were awarded for definite and limited periods to allow the government to alter the provisions of the charter and collect additional fees and taxes (Kindleberger, 1984). Without exception, these trading companies produced significant profits for their owners (Scott, 1912).

The Dutch East India Company was formed in Holland in 1602 and was granted a monopoly for trading with India (Van Loon, 1913). This enterprise was the first permanently organized joint stock company (Kindleberger, 1984). Shares of the venture began trading in Amsterdam almost immediately after the original stock subscription was completed.

More than half of the original venture capital of the Dutch East India Company was raised from the merchants of Amsterdam. In the early years of the company, the organization paid 75% dividends[1]; the high dividend level was largely the result of reckless abuse of the new trading territories. During its first 15 years, the company's dividends averaged 25% (Scott, 1912).

The market for exchange of shares was held out of doors in Holland until a building was erected for this purpose in Amsterdam in 1613.[2] Demand

---

[1]References to percent dividends throughout this chapter are always to earnings, as in dividends are 75% of earnings.

[2]The first stock market in modern history.

for the shares was stimulated by the expectation of high profits from the company's endeavors and the desire to participate in those profits by individuals excluded from the original share subscription. The demand for shares by individuals and nonmember merchants quickly increased the price of the shares by 15% (Ehrenberg, 1963).

Circulation of news of the venture by correspondents around the globe and rumors of its successes and failures increased speculation in the shares. Professional traders also used eavesdroppers and spies to glean private information. Rumors were often started depending solely on a trader's current position (Schama, 1987). Orders for the sale of a large number of shares entered by professional traders led to a flood of sale orders by frightened amateur investors and hence to a drop in share price. The professional investor/trader would profit by repurchasing the shares at a lower price (Allen and Gale, 1992). Trading was primarily in futures, and liberal settlement dates increased share volume and volatility (Ehrenberg, 1963).

The line between casual wagering and organized stock trading was often blurred. Speculators traded in hope of earning profits from short-term price fluctuations rather than from profits resulting from successful completion of the voyages.

In Holland, the Dutch East India Company monopolized that country's spice trade. In 1632, seven ships returned from India laden with spices. The cargo was sold at five times the venture's cost. In 1661, goods were sold at twice their cost. In 1672, the company's worst year during the 17th century, cargos worth in excess of 40 million guilders were brought to the republic. The average gain to the company per pound of spice was 1200% (Van Loon, 1913).

Merchant ships of the period were often accompanied on their expeditions by armed men-of-war. Although the practice originated during the Middle Ages, the foremost use of the convention was with the organized trade of the Dutch East India Company. Because of the lack of competition among the ships of the venture and the common ownership of the vessels, there was no fear of losing the monopoly rents common to single-ship endeavors of the period (Barbour, 1929).

The Dutch East India Company was not managed by a single individual; rather, the company was divided into four chambers, each representing a fixed number of shares that had been purchased by investors from a distinct geographical area. Inhabitants of other provinces could hold stock individually but had no influence on managerial policy. Each chamber sent ships in proportion to their ownership of the company; the ships and all potential profits from those ships remained the sole property of that chamber. The company had a general board of directors with 46 members, but immediate power was centered in a 17-member board of governors.

Minority stockholders holding fewer than five shares had no voice in the company's operations. These investors were allowed only to accept their dividends from the directors and express their profound gratitude for their excellent management. No shareholder meetings were held, and neither annual nor quarterly reports were issued. Also, there were no minutes kept of the meetings of the board of governors. To keep the shareholders mollified, managers, through adroit juggling, paid a high level of dividends throughout the 17th century. A share purchased at the time of original subscription produced dividends exceeding 35 times the initial purchase price during the company's first 80 years of business. During the 180 years of the company's existence, dividend payments averaged 21% annually.

The Dutch West India Company was founded in 1621, but unlike the Dutch East India Company, it was not granted a strict trading monopoly. Shareholders had a more direct influence in the company's operations. The 74-member board of directors was chosen from all owners possessing at least two shares of stock. A committee of 19 directors was given direct managerial control. The company's trade areas included the west coast of Africa, the east coast of America, and all islands between and south of the two coasts. The Dutch West India Company was unsuccessful from its inception because of competition and other exogenous factors (Van Loon, 1913).

The most important joint stock venture in Great Britain was the British East India Company, formed in 1599 as a spin-off of the Levant Company. The British East India Company was granted a charter and monopoly trading rights by an act of Parliament in 1600 (Baskin, 1988). The first agreement between a loosely organized group of merchants was for one voyage; proceeds from the sale of cargo and company assets were divided among the shareholders at the end of the voyage proportionate to their ownership (Kindleberger, 1984). The assets of the venture were liquidated at the conclusion of each voyage to prevent fraudulent practices and to ensure the proper division of proceeds to shareholders (Baskin, 1988).

The limited number of original shares was sold primarily among acquaintances. Shareholders had unlimited liability and were subject to calls for additional funds if needed. Management and ownership were completely independent, with managers chosen according to their ability and knowledge of the venture rather than their proportion of ownership in the company (Baskin, 1988). According to Scott (1912), a governor, deputy governor, and 24 committees made up the management structure of the British East India Company. The ownership of shares was transferrable through sale of the shares, but it was understood that any change of ownership would be limited to individuals known by the other stockholders (Baskin, 1988). Between 1609 and 1613, distributions of profit and principal from voyages totaled between 120 and 240% (Scott, 1912); a significant portion was paid in articles acquired during the expeditions. These divisions of principal and profits closely resembled liquidating dividends (Preinreich, 1978).

The first joint-stock shares of the British East India Company were issued in 1613 with the cost of the shares to be paid over a 4-year period. For record-keeping convenience, each share had an equal and definite value (Williston, 1888b). Four voyages were scheduled, with separate capital raised for each expedition through the installment payments required by the purchase of stock. Divisions from the company averaged 31% of share purchase price per year from its inception through 1617 (Scott, 1912) and totaled over 150% for the first 5 years after the initial joint-stock sale (Baskin, 1988).

By 1617, the company had 934 shareholders and 36 ships; seven additional voyages were scheduled. Not all voyages were profitable because of the high risk and uncertainty associated with sea voyages (Kindleberger, 1984). Depressed economic conditions in Great Britain and an outbreak of plague in London further contributed to the loss of profitability (Scott, 1912). The shares sold more than 30% below the original offering price from 1617 to 1634 because of the company's poor performance (Ehrenberg, 1963).

The minimum investment allowed in the company had increased to $100 by 1657 (Scott, 1912). Voting rights required an investment of at least $500, with smaller investors being allowed to pool their holdings to reach voting status. An investment of $1000 was required for committee membership (Williston, 1888b).

An independent appraisal of company assets was scheduled in 1664 with subsequent appraisals to occur at 3-year intervals. After each appraisal, shareholders were allowed to exchange their proportion of ownership for cash, and their shares were sold to new investors. New stockholders were required to pay an admission fee to the company in addition to the share purchase price.

Liquidation of assets at the end of each voyage proved to be inefficient since a portion of the proceeds was invariably paid in the form of commodities acquired on the voyage. The success of the company and the subsequent confidence of the shareholders in the corporation's managers led to a belief among shareholders that accountability could be accomplished exclusively through the payment of generous dividends (Baskin, 1988). This fundamental right of the shareholder to receive dividends was recognized from the initial joint stock offerings (Williston, 1888b).

A 20% dividend paid exclusively from profits was declared in 1661 and paid in 1662. Once begun, the practice of paying dividends solely from profits continued; a dividend of 20% was paid again in 1663 and 1664. The 1664 appraisal conducted after dividend payment showed a 30% undistributed capital gain. The 40% dividend declared in 1665 included the undistributed capital gain of 30% and an additional 10% dividend from profits (Scott, 1912).

The trading price of the shares varied independently of the level of dividends during this period. Despite the large dividends paid between 1665 and 1667, the shares routinely sold below par. Between 1668 and 1670, when no dividend was paid, the stock price traded above par. The turnover of shares was

**Table 2.1**

**Trading Price Range, Cash Dividends, and Stock Dividends of the British East India Company<sup>*a*</sup> (1662–1720)**

| Year | Trading price range | Cash dividend (percent) | Stock dividend (percent) |
|---|---|---|---|
| 1662–1667 | 60–80 | 150 | |
| 1668–1674 | 80–130 | 90 | |
| 1675–1682 | 130–520 | 200 | 100 |
| 1683–1691 | 150–500 | 200 | |
| 1692–1699 | 60–316 | 0 | |
| 1700–1708 | 116–278 | 66 | |
| 1709–1720 | 208–898 | 100 | |

<sup>*a*</sup>From Scott, William Robert. 1912. *The Constitution and Finance of English, Scottish, and Irish Joint Stock Companies to 1720*, Cambridge: Cambridge University Press.

small during the period, despite the well-distributed ownership; the largest holding in the company at the time was less than 1% of the total outstanding stock. This pattern was indicative of a general shareholder confidence in the firm's managers.

Dividends from 1671 through 1677 totaled 130%. In 1677, the stock price reached $245; a dividend of 40% was paid in 1678. In addition, a distribution of 0.5% was made in damaged calico. Between 1675 and 1681, dividends averaged greater than 20% each year, with total dividends for the period totaling more than 150% (Scott, 1912); the stock at the same time traded between $300 and $500 (Ehrenberg, 1963). Although impressive, these returns were not exorbitant when compared with other joint stock company dividends of the period (Scott, 1912). The 1678 appraisal value of the company exceeded $1,750,000 with more than $1,000,000 in undistributed profits. Beginning in 1681, the corporate directors instituted an annual gift to the king from corporate profits.

Table 2.1 shows the trading price, cash dividends, and stock dividends of the British East India Company between 1662 and 1720. The highest dividends paid in any single year were 50% of income, in 1680, 1682, 1689, and 1691. The British East India Company failed to pay dividends for 8 consecutive years beginning in 1692. The price of the stock showed considerable volatility during that period, trading between $60 and $900 per share (Scott, 1912).

The British East India Company also used men-of-war to protect their vessels. Private marine insurers began to provide insurance against the loss of ships involved in the expeditions. Insurance providers were more successful and reputable in Holland, and many British ships were insured by Dutch companies, despite the higher premiums charged by these firms. Premiums were highly diverse, varying from 3 to 4% in peacetime to more than 15% in time of war (Barbour, 1929).

The success of early trading companies increased the public's interest and acceptance of joint stock ventures during the 17th century (Baskin, 1988). Although stock and share dealing was largely unorganized before 1680, by the middle of the next decade a highly developed securities market had evolved (Morgan and Thomas, 1969). London coffee shops served as the first venues of security trading. Corporate activity climaxed between 1690 and 1720 (Baskin, 1988). Before 1691, only three joint stock companies existed and all three were trading companies—the East India Company, the Royal African Company, and the Hudson's Bay Company (Williston, 1888a). Increases in trade and the subsequent improvement in the general economic conditions between 1691 and 1695 precipitated the formation and issuance of stock by 100 new companies (Kindleberger, 1984). These issues included mining, banking, clothing, and utility companies (Ehrenberg, 1963).

The absence of cash dividend payments by the East India Company during the period did not discourage potential investors from purchasing shares of the joint stock companies (Scott, 1912). Speculation in joint stock issues increased to frenzied levels, and share prices, new issues, and volatility rose to unprecedented heights (Baskin, 1988). The East India Company resumed cash dividends in 1700, and the stock price increased eightfold over the next two decades (Scott, 1912). The total capitalization of joint stock companies reached $21 million by 1717, a fourfold increase in 22 years (Kindleberger, 1978). New company formation continued at a frantic pace; in the 12 months beginning in September 1719, a total of 195 new companies were formed (Kindleberger, 1984).

Trading and speculating in new and established issues continued to accelerate. Allowing investors to purchase shares for only 5 to 10% of their market price further fueled this rampant growth; shareholders were subject to future calls for the balance owed on the shares. The small down payment was justified by the belief that a new company's need for funds was a gradual process and that regular infusions of capital from the shareholder payments would increase the safety of the firm's creditors (Scott, 1912).

The South Sea Company was granted a charter in 1711 for the purpose of consolidating the national debt of Great Britain and replacing the debt with corporate stock. Secondary issues provided funds for the company to pay exorbitant dividends to original issue shareholders.

Other fraudulent practices, including income and dividend manipulations, were also common. The South Sea Company's stock price increased 10-fold before its inevitable collapse (Kindleberger, 1978). This rampant manipulation of capital and the ensuing speculation prompted Sir Isaac Newton, who lost a considerable sum of money, to remark that he could plot the movement of planetary bodies, but not the madness of man.

The debacle of the South Sea Company and the subsequent passage of the Bubble Act in 1720 greatly limited the promotion and development of joint stock companies in Great Britain over the next four decades. The Act made unincorporated joint stock companies illegal and placed severe stipulations on new company formation (Clark, 1929). After passage of the Act, corporations could not be established without an explicit charter from Parliament and the sale of shares was prohibited (Davis, 1917).

## 2.2 REVIVAL OF THE JOINT STOCK COMPANIES, 1800–1900

The dawn of the 19th century in Great Britain found a renewed investor interest in corporate securities (Kindleberger, 1984). This revival was largely the result of investor perception of railroad and canal corporations as civic improvement companies rather than parsimonious profit seekers. The perceived increase in legitimacy decreased the public's fear of fraudulent activity (Baskin, 1988). Annual dividend payments of 7–12% by publicly traded banking firms also boosted investor confidence. A price list of publicly traded securities began to be a regular feature in the newspapers of the era, and the number of issue quotes published grew rapidly (Hunt, 1936). According to Conant (1904), shares of 30 different corporations were available for purchase by investors in 1815.

A boom in English insurance company stocks occurred during the third decade of the 19th century; the rapid growth and abundant success of these companies intensified speculation in joint stock companies. At the same time, the market was inundated with new issues. The British Parliament received 250 joint stock company applications for incorporation in April 1824 alone (Hunt, 1936). And, as Kindleberger (1984) reports, 624 new companies issued stock between 1823 and 1825.

The financial collapse of 1827 led to the failure of 75% of the companies organized between 1823 and 1825; most of the others had failed by 1843 (Baskin, 1988). Joint stock banks generally emerged from the period unscathed, with the majority of the 40 banks organized between 1826 and 1833 remaining profitable and paying dividends of between 7 and 12% in 1833. Insurance companies were also generally successful; all but one of the companies organized during the boom were paying dividends to shareholders in 1843 (Hunt, 1936).

Great Britain's first railroad stock began trading in 1825. For the next decade, an average of five new railroad companies issued shares each year. In 1836, 29 railroad corporations sold stock for the first time, and in 1837, 17 additional transportation companies offered their initial sale of shares (Kindleberger, 1984).

Before 1840, most railroad stocks were marketed and traded in local markets; the majority of shareholders were not London financiers, but local investors with knowledge of the venture's benefits and profit potential (Baskin, 1988). By 1840, several of these issues were paying dividends in excess of 10% and almost all the companies paid dividends of at least 6%; by 1844, these issues had earned a positive reputation among investors for their security and profitability (Hunt, 1936).

Railroad issues experienced an almost manic boom over the 10 years that followed. The trading activity and price increases were unprecedented in British financial history. A flood of new issues were offered to investors; these shares required small initial payments for purchase. In 1847, when calls for additional capital led to panicked sale of shares by investors unable to meet those calls, the market collapsed. Of the large number of companies organized between 1844 and 1868, only 42% were still operating at the end of the period (Hunt, 1936).

Corporate financial practices of railroad companies in the middle of the 19th century were fraught with deception. Dividends were commonly declared before profits were determined and were often paid out of accumulated capital or from the proceeds of subsequent issues (Kindleberger, 1984). The aggregate nominal dividend return on railroad stocks in 1854 was 3.39% (Baskin, 1988).

The repeal of the Bubble Act in 1824 removed most of the existing restrictions on joint stock company organization but kept the requirement of parliamentary approval for incorporation. This stipulation was not lifted until an act allowing general incorporation was passed in 1856. The act also included a provision granting shareholders limited liability (Kindleberger, 1984). The share price of corporation stocks, especially the price of shares of those companies incorporated after the act's passage, rose steadily in the decade after enactment of the limited liability statute. Shares requiring full payment at purchase became the rule rather than the exception of securities of this period (Jeffreys, 1954).

The limited liability clause provided the impetus for the formation of more than 2500 new companies between 1856 and 1862 (Hunt, 1936), with concomitant rapid growth of the securities market for the next 20 years (Shannon, 1954). Unfortunately, the limited liability provision had no effect on the investor's personal risk when purchasing shares offered by joint stock companies. The average life of initial issue corporations of the period was less than 4 years (MacGregor, 1929).

The number of joint stock companies in Great Britain increased rapidly during the last two decades of the 19th century—from 1302 corporations in 1880 to 6182 in 1898 (Conant, 1904). In 1914, 76.4% of corporate earnings in Great Britain was paid to shareholders in the form of dividends (Baskin, 1988); preferred stock dividend requirements absorbed 21% of the earnings and the remaining 55% was used to pay common stock dividends. Perhaps the higher personal tax rate in Great Britain was the reason for higher dividend payments by British corporations than their American counterparts of that era (Montgomery, 1927).

# REFERENCES

Allen, Franklin, and Douglas Gale. 1992. "Stock-price manipulation." *Review of Financial Studies* 5:503–529.

Barbour, Violet. 1929. "Marine risks and insurance in the seventeenth century." *Journal of Economics and Business History* 1:561–596.

Baskin, Jonathon Barron. 1988. "The development of corporate financial markets in Britain and the United States, 1600–1914: Overcoming Asymmetric Information." *The Business History Review* 62:199–237.

Clark, Victor S. 1929. *History of Manufactures in the United States, Volume I, 1607–1860.* New York: McGraw-Hill Book Company, Inc.

Conant, Charles A. 1904. *Wall Street and the Country: A Study of Recent Financial Tendencies.* New York: Greenwood Press Company.

Davis, Joseph S. 1917. *Essays in the Earlier History of American Corporations.* Cambridge, MA: Harvard University Press.

Ehrenberg, Richard. 1963. *Capital and Finance in the Age of the Renaissance.* London: Augustus M. Kelly, Bookseller.

Hunt, Bishop Carleton. 1936. *The Development of the Business Corporation in England, 1800–1867.* Cambridge, MA: Harvard University Press.

Jeffreys, J. B. 1954. "The denomination and character of shares, 1855–1885." In *Essays in Economic History, Volume I.* E. M. Carus-Wilson, ed. London: Edward Arnold Publishers, Ltd.

Kindleberger, Charles P. 1978. *Manias, Panics, and Crashes (A History of Financial Crises).* New York: Basic Books, Inc.

Kindleberger, Charles P. 1984. *A Financial History of Western Europe.* London: George Allen & Unwin.

MacGregor, D. H. 1929. "Joint stock companies and the risk factor." *The Economic Journal* 39:491–505.

Masselman, George. 1963. *The Cradle of Colonialism.* New Haven, CT: Yale University Press.

Montgomery, Robert H. ed. 1927. *Financial Handbook.* 11th ed. New York: The Ronald Press Company.

Morgan, E. Victor, and W. A. Thomas. 1969. *The Stock Exchange: Its History and Function.* 2nd ed. London: Elek Books.

Preinreich, Gabriel A. D. 1932. "Stock yields, stock dividends and inflation." *The Accounting Review* 7:273–289.

Schama, Simon. 1987. *The Embarrassment of Riches.* New York: Alfred A. Knopf.

Scott, William Robert. 1912. *The Constitution and Finance of English, Scottish, and Irish Joint Stock Companies to 1720.* Cambridge: Cambridge University Press.

Shannon, H. A. 1954. "The Limited Companies of 1866–1883." In *Essays in Economic History, Volume I.* E. M. Carus-Wilson, ed. London: Edward Arnold Publishers, Ltd.

Van Loon, Hendrik Willem. 1913. *The Fall of the Dutch Republic,* London: Constable and Co., Ltd.

Warren, Edward H. 1923. "Safeguarding the creditors of corporations." *Harvard Law Review* 36:509–547.

Williston, Samuel. 1888a. "History of the law of business corporations before 1800." *Harvard Law Review* 2:105–124.

Williston, Samuel. 1888b. "History of the law of business corporations before 1800 (continued)." *Harvard Law Review* 2:149–166.

# CHAPTER 3

# The Evolution of the Modern Corporation in the United States of America

## 3.1 FROM THE REVOLUTION TO THE END OF THE 18th CENTURY

Business corporations in the colonies before the American Revolution were few in number and of little importance; their structure and organization were disparate of the modern firm. The New London Society United for Trade and Commerce, established in 1732, was the first U.S. business corporation, followed in 1776 by the Union Wharf Company of New Haven (originally founded in 1760). No evidence exists of the payment of dividends by these corporations before 1800; all earnings were used for expansion and the maintenance of existing assets.

The Philadelphia Contributionship for the Insuring of Houses from Loss by Fire, the first corporation with modern corporate characteristics, was chartered in Philadelphia in 1768 (Davis, 1917). This company was the only business corporation with a charter predating the Declaration of Independence (Williston, 1888a,b).

The number of both incorporated and unincorporated joint stock companies grew rapidly during the 25 years that followed the American Revolution. Several whaling, mining, and manufacturing corporations were chartered during these years.

The first banking corporations began to pay substantial dividends soon after their inception. Other joint stock companies were less successful in their efforts to pay shareholders generous dividends; some of these corporations used current earnings to fund expansions and other investment opportunities, whereas other ventures were simply unprofitable.

The first true banking corporation, one that was involved in all aspects of commercial banking, the Bank of North America, was chartered in 1781 in Philadelphia with local citizens purchasing the majority of the shares (Williston, 1888a,b). The bank was highly profitable from its beginning and paid a 4.5% dividend after 6 months of operation.[1] Dividends of 14.5% and 13.5% were paid in 1784 and 1785, respectively. Shareholder income from dividends averaged 9.4% for the next century. The Bank of New York, another early joint stock company, paid a 3% semiannual dividend from 1784 to 1791.

By 1793, over 20 banks were in operation. The shares of these stocks usually sold above par, most likely because of their generous and consistent dividend payments. Bank stocks averaged 8.6% dividends, usually paid semiannually, between 1785 and 1800 (Davis, 1917). Table 3.1 shows that dividends were paid by banking corporations on common stocks each year between 1785 and 1800.

New issue sales and share trading became commonplace. The most common method of security sale was by public auction. Speculation and an influx of European money for investment in the United States led to four semiannual upswings in stock prices between 1789 and 1791. Newspaper quotes of stock prices began to appear in 1786 and became a regular feature as early as 1789 (Davis, 1917).

Between 1783 and 1800, 74 charters were granted to corporations to enhance inland navigation. The operating results of these firms were disproportionate to the efforts. Although the canals offered increased convenience, the firms were unable to pay cash dividends to their investors. Toll bridge and water supply companies of the period also failed to pay significant dividends to their shareholders.

The 33 insurance companies chartered from 1768 to 1800 were for the most part financially prosperous. Although dividends were paid by these companies to their shareholders, the variance in the amount and the reliability of the dividend payments was much more pronounced than in the dividends received from banking corporations.

Between 1789 and 1800, eight manufacturing firms were chartered. The success of these companies was at best equal to the success of unincorporated manufacturing firms of the period. Shareholders were not rewarded with dividends; all profits were reinvested in the firm to finance growth and expansion (Davis, 1917). By the end of the 18th century, 335 American corporations existed; over 90% of these were incorporated after 1789 (Kehl, 1941).

---

[1] The dividend percentage throughout this chapter is calculated as a percentage "of the capital upon which they were declared." These figures are based on letters from the officers of the banks, bank records, wills, and older texts (Davis, 1917).

Table 3.1

U.S. Bank Stock Dividends by Year[a] (1785–1800)

| Bank | 1785 | 1786 | 1787 | 1788 | 1789 | 1790 | 1791 | 1792 | 1793 | 1794 | 1795 | 1796 | 1797 | 1798 | 1799 | 1800 |
|---|---|---|---|---|---|---|---|---|---|---|---|---|---|---|---|---|
| North America | 6.0 | 6.0 | 6.0 | 6.5 | 7.0 | 7.0 | 13.5 | 12.5 | 12.0 | 12.0 | 12.0 | 12.0 | 12.0 | 12.0 | 11.0 | 10.0 |
| New York | 6.0 | 6.0 | 6.0 | 6.5 | 7.0 | 7.0 | 10.5 | 8.5 | 9.0 | 13.5 | 9.0 | 9.0 | 13.5 | 9.0 | 9.0 | 13.5 |
| Massachusetts | 2.5 | 5.0 | 6.5 | 7.5 | 8.5 | 22.75 | 19.0 | 27.33 | 8.0 | 8.0 | 10.5 | 8.5 | 9.0 | 9.0 | 9.0 | 9.0 |
| Maryland | — | — | — | — | — | 12.0 | 12.0 | 12.0 | 12.0 | 12.0 | 12.0 | 12.0 | 12.0 | 12.0 | 12.0 | |
| United States | — | — | — | — | — | — | — | 8.0 | 7.5 | 8.0 | 8.0 | 8.0 | 9.0 | 8.0 | 8.0 | 10.0 |
| Providence | — | — | — | — | — | — | — | 7.5 | 7.0 | 7.0 | 8.0 | 8.0 | 8.0 | 8.0 | 10.5 | 10.0 |
| South Carolina | — | — | — | — | — | — | — | 9.0 | 9.0 | 15.0 | 15.0 | 7.5[b] | NA[c] | NA | NA | NA |
| Hartford | — | — | — | — | — | — | — | — | 3.5 | 3.0 | 0.0 | 0.0 | 3.0 | 3.5 | 4.0 | 4.0 |
| Union (Boston) | — | — | — | — | — | — | — | — | 8.0 | 8.0 | 8.5 | 10.0 | 10.0 | 9.0 | 9.0 | 9.0 |
| New Haven | — | — | — | — | — | — | — | — | — | — | — | 0.0 | 8.0 | 8.25 | 6.0 | 6.0 |
| Pennsylvania | — | — | — | — | — | — | — | — | — | — | — | 8.0 | 8.0 | 10.00 | 9.5 | 9.5 |
| Rhode Island | — | — | — | — | — | — | — | — | — | — | — | 5.5 | 8.0 | 8.0 | 10.0 | 10.0 |

[a]From Davis, Joseph S. 1917. *Essays in the Earlier History of American Corporations*, Cambridge, MA: Harvard University Press.
[b]For 6 months.
[c]Not available.

Practically no general statutes governing corporations existed before 1800. Corporations and investors relied on English precedents to determine the legality of corporate operations (Davis, 1917). No specific provisions in the charter protected the interests of the firm's creditors—these creditors were safeguarded only by existing common law principles (Warren, 1923).

Of paramount importance to American dividend law was the Bank of England charter of 1694. When writing the charter of the Bank of the United States, Alexander Hamilton copied large sections of the charter verbatim. The only significant change in the charter was the assignment of liability for incurred indebtedness because of excess dividend payments. In the original charter, *shareholders* were liable for the debts; in the U.S. charter, the *board of directors* was held accountable for the indebtedness. The same policy of board of director liability was followed in subsequent bank charters (Kehl, 1941). Although corporate statutes varied from jurisdiction to jurisdiction, this liability of the board of directors was held across the United States (Briggs, 1933). At the same time, shareholder liability was unlimited (Clark, 1929a).

The 1781 charter of the Bank of North America granted the board of directors the power to regularly pay the "appropriate" amount of dividends out of corporate profits. The 1784 charter of the Bank of New York contained a similar clause. The 1790 Bank of the United States charter was the first to specify the payment of semiannual dividends from *profits* (Davis, 1917).

## 3.2 THE 19th CENTURY

The 19th century marked an increasing need for equity capital coupled with the recognition of the importance of a consistent dividend stream. This awareness of the importance of dividends, however, led to less than legitimate financial practices by managers of joint stock companies when corporate profits proved to be insufficient to continue dividend payments at already established levels. The number of both incorporated and unincorporated joint stock companies grew rapidly following the American Revolution.

The first banking corporations began to pay substantial dividends soon after their inception. Other joint stock companies were less successful in their efforts to pay shareholders generous dividends; some of these corporations used current earnings to fund expansions and other investment opportunities while other ventures were less than profitable. By the beginning of the 19th century, dividends had become symbolic liquidations rather than distributions of net profits.

Between 1800 and 1823, 557 manufacturing corporations were incorporated in the United States with over half of the new corporations based in New York or Massachusetts.

After the War of 1812, profits of manufacturing corporations increased significantly. The allure of increasing profits enticed outside investors to contribute capital to these ventures. Equity sales became the textile mills' most important source of capital in the first half of the 19th century (Davis, 1917).

Cotton manufacturing corporation dividends during the period averaged 5.5%, while the textile mill dividends averaged almost twice that rate. Textile makers paid dividends of between 10 and 20% during the War of 1812 (Clark, 1929a). Up to this time, many of the textile mills had been closely held.

Share par values ranged from $25 to $1000 per share (Clark, 1929a). Despite these advances, only a few U.S. financial firms were capitalized in excess of $500,000. The majority of manufacturing and other industries' firms had less than $50,000 capital (Davis, 1917).

Public offering of U.S. corporate issues in Great Britain commenced during the early 19th century. Shares of existing corporations, as well as new issues, were sold through investment bankers with offices both in the United States and Great Britain (Carosso, 1970).

Before the Civil War, individuals seeking investment opportunities generally bought real estate. Equity share investment opportunities were limited primarily to railroad stocks. The only industrial stocks available to investors were coal and textile firms (Navin and Sears, 1955). Before 1890, the Pullman Palace Car Company was the only manufacturing firm traded on the New York Stock Exchange. Its close association with the prosperous railroad industry caused investors to consider the company more of a railroad firm than an industrial firm (Baskin, 1988).

The temporary shutdown of many of the mills for 2 years following the War of 1812 was followed by payment of between 6 and 8% dividends for the next 10 years. The losses and lack of dividends during the panic of 1837 were offset by dividends averaging 13.33% for the 3 years following the recession.[2] Textile dividends averaged 7.6% between 1825 and 1830 and 14.5% between 1831 and 1860.

The beginning of the Civil War brought another increase in profitability and a further increase in northeast textile mill dividends. Dividends increased from 8% in 1860 to between 10 and 20% the following year. One textile mill paid a 66% dividend to its shareholders in 1861. Textile firms paid dividends of 25 to 50% in 1865, the most profitable year in the industry's history (Clark, 1929b).

Early offerings of U.S. railroad company shares were primarily to local investors who had a reasonably accurate profit expectation. The sale of equities provided most of the capital raised for railroad construction in areas with a high population density and a large number of potential investors. This practice was especially common in New England. In contrast, western U.S. railroads were

---

[2]The causes of the panic of 1837 were both financial and commercial; British exporters allowed American importers to pyramid credits; obligations coming due were "paid" by substituting other obligations with longer maturities. When a recession in the United States slowed cash flows, many manufacturers could not meet credit obligations and were forced out of business. Large manufacturers were affected more severely than small companies (Clark, 1929a).

financed primarily with mortgage bonds because of a lack of potential investors (Baskin, 1988).

Nevertheless, before 1865, equity was the most important source of capital for manufacturing corporations. The need for investment capital was greatest when the firm was least able to find funds—during initial organization. Legal restrictions against stock issues at less than par and the average proprietor's aversion to dilution of ownership and managerial control limited the ability of most firms to raise equity capital. Thus, most manufacturing firms before 1880 remained closely held. In the textile industry, 75% of the shares of the 11 largest mills of the period were held by fewer than 750 investors (Davis, 1917).

By the beginning of the 19th century, dividends had become more than mere distributions of net profits; they were also *symbols of continuity*. A desire to provide investors with a consistent dividend stream led to less than legitimate financial practices by the managers of joint stock companies when corporate profits proved to be insufficient to continue dividend payments at established levels.[3] Consequently, to attract investors and to protect creditors, corporate charters began to include provisions addressing dividend payments. Most notable of these were the profit rule, the capital impairment rule, and the insolvency rule.

Around 1800, special charters began to provide a remedy against capital impairment caused by the declaration and payment of a dividend. Although the profit rule and the capital impairment rule became common in U.S. corporate charters before 1825, dividend policy continued to be governed by special clauses in each corporate charter. The first general dividend statute, enacted in New York in 1825, made it unlawful to pay dividends except out of corporate profits. The corporation's board of directors was liable for damages if the law was violated. This statute was widely copied by other states.

A third general rule, the insolvency rule, was first adopted in Massachusetts in 1830. This rule prohibited the declaration or payment of a dividend if the firm was insolvent, or if the payment *would make* the firm insolvent. As with the profit rule, the corporation's board of directors was held accountable for the violation of this rule. This rule, too, was readily adopted by other states (Kehl, 1941).

Following the Civil War, the majority of northern manufacturing companies paid regular dividends. The Lowell Company, the premier textile manufacturer in New England, paid on average 18% dividends during the decade following the war. Despite their closely held nature, these companies continued to pay significant dividends. Dividend payments for all textile manufacturers averaged almost 8% per year until the beginning of the 20th century, despite the temporary suspension of dividends by many companies following the panic of 1874.

---

[3]It was common practice for banks to set aside stock for state governments and governmental officials to purchase. Early companies also paid dividends from capital rather than earnings.

Post-Civil War inflation was dominated by a persistent premium on gold. Economic problems in Europe caused the tightening of European lending to railway builders. Railways had been overbuilt into new territories that were unable to generate enough traffic to cover fixed charges. Overabundant farm production led to an agricultural glut and a decline in agricultural product prices. The purchasing power of rural buyers decreased as well as the demand for manufactured goods. The lack of demand caused decreased production (and employment) by the manufacturing sector. The failure of brokerage houses and railway companies added additional fuel to the panic of 1874 (Clark, 1929b).

During the decade following the Civil War, manufacturing production increased twice as fast as the population (Clark, 1929b). At the same time, the general lack of publicly available financial information required investors to value industrial securities solely using their dividend history. The dawn of the 20th century brought a further change in American business. The percentage of manufactured goods being exported had tripled during the 35 years following the Civil War to over 30% of all manufactured products (Conant, 1904).

Investor confidence in industrial firms increased significantly at the end of the 19th century because of the payment of high dividends by nearly all issues almost immediately after their inception (Faulkner, 1924). At the same time, railroad bond interest rates declined from 7 to 3.5% (Conant, 1904). Dividends were frequently paid out of capital by these newly organized firms and the use of capital for dividend payment by firms in financial distress was common (Faulkner, 1924). These extravagant dividend payments led to financial distress and bankruptcy by many of the firms (Baskin, 1988).

The majority of the other manufacturing firms of the period were small partnerships or closely held corporations. Many firms remained family owned, even the larger manufacturers, such as Singer and McCormick. However, ownership in New England textile firms started to be more widely disseminated, with shares primarily trading on the Boston Exchange. The shares were regarded as investment grade securities and were often used as loan collateral.

Marshall Field and Company, Macy's, and other large department stores of the period were all partnerships. Sears, Roebuck and Company, Woolworth, Montgomery Ward, and The Great Atlantic and Pacific Tea Company were all in their infancy during this period; of these, only Montgomery Ward was incorporated.

Most of the extractive companies of this era were small partnerships. Homestake Mining and Standard Oil were peculiarities, as were a few large, publicly traded copper and iron mining firms. Standard Oil paid dividends ranging from 5.25 to 30% during the last 20 years of the 19th century (Faulkner, 1924).

The first industrial firms to attract public interest were in the processing industries, especially sugar and oil refining. The trust form of organization used by many of the firms in these industries foreshadowed the modern corporate merger. Trust formation began when the majority of oil companies deposited their securities with a group of trustees with the expressed goal of controlling production, *de facto* decreasing output. The managers of the member firms of the trust would coordinate their commercial strategy to meet joint objectives. A few of the individual corporations remained independent. In addition, cotton, whiskey, and sugar refining trusts were formed during this period.

The rise of industry trusts increased investor interest in the securities markets reflected in the increase in trading activity. The first signs of smoothing corporate dividends were evident, and specialized uses of preferred stock and no-par common stock increased.

Although the shares of the Standard Oil trust were closely held, shares of other trusts were actively traded. Very little information about earnings or operations was available to investors, however. Trusts commonly sold preferred stock secured by fixed assets and backed by earning capacity, whereas common shares embodied the risk, uncertainty, and anticipated growth of the enterprise. The average volume of shares in the trusts dwarfed other issues; during the last half of 1889, an average of 150,000 trust shares exchanged hands each week compared to only 2000 shares of the Pullman Car Company, one of the largest firms of the era (Navin and Sears, 1955).

In 1890, fewer than 10 industrial stocks were traded and quoted on the New York Stock Exchange. This number increased to more than 30 issues around the crash of 1893 and to over 200 by 1897. Industrial securities of the period were concentrated in the manufacturing, distributive, extractive, and processing industries.

The Dow Jones Industrial Average began to be reported in the middle of this decade, followed by the publication of *Moody's Industrial Security* in 1900.

Financial information other than the firm's capitalization and dividend record was frequently unavailable to investors in the early 20th century. Utility, financial, and railroad corporations generally provided more detailed data than other companies of the period. Before World War I, managers generally ignored demands by shareholders for greater and better disclosure of information (Hawkins, 1963).

The New York Stock Exchange, Investment Bankers Association of America, public accounting firms, and the U.S. government began to require increased disclosure from publicly held corporations. The New York Stock Exchange lacked stringent regulations for securities during the 19th century (Michie, 1986). When the 1869 requirement for annual report publication by listed corporations was first instituted, most managers largely ignored it. Over time, the exchange sought to increase requirements for disclosure. Quarterly reports were not required until 1926 (Hawkins, 1963).

Returns from industrial firms' shares began to surpass railroad company stock returns after the Civil War. The extreme volatility of the market immediately following the war decreased during the last 15 years of the century (Smith, 1923). Between 1872 and 1899, the income to investors from industrial and utility common stock was greater than the income provided by railroad bonds (Snowden, 1990). Overall, industrial stocks fared better than railroad stocks in the depression of the last decade of the 19th century. The three largest industrials of the time paid dividends throughout the depression. Only General Electric (GE) failed to pay dividends. GE's suspension of dividends was the result of planned retention of cash by corporate management rather than the consequence of a lack of earnings (Navin and Sears, 1955).

## 3.3 THE EARLY 20th CENTURY

From 1900 to 1920, the return on investment in industrial, utility, and railroad common stocks exceeded the return from railroad bonds of the same period (Smith, 1959). Corporate dividends before 1920 did not reflect the cyclical economic influences shown by stock prices (Snowden, 1987).

Dividend payment and stock price trends moved in opposite directions during the first 20 years of the 20th century in contrast to the positive relationship shown before 1900 (Van Strum, 1927). After 1900, consistently strong earnings by corporate America led to a gradual increase in dividends, but the increased earnings precipitated by World War I were not reflected by increased dividends (White, 1990). However, the aggregate dividend payment by American corporations during the first two decades of the 20th century increased more rapidly than nominal stock prices (Snowden, 1990).

Smoothing of dividends by corporate management, as a common practice, did not commence until after 1920 (Van Strum, 1925). The increased variability of dividends during the period is a potential explanation for the extreme volatility of stock prices during this era (Baskin, 1988). Nevertheless, attempts by professional traders to manipulate share prices might have equally contributed to the increased price volatility during this period (Allen and Gale, 1992).

The mean return from common stock dividends between 1871 and 1925 was 5.17%. Average share dividends exceeded 8% in 1918, whereas returns fell to less than 4% in 1886, 1890, 1898, and 1906–1907. Table 3.2 shows the average dividend income per share by year from 1871 through 1919.

## 3.4 THE ORIGINS OF NO-PAR STOCK ISSUES

Shares of stock were originally issued with a minimum fixed value called par that was defined as the valuation of the participation in the rights of ownership. Initial investors were required to pay in cash at least the par value to

**Table 3.2**

**Dividend Income on Common Stocks by Year[a] (1871–1919)**

| Year | Dividend income (percent) | Year | Dividend income (percent) |
|---|---|---|---|
| 1871 | 5.57 | 1896 | 4.17 |
| 1872 | 5.17 | 1897 | 4.38 |
| 1873 | 5.07 | 1898 | 3.81 |
| 1874 | 7.37 | 1899 | 4.10 |
| 1875 | 6.35 | 1900 | 4.35 |
| 1876 | 6.47 | 1901 | 4.45 |
| 1877 | 5.32 | 1902 | 4.02 |
| 1878 | 5.39 | 1903 | 4.10 |
| 1879 | 6.24 | 1904 | 4.54 |
| 1880 | 5.24 | 1905 | 4.19 |
| 1881 | 4.98 | 1906 | 3.95 |
| 1882 | 5.12 | 1907 | 3.98 |
| 1883 | 5.54 | 1908 | 6.02 |
| 1884 | 5.97 | 1909 | 5.34 |
| 1885 | 5.34 | 1910 | 4.16 |
| 1886 | 3.78 | 1911 | 5.09 |
| 1887 | 4.14 | 1912 | 5.22 |
| 1888 | 4.17 | 1913 | 5.25 |
| 1889 | 4.28 | 1914 | 5.03 |
| 1890 | 3.85 | 1915 | 5.61 |
| 1891 | 4.72 | 1916 | 6.39 |
| 1892 | 4.43 | 1917 | 7.48 |
| 1893 | 4.12 | 1918 | 8.58 |
| 1894 | 4.40 | 1919 | 6.37 |
| 1895 | 4.53 | | |

[a]From Wilson, Jack W., and Charles P. Jones. 1987. "A Comparison of Annual Common Stock Returns: 1871–1925 with 1926–85." *The Journal of Business* 60:239–258.

protect the creditors of the corporation (Berle and Means, 1932). Later, property, services, and intangibles of equal value became acceptable substitutes. This legal dilution of par value originated when management was allowed to value noncash equivalents to be used for payment of par. Owners wishing to sell their shares, however, could not collect par value from the corporation even if that amount had been paid in full in cash. The shares' current trading price on the exchange was the maximum price per share available to the shareholder (Dewing, 1926).

Par value also provided the investor an approximate valuation of the corporation even with the crude accounting methods of the period (Baskin, 1988). Railroad and industrial shares were commonly issued with a par value of $100; early railroad shares had a par value of $50 (Montgomery, 1927); and copper mining shares were often issued with a $25 par value. Other mining stocks were issued with par as low as $1.

Shares designed to participate in earnings only but not representing ownership in corporate assets began to be issued without a par value in the first decade of the 20th century. Capital stock taxes were levied on the shares assuming a par value of $100. Subsequent offerings were issued with low par values— $1 or $5—bearing little relation to the historical contribution (Dewing, 1926).

The New York Bar Association began lobbying for legal issuance of no-par stock before the beginning of the 20th century. Par value was criticized for causing confusion among investors and for unfairly pegging the value of the shares to their par value. The trading price of par value shares tended to gravitate toward par. Others criticized par value because of the difficulty of assessment of the economic value of the firm. The decline of trading price below par value would have enabled new shareholders to purchase the shares at a discount compared to original investors paying par for the stock. Proponents argued that the retention of par value would maintain the distinction of capital and profits to be used for dividend payment and would provide a "true" value for investors to use in their analysis of an issue (Dewing, 1926).

The issuance of no-par stock was first legalized in New York in 1912 (Berle and Means, 1932). By 1919, 27 New York Stock Exchange (NYSE) corporations had issued no-par stock; by 1924, the number had increased to 189 (Montgomery, 1927). By 1923 more than 20 states followed this precedent and allowed the issue of no-par stock. By 1927 almost all states allowed the issuance of no-par shares (Dewing, 1926).

## 3.5 THE BOOM AND THE BUST

Until 1920, common stock was not viewed as an investment grade security. Conservative private and institutional investors purchased only railroad bonds and industrial preferred stock. Around this time, security analysts began recommending the purchase of common stock as an inflation hedge. The increasing short-term volatility of stock was balanced by the benefits of superior returns over the long term (Snowden, 1990).

Shareholder rolls of American corporations increased dramatically in the first three decades of the 20th century (Carosso, 1970). The number of corporate shareholders rose from 500,000 in 1900 to 2 million in 1920 to over 10 million by 1930 (Baskin, 1988). Share ownership was no longer just for the very wealthy. The most dramatic increase was among investors not in the top income bracket, who became shareholders in record numbers during this time. The percentage of share ownership by these individuals increased from 43% in 1916 to 63% in 1921.

The increase in ownership was the result of customer ownership campaigns and employee stock ownership plans. The decrease of ownership among the wealthy was attributed to high dividend tax burdens, a decrease in the World War I surtax following the end of the conflict (Means, 1930), funds available for investment from Liberty Bond maturation, and a decrease in the commission rate on smaller share purchases (Carosso, 1970).

Average dividends paid by corporations increased threefold from 1871 to 1929 (White, 1990). In 1920, share prices were low and dividend yields were relatively high. The market began a long rise in mid-1921 with only minor corrections in 1924 and 1926 (Galbraith, 1954). Total yearly share volume increased 500% between 1921 and 1928 (Klingaman, 1989). The bull market beginning after World War I was largely the result of the public's expectations of continued dividend increases, expectations exceeding what the actual increases turned out to be (Galbraith, 1954). Growth in corporate earnings averaged 9% per year from 1922 to 1927, whereas dividend growth averaged 7% (Fisher 1930; White, 1990). In 1927, $1.5 billion was paid in dividends (Wilbur, 1932).

As American businesses prospered in the 1920s, stock values increased. Within a 5-year period, stock prices rose threefold (Erickson, 1972). Share volume also increased 250% between 1927 and 1929, paralleled by a decrease of bond offerings of 38% (Carosso, 1970).

Trading volume in railroad stocks fell in relation to that of industrial and, especially, utility shares (White, 1990). In 1927, the bull market began in earnest; by 1928, buy orders overwhelmed the capacities of the brokerage houses (Galbraith, 1954). Trading hours on the NYSE were shortened in hope of decreasing trading volume (Carosso, 1970).

As share prices continued to increase, corporate managers began to slow dividend increases in an attempt to retard investor speculation and enthusiasm. Other managers warned the public of the overvaluation of company shares and the unrealistic nature of their expectations (White, 1990). Analysts warned of the impending crash; professional financiers and traders began to quietly withdraw their funds from the market (Erickson, 1972). Other, smaller investors heeded few of these cautions and share prices continued to increase rapidly, outpacing dividend increases (White, 1990).

March 1928 marked the beginning of a "speculative mania" (Galbraith, 1954). Novice and seasoned investors alike purchased stocks with their savings believing that stock prices would increase indefinitely (Erickson, 1972). On March 5, General Motors (GM) stock increased in price $5 and had risen $10 by the end of the week. Radio Corporation of America (RCA) increased $13 the same week. Despite the common favoritism shown to these issues by speculators, the stocks were dissimilar. GM had recently promised to increase dividends and investors expected the recent increases in earnings to continue. RCA, however, had not yet paid a dividend nor would the firm pay dividends for many years to come (White, 1990).

Speculative stocks of infant industries—radio, airplane, and movie corporations—paying little or no dividends enjoyed the greatest increase in price (Carosso, 1970), not unlike the *fin de siécle* techno boom. The stable dividend paying railroad stocks languished during the boom. The average dividend per share increased to $5.97 in 1928 (White, 1990).

During September 1929, the 240 leading issues of the NYSE lost 2.8 billion dollars in market value (Klingaman, 1989). The stock market decline beginning in 1929 by no means can be logically explained by dividend decreases, however. Total dividends increased to $2.6 billion in 1929 (Wilbur, 1932). Dividend increases averaged slightly less than 8% per year for the decade with the average dividend paid to common shareholders doubling in less than 10 years (Brittain, 1966). Quarterly dividends continued to rise in late 1929, increasing 12.8% in the third quarter and 11.6% in the fourth quarter.

Although slowed, dividend increases and stock prices gave no indication of the imminent recession (White, 1990). Bear raids were not the cause of the drastic fall in prices either, but other forms of stock price manipulation were common. Trading pools—investor groups that purchased blocks of stocks, circulated rumors that led to price increases, and sold their blocks at a profit—were the order of the day (Allen and Gale, 1992).

Dividend payments exceeded net income from 1922 to 1933; the shortfall in income was paid from accumulated surplus (Sage, 1937). The average dividend yield on all NYSE stocks from 1921 to 1930 ranged from a low of 3.5% to a high of 9%. Blue chip issue yields from 1897 to 1930 ranged from a low of 2% immediately preceding the crash to a high of 7.5% (Sloan, 1931).

In 1931, the management of General Motors announced that all earnings should be paid as dividends in poor economic times and that, if a corporation is sound, the use of accumulated surplus to maintain the dividend is justified (Wilbur, 1932). Shareholders began to lobby Congress to decrease corporate retained earnings and increase dividend payments. The Revenue Act of 1934 threatened to tax undistributed corporate earnings, heavily, and, indeed, The Revenue Act of 1936 did levy a tax on retained earnings. In response, many corporations increased dividends or declared special dividends (Sage, 1937) despite profits dropping 22% below their 1926–1929 average (Jaeger, 1972).

Managers were thankful to have an excuse for increasing dividends. The large number of business failures early in the decade had seriously shaken shareholder faith in corporate management, and according to Graham and Dodd (1934), many managers believed that increasing dividends was a low cost instrument of restoring investor faith.

The increase in dividends totaled over $1.1 billion in 1936 and 1937, one-third greater than expected by financial mavens (Lent, 1948). Large corporations in the United States distributed more than 80% of their earnings as dividends in 1937. Despite the increases, the ratio of net dividend to net profit after tax (the dividend payout ratio) fell to 35% during 1929–1947. Although corporate profits were 90% greater in 1946 and 1947 than in 1929, the aggregate dividend payout was only 3% greater (Brittain, 1966).

## 3.6 POST-WORLD WAR II

During World War II, corporate cash dividends were paid using Liberty bonds (Preinreich, 1978). Dividend increases averaged 6% per year in the 15 years following the end of World War II, whereas after-tax net profits increased on average 2% per year during the same period (Brittain, 1966).

The dividend payout ratio increased to its highest level during the 20 years following World War II (Brittain, 1966). The dividend payout ratio in the electric utility industry showed exceptional stability from 1947 to 1959. Individual firm ratios were much more volatile during the period (Dhrymes and Kurz, 1964).

In the 15 years following World War II, corporate dividend policy in the United States (and Great Britain) remained relatively unchanged. Dividend payout levels stayed relatively constant. Dividends increased an average of 6% each year, and the aggregate dividend payout ratio increased to levels comparable to the payout levels following World War I (Brittain, 1966). A state of "inertia" had developed in the payment of corporate dividends (Dhrymes and Kurz, 1967).

The dividend rate was relatively unaffected by the high levels of inflation that characterized the American economy during and immediately following the war in Viet Nam, showing only a slight increase during these years. As Ibbotson and Sinquefield (1982) argue, the consistent level of dividend payment is evidence of management's continued effort to "smooth" dividends, as a matter of policy.

Then came the 1980s and the 1990s. The stock market took off gangbusters for reasons that are not the topic of this book. The NASDAQ and OTC market established at the beginning of the 1970s continued to attract young, growth-intensive firms and gained more and more prominence. The incredible growth in wealth of the stock market is depicted, respectively.

One must remember that dividend yields, i.e., cash dividends paid in the year divided by an index (either a stock price or an absolute value of a popular market index), can be affected nine ways (Table 3.3).

What happened during these two decades was that after a relatively slow growth during the 1980s (which was temporarily wiped out by the crash of the market in 1987, and quickly regained thereafter) there was an unprecedented

**Table 3.3**

**Dividend Yields**

| Numerator | Denominator | Change in the denominator | Net effect on yield |
|---|---|---|---|
| Goes up | Unchanged | | Goes up |
| Goes up | Goes down | | Goes up |
| Goes up | Goes up | Proportionally less than the numerator | Goes up |
| Goes up | Goes up | Proportionally the same | Unchanged |
| Goes down | Goes down | Proportionally more than the numerator | Goes up |
| Goes down | Goes down | Proportionally the same | Unchanged |
| Goes down | Goes down | Proportionally less than the numerator | Goes down |
| Goes down | Goes up | | Goes down |
| Goes down | Unchanged | | Goes down |

growth during the last decade of the century. As a consequence, dividend yields, which were from 2.5 to 4.5% during the 1980s, declined further, with many giants of the American stock markets paying either no or very little dividends. It seemed that Black's (1990, p. 5) prophecy that ". . . dividend that remain taxable will gradually vanish" finally came true.

In fact, as discussed in Chapter 1, *The Economist* article "Shares without the Other Bit," says this:

> In the 1950s, nine out of ten American companies paid dividends. Today only one in five does (see chart). Dividends are disappearing so fast in America that Eugene Fama and Kenneth French, professors of finance at the University of Chicago and the Massachusetts Institute of Technology, respectively, have looked into the phenomenon.

The chart in the article is titled "Unyielding" and shows how dividend-paying firms declined from over 80% in the 1950s to less than 20% by 1998. The decline in numbers was also accompanied by a concomitant decline of yields. This was so not just because proportionally more unprofitable or growth-oriented firms were traded in the American stock markets that paid no, or very little, dividend, but also because the decline of dividend paid by older, much profitable firms.

> Even so, there is a puzzle about the disappearing dividend. It is not just growth companies that are opting out of dividends, but all companies, including those enjoying healthy flows of free cash. Among very profitable companies, only 32% pay dividends, half the proportion that did 20 years ago. And even diehard dividend-payers are changing their minds. J.P. Morgan, an investment bank, estimates that the dividend pay-out of America's 500 largest companies has fallen from over half of profits in 1990 to about a third now (*The Economist*, p. 93).

Discarding a whole series of conjectures for the reasons of the "puzzle" of disappearing of dividends, among which perhaps the most dominating and convincing the contention of share buyback, *The Economist* concludes:

But it may mean that they [dividends] have become less relevant. For most of the century, before the bull market of the 1990s, the dividend yield was one of the most watched measures in the stockmarket. Whenever it dropped to 3% or less, traders assumed the market was overvalued and sold their holdings. Yet today the dividend yield on the S&P 500 shares is 1.2%. Optimists might argue that, since dividends no longer play the role they once did, this does not, of itself, mean the market is wildly overvalued. But, given the uncertainty over precisely what role dividends now play, to say nothing of the market's heady levels, that is scarcely reassuring.

Let us just stop here for a moment and take stock of what evolved during the go-go decade of the 20th century's *fin de siécle*. If we take *The Economist* assessment as reasonably descriptive, then dividends became less relevant as a measure of value. At the same time, the immateriality of this relevance does not mean that the market is "wildly overvalued." Conclusion: dividends, once the litmus test of rational valuation, should not be considered as such.

However, this also necessarily means that all the "rational," academic models, models based on the tenets of the *homo economicus,* necessarily rely on unobservable factors and that the evolution of dividend practices, which one may call dividend policies of firms, must be part and parcel of model building. Ergo, there cannot be universally "true" dividend models because they are subject to both temporal and spatial vagaries.

This is not the end of the story, however. The end of the century decade came to a crashing halt with the burst of the techno bubble in early 2001. The NASDAQ index went down from over 5000 to below 2000, and the DJIA, although not the same crash and burn, nevertheless lost a good 25% of its value by mid-September 2001. The *Wall Street Journal* (8/21/2001), in an article titled "Dividends, Not Growth, Is Wave of Future," had this to say:

> If the 1990s were about clocking capital gains, I suspect the current decade will belong to yield investors. The reason: Stocks may return just 8% a year and possibly less, so why not skip some of the uncertainty and claim your reward in cash?

> "A little more than a year ago, people laughed at dividends," recalls Jeremy Siegel, a finance professor at the University of Pennsylvania's Wharton School. "In the future, I believe that more attention will be paid to dividends and current earnings and less to growth."

> The first three months of 2000 saw a continuation of the late 1990s technology stock frenzy. But since then, pursuing yield has paid off handsomely. Bonds have posted healthy gains. Real-estate investment trusts have been big winners.

NETFOLIO Inc., which describes itself as ". . . a registered investment adviser that offers custom-designed stock portfolios (personal funds) to individuals at a fraction of the cost of the typical mutual fund" in its website (www.netfolio.com),[4] offers some interesting reading regarding dividend yields.

[4]Netfolio discontinued its services on September 14, 2001.

After brief technical explanations about what dividend yield is and where to find data about dividend yields, NETFOLIO goes on to interpret dividend yields.

- A company that sports a higher yield in effect is providing you with a safety net. If the price of its stock falls too far, investors will rush in to buy it for no other reason than to capture its high yield, thus pushing its stock price back up.
- Stocks with higher yields tend to have greater upside potential. Imagine that you are choosing between two companies that are identical in all respects except that the first's dividend yield is 2% and the second's is 4%. This second company's stock would have to double in price just to bring its yield down to where the first one is already!

Especially the second bullet point rings untrue. First, as shown earlier, dividend yield can decline in any of three cases, and not just increase in the price of the stock. Second, as Graham and Dodd taught the investment public, if of two otherwise identical firms one pays less dividend than the second, the latter firm's price reflects lower price-earning multiple, meaning higher risk, with other things being equal (which is the assumption of NETFOLIO).

Then they refer to the Fama and French study, mourning the dividend decline phenomenon, but speculating like some others in *The Economist*'s piece that stock repurchases replaced dividend payments (a hypothesis rejected by *The Economist* as a plausible explanation).

After some creative and rather suspicious accounting, NETFOLIO concludes that $10,000 invested in 1979 in the top 10 dividend-paying stocks would have yielded an annualized return of 14.68% vis-à-vis a 16.17% return on the S&P 500 index. Further, that "on a risk-adjusted basis, in fact, the dividend yield strategy over these 21 years actually comes out ahead of the S&P 500." Of course, this calculation is feasible only when one disregards the tax that had to be paid on dividends, just as in case of a costless and nontaxable dividend reinvestment plan.

So, we have a complete reversal of policy in a matter of a few years. Or do we? Wait until the next cycle of the stock market comes about. But this is what makes dividends and dividend policy the most intriguing and research-inviting topic of financial economics.

# REFERENCES

Allen, Franklin, and Douglas Gale. 1992. "Stock-price Manipulation." *Review of Financial Studies* 5:503–529.

Baskin, Jonathon Barron. 1988. "The development of corporate financial markets in Britain and the United States, 1600–1914: Overcoming asymmetric information." *The Business History Review* 62:199–237.

Berle, Adolf A., and Gardiner C. Means. 1932. *The Modern Corporation and Private Property*. New York: The MacMillan Company.

Black, Fisher. 1990. "Why firms pay dividends." *The Financial Analysts Journal* 46:5.

Briggs, L. L. 1933. "Dividends and the general corporation statutes." *The Accounting Review* 8:130–144.

Brittain, John A. 1966. *Corporate Dividend Policy*. Washington: The Brookings Institution.

Carosso, Vincent P. 1970. *Investment Banking in America, A History*. Cambridge, MA: Harvard University Press.

Clark, Victor S. 1929a. *History of Manufactures in the United States, Volume I, 1607–1860*. New York: McGraw Hill Book Company, Inc.

Clark, Victor S. 1929b. *History of Manufactures in the United States, Volume II, 1860–1893*, New York: McGraw Hill Book Company, Inc.

Clements, Jonathan. 2001. "Dividends, no growth, is wave of future." Wall Street Journal 8/21/2001.

Conant, Charles A. 1904. *Wall Street and the Country: A Study of Recent Financial Tendencies*. New York: Greenwood Press Company.

Davis, Joseph S. 1917. *Essays in the Earlier History of American Corporations*. Cambridge, MA: Harvard University Press.

Dewing, Arthur Stone. 1926. *The Financial Policy of Corporation*. 2nd ed. New York: The Ronald Press Company.

Dhrymes, Phoebus J., and Mordecai Kurz. 1967. "Investment, Dividends and External Financing Behavior of Firms." In *Determinants of Investor Behavior: A Conference of the Universities—National Bureau Committee for Economic Research*. Robert Ferber, ed. New York: National Bureau of Economic Research.

*The Economist*. 1999. "Shares without the other bit." November 20:93.

Erickson, Erling A. 1972. "The great crash of October, 1929." In *The Great Crash Revisited: Essays on The Economics of the Thirties*. Herman Van Der Wee, ed., The Hague, Netherlands: Martinus Nijhoff.

Faulkner, Harold Underwood. 1924. *American Economic History*. New York: Harper and Brothers.

Galbraith, John Kenneth. 1954. *The Great Crash 1929*. Boston, MA: Houghton Mifflin Co.

Graham, Benjamin, and David L. Dodd. 1934. *Security Analysis*, New York: Whittlesey House.

Hawkins, David F. 1963. "The development of modern financial reporting practices among American manufacturing corporations." *The Business History Review* 37:135–168.

Ibbotson, Roger G., and Rex A. Sinquefield. 1982. *Stocks, Bonds, and Inflation; The Past and the Future*. Charlottesville, VA: The Financial Analysts Research Foundation.

Jaeger, Hans. 1972. "Business in the great depression." In *The Great Crash Revisited: Essays on The Economics of the Thirties*. Herman Van Der Wee, ed. The Hague, Netherlands: Martinus Nijhoff.

Kehl, Donald. 1941. *Corporate Dividends*. New York: The Ronald Press Company.

Klingaman, William K. 1989. *1929 The Year of the Great Crash*. New York: Harper and Row.

Lent, George E. 1948. *The Impact of the Undistributed Profits Tax 1936–1937*. New York: Columbia University Press.

Means, Gardiner C. 1930. "The diffusion of stock ownership in the United States." *The Quarterly Journal of Economics* 44:561–600.

Michie, Ranald C. 1986. "The London and New York stock exchanges, 1850–1914." *The Journal of Economic History* 46:171–187.

Montgomery, Robert H. ed. 1927. *Financial Handbook*. 11th ed. New York: The Ronald Press Company.

Navin, Thomas R., and Marian V. Sears. 1955. "The rise of a market for industrial securities." *The Business History Review* 29:105–138.

"NETFOLIO University: Dividend Yield."
http://www.netfolio.com/info/netfolio_university/dividend_yield.jsp

Preinreich, Gabriel A. D. 1932. "Stock yields, stock dividends and inflation." *The Accounting Review* 7:273–289.

Sage, George H. 1937. "Dividend policy and business contingencies." *Harvard Business Review* 15:245–252.

Sloan, Laurence H. 1931. *Everyman and His Common Stocks.* New York: McGraw-Hill Book Company, Inc.

Smith, Edgar Lawrence. 1959. *Common stocks and business cycles.* New York: The William-Frederick Press.

Snowden, Kenneth A. 1987. "American stock market development and performance, 1871–1929." *Explorations in Economic History* 24:327–353.

Snowden, Kenneth A. 1990. "Historical returns and security market development, 1872–1925." *Explorations in Economic History* 27:381–420.

Van Strum, Kenneth S. 1925. *Investing in Purchasing Power.* New York: Barron's.

Van Strum, Kenneth S. 1927. *Forecasting Stock Market Trends.* New York: Barron's.

Warren, Edward H. 1923. "Safeguarding the creditors of corporations." *Harvard Law Review* 36:509–547.

White, Eugene N. 1990. "When the ticker ran late: the stock market boom and crash of 1929." In *Crashes and Panics: The Lesson From History.* Eugene N. White, ed., Homewood, IL: Dow Jones-Irwin.

Wilbur, Donald E. 1932. "A study in the policy of dividend stabilization." *Harvard Business Review* 10:373–381.

Williston, Samuel. 1888a. "History of the law of business corporations before 1800." *Harvard Law Review* 2:105–124.

Williston, Samuel. 1888b. "History of the law of business corporations before 1800 (continued)." *Harvard Law Review* 2:149–166.

Wilson, Jack W., and Charles P. Jones. 1987. "A Comparison of Annual Common Stock Returns: 1871–1925 and 1926–1985." *The Journal of Business* 60:239–258.

# CHAPTER 4

# 200 Years of Dividend Practices

## 4.1 INTRODUCTION

At the genesis of the modern corporation, dividends were liquidating dividends. The enterprise was a ship, financed by a group of investors, cargo of which and the vessel itself were sold at the successful completion of the voyage. The proceeds of the sale were distributed equally among the partners of the venture. The sale not only solved the problem of accounting for income, but also eliminated any question of measurement of value by the market place. Naturally, this convenient solution had its economic drawbacks. Specifically, that the nexus of contracts—experience and managerial skill that could have been accumulated, had the enterprise continued—was lost.

Once this shortcoming was realized, the idea of the going concern was quickly espoused. Accordingly, professional stewards were retained and the chain stretching from owners to managers was lengthened. One necessary outcome of this development has been the retention of some or all of the periodic earnings of the business to finance future activities. This, of course, created the problem of measuring income, both for tax as well as for distribution purposes, a problem with which the accounting profession is still grappling.

It also created the concept and use of a "market" that is supposedly better able to measure the "true" value of the business than accountants can. This, too, developed its own set of problems with which modern finance's research has been grappling since the early 1950s.[1]

---

[1] Issues related to the paradigm of market efficiency (aka modern finance) in its three forms: informational, allocational, and liquidity efficiency. In fact, the very subject of dividends and dividend policy is a subset of the as of yet unresolved problems of modern finance.

Corporate dividend payments to shareholders began more than 300 years ago and have continued as an acceptable, if not required, activity of corporate managers, despite the apparent contradictory economic nature of these payments. As noted at the beginning of Chapters 2 and 3, the original payments to joint stock company shareholders in Holland and Great Britain were liquidating distributions of capital and profit that terminated the joint stock enterprise's existence. Later payments were limited to the net profits of the undertakings that permitted a more efficient use of investment capital and gave the firms perpetual existence.

Over the better part of the late 20th century the payments have become symbolic liquidations solely determined by managers; dividends are paid to shareholders from a combination of profits from the current period and earnings retained in previous profitable periods. Although largely symbolic, the continued importance of a consistent and significant dividend payment to maintain shareholder contentment remains a managerial priority.

It seems that the corporation progressed from its original liquidating dividend, to distribution of all profits (retaining some capital), to a token dividend payment, the size and frequency of which are left to the discretion of management. At the same time, alternative schemes of distribution (such as repurchase of stock, green mail, etc.) and quasi-distributions (such as stock dividends and splits) have been devised and accepted. These subjects are discussed in later chapters of this book.

Clearly, this evolution could not have occurred in a vacuum. It has been paralleled, if not precipitated, by the systematic removal of the owners from management, i.e., the separation of control from ownership. Hence, it is not totally illogical to presume that the payment of dividends, especially those that are undoubtedly symbolic (because of their magnitude relative to the value of the share itself), is a ritual performed by managers to show good faith toward the owners.

Adam Smith is perhaps the first to express this view. He thus became the forerunner of the school of thought that defines dividends as "hush money to the shareholder."

> This court, indeed, is frequently subject, in many respects, to the control of a general court of proprietors. But the greater part of those proprietors seldom pretend to understand anything of the business of the company, and when the spirit of faction happens not to prevail among them, give themselves no trouble about it, but receive contentedly such half-year or yearly dividend as the directors think proper to make to them. The directors of such companies, however, being the managers of other people's money rather than their own, it cannot well be expected that they should watch over it with the same anxious vigilance with which the partners in a private copartnery frequently watch over their own (Smith, 1937, p. 264).

The importance of significant dividend payments to maintain shareholder satisfaction was recognized early by corporate managers. Less than ethical practices were often used to continue dividend payments, and the payments were often paid solely from retained earnings during unprofitable periods of company operations.[2] The lack of financial information available to investors in the late 19th and early 20th centuries magnified the importance of a history of consistent dividend payments. Shareholders and analysts often used this information as their primary input when valuing firms.

If one embraces the "hush-money" point of view, one cannot escape the inevitable conclusion that today there is no pure economic rationale to dividends. Yet, it is also an inescapable fact that the market reacts positively to dividend increase announcements and negatively to announcements of reduction or elimination of dividends, which is generally referred to today in academia as "the dividend puzzle" (Black, 1976, 1990). Ironically, the laymen press used the metaphor, precisely to the opposite, the disappearance of dividend as was reported toward the end of the previous century (*The Economist*, 1999).

One must also not forget that there are institutional consequences for *not* following a certain dividend policy, such as removal from legal listings, analysts' reports, and "buy" "sell" recommendations that may influence dividend policy decisions. Black (1990) mentioned some of these as reasons for the love of dividends by shareholders, implying that the "rationality" is a conditioned reflex, so to speak. These repercussions, although not directly related to any economic logic posited thus far in the academic literature, are certain to influence the price of the stock. Consequently, these institutional aspects turn, as much as it may sound paradoxical, to an "economic logic," influencing, most notably perhaps, short-term outcomes, a knee-jerk reaction of sort. However, as already noted at the end of the previous chapter, "trends" of dividend policy are influenced temporarily and spatially.

Quite puzzling as well is the emergence of well-recognizable patterns of dividend policy in the course of the present century. The phenomenon of "income stocks" (mostly public utilities and certain car manufacturers) that pay high cash dividends, fixed dollar dividends, fixed payout of earnings and steadily increasing dividends, and industry "norms" are all among the recognizable patterns. The wealth maximization principle that has been the foundation of the majority of the academic models of dividends, because of its ideological base of the methodology of financial economics, cannot account for such details. It follows then that universal applicability is a misleading, and delusional, presumption. Nor can or will these models accommodate a rationale that is not purely economic, or inconsistent with the wealth maximization principle.

At the opposite end of the spectrum are firms that either never paid dividends from the start (many of the new internet firms) or quit paying dividends

---

[2]During the S&L crisis of the late 1980s early 1990s, banks were still paying dividends on their way to bankruptcy court.

altogether. Over all, as *The Economist* (1999) reported, dividend payments declined across the board. Strangely, this is what *The Economist* now calls "the dividend puzzle," although academe got used to calling the very payment of dividends the same name.

Five decades of academic research set about unraveling the mystery of dividends and, to a much smaller extent, dividend policy, without much success. Sections II and III of this book examine this research, what it accomplished, and what remains still a mystery.

## 4.2 DIVIDEND PATTERNS

From liquidating dividends to token (perhaps hush money) dividends and anything in between, this is the story of dividend patterns that evolved during emergence of the modern corporation.

As stated earlier, the corporation originated as a single venture. At its termination, the enterprise was liquidated and the proceeds were divided among the "shareholders" in proportion to their original investment in the venture. Soon, it was realized, however, that there is real economic value in retaining the expertise and experience that were gained in every voyage. The "cost" of this retention had been the accounting and other problems associated with measuring income and distributing capital among the owners in such a way that it would not adversely affect the total value of their holding. It also created an ever-widening gap between the owner and the manager, a gap that necessarily required bridging with tokens and gestures of reliability.

Although the payment of dividends in any fashion other than a liquidating dividend instead of total liquidation is still liquidation, however partial, corporate managers quickly realized that shareholders like dividends, and they lent a hand in conditioning them to like dividends, not unlike getting babies "hooked" on sugar as a pacifier.

Throughout most of this century, the major promoters of the notion that dividends are good for the shareholders were financial analysts and other financial mavens. This in turn created two not necessarily desirable patterns: the use of dividends for fraudulence as a means to increase confidence in otherwise failing management and the "love" of dividends by the shareholder. Both of these patterns are at variance with the notion of economic savvy/rationality that, sadly, is an axiom on which most of the academic models that had been posited to explain dividends as a practice, were based.

Nevertheless, some clear patterns of dividend payments emerged, especially in the second half of the 20th century. The most commonly practiced pattern is the fixed quarterly amount, turning common stock, at least partially, into a fixed income instrument. Several studies, starting as early as Lintner (1956), found that management is reluctant to increase dividends unless they feel that they can support the increase indefinitely in the future.

Another distinct pattern, practiced by much fewer firms, is the constant-earning payout ratio. This, of course, is necessarily an unequal amount paid each quarter, and sometimes translates to no dividends at all. This pattern resembles a fixed-income security with a minimum nominal yield, which may increase if income is higher than expected, not unlike an income bond.

The liquidating dividend, one of the so-called "shark repellents," to discourage corporate takeover, is another "pattern." In this case, the firm pays its shareholders an unusually high cash payment, which it cannot possibly maintain, in order to drain out cash that might have made it an attractive target for takeover in the first place.

Then, there is the pattern of no dividend. Although it is not a new practice, it is becoming popular with the new era of internet stocks. These stocks sell for an incredibly high P/E multiple, yet either they do not have the cash to pay dividends or they reinvest their earnings into growth opportunities, real or imaginary.

Later chapters of this book return to these patterns in the framework of academic theories that evolved around them, or attempt to rationalize them.

## 4.3 DIVIDEND REINVESTMENT PLANS (DRIPs)

One of the most fascinating developments regarding dividend-paying patterns is the emergence of dividend reinvestment plans (DRIPs). The idea is to give the shareholder an option to reinvest cash dividends (declared for the quarter) in the stock of the firm. The shareholder, however, is responsible for the payment of income tax, as if the dividend has been actually received. By their mere existence, in a practical sense, DRIPs are the empirical refutation of the bird-in-the-hand models (Tables 4.1 and 4.2).

DRIPs have their roots in the late 1920s and 1930s, offered first by mutual funds. The first exchange-listed firm to develop a formal dividend reinvestment plan was the Lehman Corporation in 1957. Since then, DRIPs became popular and today we have over 1500 DRIPs or dividend purchase plans, representing all walks of life in corporate America. Extensive literature about DRIPs can be found on the web. The best-known web sources of information are www.dripcentral.com, www.dripinvestor.com, and www.netstockdirect.com.

In practicality, the DRIP allows small investors to use dollar averaging, bypassing the broker and saving on possibly high brokerage fees. There are several more advantages to DRIPs both to the shareholder and to the firm, which are discussed in more detail in a later chapter. Suffice to say here that not all DRIPs

Table 4.1

**DRIP Characteristics by Industry Groups**[a]

| DRIP characteristics | Numbers by group | | | Total |
| --- | --- | --- | --- | --- |
| | Industry | Financial | Utilities | |
| Management | 119 | 51 | 30 | 200 |
| Agent | 3 | 11 | 12 | 26 |
| Company | 116 | 40 | 18 | 174 |
| No load | 119 | 51 | 30 | 200 |
| Yes | 4 | 0 | 5 | 9 |
| No | 115 | 51 | 25 | 191 |
| Discount | 119 | 51 | 29 | 199 |
| Yes | 15 | 13 | 3 | 31 |
| No | 104 | 38 | 26 | 168 |
| Fees | 119 | 51 | 30 | 200 |
| Yes | 91 | 36 | 26 | 153 |
| No | 28 | 15 | 4 | 47 |
| Safekeeping | 119 | 51 | 30 | 200 |
| Yes | 119 | 51 | 30 | 140 |
| No | 119 | 51 | 30 | 60 |
| Foreign | 119 | 51 | 30 | 200 |
| Accept | 84 | 30 | 24 | 138 |
| Does not accept | 35 | 21 | 6 | 62 |

[a]From Alexander (1994).

---

Table 4.2

**Sample Variables and DRIP Factors**

| Financial data variables | DRIP characteristic factors |
| --- | --- |
| Last dividend | Management |
| ROE |   1 = Agent-administered plan |
| NS/CA |   2 = Company-administered plan |
| NS/TA | OCP (purchase of additional shares) |
| P/E ratio |   1 = No |
| Profit margin |   2 = Yes |
| $SG_5$ | Discount |
| CA/CL |   1 = Company does offer a discount |
| EPS |   2 = Company does not offer a discount |
| ROA | Fees |
| NWC |   1 = Company does charge fees |
| LTD/EQ |   2 = Company does not charge fees |
| RP | Safekeeping |
| IO |   1 = Company does allow safekeeping |
| BETA |   2 = Company does not allow safekeeping |
| ME/BE | Accept foreign |
| MV |   1 = Company does allow foreign |
| |   2 = Company does not allow foreign |
| | Enrollment |
| |   1 = Current shareholders only |
| |   2 = Anyone |

share the same advantages, and, more often than not, certain fees apply that put into question the real savings, vis-à-vis brokerage costs.

In addition, DRIPs have their disadvantages, too, the most obvious of which is the tax obligation. Although it seems that there are some real and imaginary monetary benefits to DRIPs, the real cash outflow of taxes is indisputably present. Because of the intriguing theoretical and practical aspects of DRIPs, we will return to this topic in great detail, including our original research in the next chapter of this book.

## 4.4 CONCLUSION

Throughout the history of the modern corporation, dividend payment patterns and trends emerged. Some of the patterns disappeared and they are the relics of a past that no longer have any significance in the American corporate world of the 21st century. Some trends, as discussed in this chapter, although alternately appearing and disappearing, were more than ephemeral. The fact remains, however, that the majority of dividend models developed by academia so far and many of the explanations of the dividend rationale remain divorced from the evolution that is part and parcel of the dividend "puzzle."

For instance, one of the academic favorites of dividend rationale is the so-called signaling hypothesis. That is, firms signal their good fortunes to the market by increasing dividend payments. However, if we observe trends and reversals of trends (which we may call "runs"), what is really the signal? And what is the meaning of the signal at least to some of the real or potential investors? Is it really a signal of good fortunes, the knowledge of which would not be forthcoming to the shareholder and the market *sans* a dividend increase, or is it a signal that the firm reaches a point where it has to liquidate at least some of its earning assets because it cannot do any better?

The following chapters discuss this and many other issues that both intrigued academe and left it behind and detached without a clear-cut answer.

## REFERENCES

Black, Fisher. 1976. "The dividend puzzle." *The Journal of Portfolio Management* 2:5–8.

Black, Fisher. 1990. "Why firms pay dividends." *The Financial Analysts Journal* 46:5.

*The Economist.* 1999. "Shares without the other bit." November 20:93.

Lintner, John. 1956. "Optimal dividends and corporate growth under uncertainty." *The Quarterly Journal of Economics* 78:49–95.

Smith, Adam. 1937. *The Wealth of Nations.* New York: Random House, Inc.

# CHAPTER 5

## Dividend Reinvestment Plans:
## A Puzzle within the Puzzle

### 5.1 INTRODUCTION

One of the fascinating developments regarding dividend-paying patterns is the emergence of dividend reinvestment plans (DRIPs).

DRIPs have their roots in the late 1920s.[1] According to Cherin and Hanson (1995), the first DRIPs were developed by mutual funds in the 1920s and 1930s. The first exchange-listed firm to develop a formal DRIP was the Lehman Corporation in 1957. Since then, many other financial services industry members have followed suit. In 1968, Allegheny Power Corporation was the first nonfinancial firm to institute a DRIP. Citibank administered the DRIP. Soon, several other public utilities followed suit.

At the time of this writing, more than 1500 firms with DRIPs, representing all walks of life in corporate America, are listed on the internet.[2] In practicality, the DRIP allows small investors to use dollar averaging, bypassing the broker and saving on possibly high brokerage fees.

Theoretically, the mere existence of DRIPs raises serious doubt that the firm exists solely for the purpose of providing dividends to the shareholder. The growing popularity and proliferation of DRIPs also quickly dispense with the plethora of academic bird-in-the-hand models discussed earlier in this book. The mere exis-

---

[1]Much of the discussion in this section is based on Cherin and Hanson (1995) and on an unpublished, graduate research paper by Kim Edwards.

[2]The best-known web sources for information on DRIPs are www.dripcentral.com, www.dripinvestor.com, and www.netstockdirect.com.

tence of DRIPs is a clear indication that there cannot be a universal law regarding dividends, both as a phenomenon and as a matter of corporate policy.

From the point of view of the shareholder, here are some of the more obvious positive features of DRIPs:

- Give investors the opportunity not only to reinvest dividends, but also to make "optional cash purchases" (within limits)—"optional cash payment" or "stock purchase" plans.
- Price shares bought with reinvested dividends and, in some cases, with optional cash contributions, at a discount of anywhere from 3 to 10% (with a mode of 5%) off the market price—"discount" plans or DDRIPs.
- Allow bondholders and preferred stockholders to reinvest coupon payments and preferred dividends in the firm's stock.
- Permit customers of the business to contribute through billing systems and savings accounts.
- Have all associated transaction costs paid by the firm—the so-called "subsidized" plans.
- Allow participants to buy fractional shares.
- Meet reinvestment demand through buying shares on the open market ("market purchase" plans).
- Meet reinvestment demand through the reissue of treasury stock.
- Meet reinvestment demand through the issue of new shares ("original issue" or "new issue" plans). Frequently, the issue price is determined by averaging the closing prices for the 5 days preceding the date of reinvestment.
- Enable investors to reinvest part of their dividends and take part in cash ("split-share" plans).
- Provide safekeeping facilities for stockholders who want to leave their shares with the plan administrator.
- Offer a "book-entry" structure that eliminates the need for certificates as evidence of ownership and facilitates the administration of a DRIP (Cherin and Hanson, p. 60).

As shown later, not all plans share the same advantages, and, more often than not, certain fees apply that put into question the real savings, vis-à-vis brokerage costs.

Cherin and Hanson (1995), citing several sources, count the following as attractive features of DRIPs for a would-be shareholder.

- The benefits of "forced" dollar-cost averaging. Cash dividends are conveniently reinvested at regular intervals.
- Compounded growth each time dividends are reinvested.
- Low-cost participation. Buying stock through a DRIP is less expensive than buying it through a broker because economies of scale are

employed when it is bought through the plan agent. Furthermore, in general, the firm bears the brokerage and administrative costs that an investor would normally pay to acquire shares.

- The ability to begin or end participation at any time.
- Full investment of funds. DRIPs accommodate the full use of funds through the ownership of fractional shares.
- Shares sold at a discount. Some plans offer participants a discount (5% is the most common) on shares purchased with dividends, and, at times, additional cash. Obviously, the investor can purchase more stock with available funds.
- Simple record keeping. The plan administrator/agent, usually a bank, sends the investor periodic statements cataloging all plan transactions.
- Tax information and custodial service.
- No gaps between dividend payment and reinvestment and no chances for consumption (i.e., forced savings) (p. 61).

The story of finance, like everything else related to *human behavior*, involves the bundling of the liked with the disliked, the preferred with what should be avoided, and the good with the bad. DRIPs are no exception, and they do have their disadvantages.

The most obvious disadvantage of the DRIP from the shareholder's point of view is the tax aspect. Taxes must be paid, out of pocket, for the reinvested dividends, and records must be kept concerning the timing and purchase price of the shares. Also, although many plans exclude certain shareholders, either by choice (those who prefer cash) or by rule (e.g., foreign investors), all shareholders nevertheless share the costs of administering the plan.

Advantages for the firm include:

- Increased retention of internally generated capital.
- The reduced cost of financing through savings of flotation costs.
- Investor loyalty through the development of a steady ownership base.

Disadvantages of the DRIP are the costs associated with administration of the DRIP, dilution of earnings, and possible lack of participation.

Technically, there are three types of DRIP plans:

1. Treasury DRIPs that are designed to sell shares from the firm's treasury stock.
2. Market DRIPs that are set up as a service to shareholders and provide no "new" cash to the firm.
3. Combination DRIPs.

Treasury and combination DRIPs require the issuance of a prospectus.

The characteristics that differentiate one DRIP from another, and *de facto* determine the real economic cost/value of the DRIP, are:

- Discounts (if any) offered.
- The fees charged.
- Optional share-purchase provisions (OSP).
- Shareholders' status.
- Management of the plan (inside or outside).
- Enrollment requirements.
- The availability of safekeeping.

Because the major advantage of the DRIP is the possibility of bypassing the financial intermediary, almost all DRIPs offer an OSP. OSPs may vary, however, as to the amount that can be invested (which can be from $50 to $150,000) and the time interval in which the shareholder can exercise it (weekly, monthly, quarterly, etc.).

Most plans do not charge a "commission" per se; however, many charge "fees" under different pretenses. These fees can be for dividend reinvestment, for optional cash investment, for certificate issuance, for the selling of shares, or for termination of an account.

The fees for dividend reinvestment are usually either set as a percentage of the reinvestment amount or as a fixed dollar amount. The usual percentage ranges from 3 to 10%. The most common dollar amount is between $3 and $5. The optional cash investment fees range from $0.025 to $2.50 per share plus the broker's commission. The most common range for the fees on certificate issuance is $5.00 to $15.00. The selling fee may be either the broker's commission or a fixed amount that can range from $0.03 to $15.00 per share. The charge for the termination of an account can range from $0.03 to $2.50 to $25 per share plus the broker's commission (Alexander, 1994, p. 11).

Some plans offer discounts that can be on either dividend reinvestment or OSP. Commonly, discounts range between 3 and 5%. As strange as it may seem, some plans apply fees and, at the same time, provide discounts. The variation of fees/discounts, and their respective magnitude, brings into question the real opportunity costs of buying the shares via the DRIP or through a deep-discount broker or day trading on the internet.

An outside third party administers the majority of DRIPs. The administrators are usually banks, most notably the Bank of Boston, First Chicago Trust Co., RM Trust Co., and Bank of New York.

Enrollment requirements cover current shareholders or anyone who wishes to invest in the firm. Some of the bigger firms that allow "open enrollment," more recently referred to as dividend purchase plans (or DPP), and in the parlance of Carlson (1995), no-load stocks, include AFLAC, Dial Corp., Exxon, Johnson Controls, Texaco, and Mobil. These, however, require a minimum investment of $50 to $1000.

The October 1998 issue of *Kiplinger's Personal Finance Magazine*, in an article titled, "Who Shot DRIPs?" lists 25 *investor-unfriendly* companies, whose DPP is inordinately costly to the small investor. For current investors, only DRIPs may require a minimum of shares to be held by the investor before joining the plan.

The costs associated with either the DRIP or the DPP are on the buy, on the sell, or on both sides. In many instances, buying the shares in either plan is low cost or no cost, but selling the shares may be extremely costly. For instance, the cost to sell $250 of Wal-Mart shares is $20.41, in excess of 8%.

## 5.2 DRIPs LITERATURE

The popular, or practitioner, literature on DRIPs is quite voluminous. It is dedicated to the discussion of (mostly) the benefits and (some of) the disadvantages of the DRIP from the point of view of the individual investor. The reader interested in good reviews of this literature should look at Carson (1992, 1995, 1996).

The academic literature is scant on DRIPs because its thrust, in one way or another, is to fit the phenomenon into the straitjacket of one or another cherished, or currently in vogue, dividend theory. Bierman (1997), however, lumps DRIPs together with the "dividend puzzle," using the idiom as it was originally intended by Black (1976).

A convenient taxonomy of the academic literature puts DRIPs in four categories: (1) event studies, (2) Raising new capital/rights offerings, (3) agency costs/problems, and (4) capital structure.

### 5.2.1 EVENT STUDIES

Peterson *et al.* (1987) studied the effect of SEC filings for new shares by utilities before May 1981, utilities after July 1981, which received preferential tax treatment,[3] and nonutilities. They found no significant average abnormal returns for nonutility firms. However, they found significant abnormal returns for before and tax law change utilities; the former negative and the latter positive on the day after registration for the plan.

Chang and Nichols (1992) also studied the effect of the 1981 tax legislation. Their evidence is consistent with Peterson *et al.* (1987) results regarding qualifying utilities. Chang and Nichols (1992) also found increased DRIP participation for qualifying utility firms after the tax reform.

---

[3]Internal Revenue Code Section 305(e) created tax deferral for DRIPs of qualifying utilities.

In contrast with Peterson *et al.* (1987), Allen (1991) found negative reaction to the announcement of DRIP initiation for industrial firms.

We must emphasize that event studies are very "fragile" in the sense that it is not uncommon to find contradictory evidence, given the model from which "abnormal returns" are derived.[4] Therefore, their results should not be taken unheeded.

## 5.2.2 RAISING NEW CAPITAL/RIGHTS OFFERINGS

Finnerty (1989) and Scholes and Wolfson (1989) argued the importance of the DRIP in the process of raising new capital. DRIPs provide an investment banking function in raising additional capital for a firm. The method is less costly than through traditional investment banker methods.

Eckbo and Masulis (1992) studied a large sample of equity offerings via rights offerings and standbys. They found that 54% adopted new issue DRIPs between 1973 and 1981, whereas only 28% of firm commitment issuers used new issue DRIPs. They concluded that DRIPs are tantamount to periodic rights issues of new shares. Eckbo and Masulis surmised that the wide use of DRIPs by firms that formerly utilized rights offering/standbys will lead to the disappearance of equity offerings through rights offering/standby methods.

## 5.2.3 AGENCY COSTS/PROBLEMS

Saporoschenko (1996) argued that firms with growth potential are more likely to use treasury and combined DRIPs because of their need for outside funding. Regarding monitoring, firms that issue treasury and combined plan DRIPs bypass outside monitoring, part and parcel of other equity types. With respect to information asymmetries, Saporoschenko pointed out that

> . . . since treasury and combined DRIP's are comparable to rights offering, firms issuing DRIP's should be confident of high subscription rates (this may be a reason why some firms, offer discounts of shares purchased through DRIP's) and relative undervaluation.

[4]Abnormal returns are nothing else but error terms of a regression structure in which the rate of return on a stock is the dependent variable. As such, they are a dustbin of many "effects" and/or misspecification of the theoretical model from which they are derived or the violation of one or more of the basic assumptions of the regression itself. Also, the periodicity of the returns and the pinpointing of the date in which the phenomenon studied becomes public knowledge are critical for the results. In fact, event studies are a cottage industry in which academics see, unfortunately, a quick and easy way to gain a publication record or to prove a cherished theory/hypothesis.

These conjectures are based on the validity of the findings of Eckbo and Masulis (1992) and Smith (1977) that the lower direct flotation costs make rights offerings a substantially less expensive method of equity issuance than going through an underwriter/investment banker.

Saporoschenko (1996) also looked at the small firms effect. He surmised that smaller firms should benefit more from the alleviation of informational asymmetries via the use of DRIPs.

Steinbart and Swanson (1998) studied the reasons for firms amending their DRIPs to allow investors to make initial purchases of their stock. Their study sought to clarify if firms offer no-load DRIPs for economic or agency purposes. Through telephone interviews, investor relations' representatives of firms were asked for the reasons why they were selling "no-load" DRIPs. The prospectuses of these firms were also studied to find out the source of the shares that would be issued through "no-load" DRIPs. Results showed that firms offer "no-load" DRIPs to broaden their shareholder base. The authors concluded that the objective of broadening shareholder base is consistent with agency-related explanations.

### 5.2.4 CAPITAL STRUCTURE

Dubofsky and Bierman (1988) found significant positive returns for discount DRIPs, which returns they attribute to the firm's efforts to move toward a less risky (less levered) capital structure. This is consistent with the results obtained by Perumpral *et al.* (1991), who examined the announcement month of DRIPs. Dubofsky and Bierman (1988) also asserted that internally generated capital (in stark contrast to the braggadocio of the free cash flow hypothesis) and reduced transaction costs created by the DRIP convey positive information. Also, the net effect is reduced brokerage costs and other transaction fees.

## 5.3 DRIP CHARACTERISTICS

As stated earlier, DRIPs differ with respect to a number of distinct factors. Also, in recent years a new form of the DRIP, called the direct purchase plan (DPP), has evolved. This form is *de facto*, a circumvention of the original intention and logic of the DRIP by making the DRIP more expensive to the small investor. The distinction between the DRIP and the DPP, however, manifests itself only in the values that one or another factor in the plan, either DRIP or DPP, have.

The remainder of this section shows some preliminary results from ongoing research by Chiang, Frankfurter, and Kosedag comparing firms that have a DRIP

**Table 5.1**

**DRIP Characteristics/Definitions**

| Number | Item | Value |
|---|---|---|
| | Covenants | |
| 1 | MININSH = minimum initial shares required | Quantity |
| 2 | CASHD = cash dividends | Binary; yes = 1 |
| 3 | DRIOPT = dividend reinvestment option | Binary; yes = 1 |
| 4 | IRA = IRA option | Binary; yes = 1 |
| 5 | OCP = optional cash purchase | Binary; yes = 1 |
| 6 | ACH = direct debit from bank | Binary; yes = 1 |
| 7 | DISC = discount | Binary; yes = 1 |
| 8 | LAH = loans against holding | Binary; yes = 1 |
| 9 | AF = open to/accept foreigners | Binary; yes = 1 |
| 10 | ADR = Non-U.S. deposit receipt | Binary; yes = 1 |
| 11 | RSA = requires special affiliation | Binary; yes = 1 |
| 12 | MINOCP = minimum optional cash purchase | $/year |
| 13 | MAXOCP = maximum optional cash purchase | $/year |
| | Fees | |
| 14 | OCP Fee | $ amount |
| 15 | PUCOM = commission—purchase | $/share |
| 16 | SALESCOM = commission—sales | $/share |
| 17 | SALESFEE = sales fee | $/share |
| 18 | TERMFEE = termination fee | $/share |
| 19 | ENROLFEE = enrollment Fee | $ amount |
| 20 | SKINSUR = safekeeping/insurance | $/share |
| 21 | NSF = not sufficient funds | $/share |
| | Additional factors | |
| 22 | PTYPE = plan type | Registered dividend reinvestment plan = 1; anyone = 0 |
| 23 | E = enrollment | Current shareholders only = 1; anyone = 0 |
| 24 | MNG = management type | Company-administrated plan = 1; agent-administered plan = 0 |

and firms that do not have a DRIP or a DPP (what we will refer to subsequently as no-DRIP firms). The reader should note that this material is both preliminary and proprietary, and it is included here by permission of the authors of the study. Thus, quoting these results should be strictly with the written permission of the aforementioned authors.

The study involves a random sample of 214 DRIP firms. In the project, 24 factors are presented, which were found for one or more firms in this particular sample. The different DRIP factors/conditions are shown in Table 5.1.

Table 5.1 shows the factor definitions and the factor names that are used in the study, the possible values these factors can take, and any additional expla-

**Table 5.2**

**DRIP Firms Descriptive Statistics**

| Number | Factor | Number of observations | Minimum | Maximum | Mean | Standard deviation |
|--------|--------|------------------------|---------|---------|------|--------------------|
| 1 | MININSH | 163 | 1 | 100 | 2.8098 | 9.8417 |
| 2 | CSHDIV | 214 | 0 | 1 | 93.93% | 23.94% |
| 3 | DRIOPT | 214 | 0 | 1 | 96.73% | 17.83% |
| 4 | IRA | 214 | 0 | 1 | 6.54% | 24.78% |
| 5 | OCP | 214 | 0 | 1 | 95.79% | 20.12% |
| 6 | ACH | 214 | 0 | 1 | 21.50% | 41.18% |
| 7 | DISC | 214 | 0 | 1 | 47.66% | 50.06% |
| 8 | LAH | 214 | 0 | 1 | 0.47% | 6.84% |
| 9 | AF | 214 | 0 | 1 | 97.20% | 16.55% |
| 10 | ADR | 214 | 0 | 1 | 4.67% | 21.16% |
| 11 | RSA | 214 | 0 | 1 | 1.40% | 11.78% |
| 12 | MINOCP | 213 | 0 | $600.00 | $50.56 | $89.74 |
| 13 | MAXOCP | 207 | 0 | $480,000.00 | $52,136.23 | $66,293.22 |
| 14 | OCPFEE | 143 | 0 | $7.50 | $0.58 | $1.54 |
| 15 | PUCOM | 143 | 0 | $0.25 | $0.01 | $0.04 |
| 16 | SALESCOM | 47 | 0 | $0.25 | $0.10 | $0.05 |
| 17 | SALESFEE | 64 | 0 | $15.00 | $7.16 | $5.69 |
| 18 | TERMFEE | 72 | 0 | $15.00 | $2.57 | $5.24 |
| 19 | ENROLFEE | 143 | 0 | $15.00 | $0.87 | $2.74 |
| 20 | SKINSUR | 109 | 0 | $10.00 | $0.33 | $1.46 |
| 21 | NSF | 13 | 0 | $25.00 | $17.69 | $10.33 |
| 22 | PTYPE | 214 | 0 | 1 | 76.17% | 42.71% |
| 23 | E | 163 | 1 | 1 | 100.00% | 0.00% |
| 24 | MNG | 202 | 0 | 1 | 7.43% | 26.28% |

nations if needed. The factors are numbered, arbitrarily, 1–24 for the sake of convenient comparison between Table 5.1 and Table 5.2.

Table 5.2 presents the simple sample statistics of the factors. Note that not all factors are present for each of the 214 DRIP firms in the sample.

The figures in Table 5.2 for the binary factors are in percent form. The figures that represent dollars, either total/year or share, are presented as currency.

It is shown for this sample that over 90% of the DRIP firms

- Pay a cash dividend
- Have dividend reinvestment options
- Extend the possibility of optional cash purchases of the stock
- Open their plan to foreign investors
- Do not have an IRA
- Do not provide loans against the reinvested dividends

- Have no ADR[5] (because they are domestic firms)
- Do not require any special affiliations
- The plan is administered by an agent

Also, almost half the plans offer a discounted share price, and over 75% are registered dividend reinvestment plans.

Fees are just averages, and as such they are quite misleading because one must look at the specific combinations of fees with other factors (such as discounted share price, for instance). The other two factors that are interesting are the figures for the minimum, maximum, and average dollar investment required by OCP. The minimums range from zero to $600 with an average of $50.56, whereas the maximums are from zero to $480,000 with an average of $52,136.23. It seems that some of the OCPs are designed for the large investor who most likely will benefit from bypassing the broker in a large deal.

Chiang, Frankfurter, and Kosedag aim to study financial and market differences, if any, between DRIP and no-DRIP firms with this sample, using accounting and market variables. These variables are, admittedly, arbitrary. However, the very same variables are used, and quite often, in studies that are designed to discover relationships in data when no clear, well-defined, or commonly accepted economic hypotheses are present. The following are the 13 variables studied and their respective definitions.

## VARIABLES AND DEFINITIONS

CASHDIV     The amount of the last dividend paid by the firm.

ROE         Return on equity (net income/total equity) from the firm's balance sheet and income statement.

ROA         Return on assets or return on investment (net income/total assets) from the firm's balance sheet and income statement.

EPS         Earnings per share from the firm's balance sheet and income statement.

PE          Earnings multiple (the ratio of stock price to earnings) from the firm's income statement and the price of the stock at close of the market on 31/12/2001.

NSTA        Asset turnover (net sales/total assets) from the firm's balance sheet and income statement.

NPM         Net profit margin (net income/sales) from the firm's most recent income statement.

CACL        Current ratio (current assets/current liabilities) from the firm's balance sheet.

[5]American depository receipts.

SAGR        Five-year sales growth: $([S_t/S_{t-4}])^{1/5} - 1.0$, where $t = 2001$.

NWC         Net working capital (total current assets less total current liabilities).

LTDEQ       Leverage as of book (long-term debt/total equity) from the firm's balance sheet.

IO          Institutional ownership as a fraction of total ownership.

Beta        The response of the firm's stock price to the market as per the ubiquitous Sharpe (1963) market model.

Data are obtained from COMPUSTAT and represent accounting information and/or market data as of December 31, 2001. Beta is available directly from COMPUSTAT, where it is calculated from 60 monthly observations of rate of return on the firm's stock and the S&P 500 Index.

Chiang, Frankfurter, and Kosedag try to match the DRIP firms with no-DRIP firms by a random selection of size and industry, as close as possible. In this effort, because of missing data or other reasons, not all the factors are present for all the firms initially selected from either the 214 DRIP or the no-DRIP firms. This is why *all* the accounting/market variables have less than 214 observations. In fact, the highest number of pairings is for ROA and NPM (173) and the fewest for PE (68). Regardless, the number of observations is still sufficient to consider the data as representative.

Table 5.3 presents the simple sample statistics of DRIP and no-DRIP firms. For each variable defined, Table 5.3 shows the DRIP values of mean, number of observations, standard deviation, and standard error in the first row and the same values for the no-DRIP firms in the second row. The last column of Table 5.3 is the simple correlation coefficient between the DRIP and the no-DRIP firm for a particular variable. An asterisk marks the simple correlations that are significantly different than zero at the 0.01 level of confidence.

It seems that all significant correlations are positive, with the highest being the correlation of turnover (net sales/total assets), a traditional measure of managerial effectiveness (how many times the total investment in the firm can generate sales).

Next in magnitude of correlation are NWC (0.576) and Beta (0.435) measures of liquidity and operating risk, respectively.

The two negative correlations (ROE = −0.065, ROA = −0.074) do not differ significantly from zero. It is safe to say that the two samples have little in common regarding these two measures of profitability. Positive correlations that do not differ significantly from zero are EPS (0.056) and PE (0.075) which are, interestingly, also traditional measures of profitability. Perhaps then it would be safe to say that as far as profitability is concerned, the two samples do not move in lock steps. It would be interesting to look at the reasons for this lack of co-movement as a prime subject of future inquiry.

**Table 5.3**

**Paired Samples Statistics of DRIP and No-DRIP Firms**

| Variable | Mean | Number of observations | Standard deviation | Standard error of mean | Correlation |
|---|---|---|---|---|---|
| CASHDIV | 0.9981 | 172 | 0.9076 | 0.0692 | 0.337★ |
|  | 0.7805 |  | 0.7054 | 0.0538 |  |
| ROE | 9.2002 | 172 | 18.2611 | 1.3924 | −0.065 |
|  | 3.1227 |  | 60.1170 | 4.5839 |  |
| ROA | 2.7826 | 173 | 4.9324 | 0.3750 | −0.074 |
|  | 2.0370 |  | 6.3833 | 0.4853 |  |
| EPS | 0.9774 | 82 | 2.6863 | 0.2967 | 0.056 |
|  | 1.3741 |  | 3.3371 | 0.3685 |  |
| PE | 26.3009 | 68 | 44.5266 | 5.3996 | 0.075 |
|  | 30.0834 |  | 54.6549 | 6.6279 |  |
| NSTA | 0.6625 | 171 | 0.6709 | 0.0513 | 0.688★ |
|  | 0.6410 |  | 0.6908 | 0.0528 |  |
| NPM | 9.2787 | 173 | 14.8661 | 1.1303 | 0.316★ |
|  | 15.0702 |  | 123.1780 | 9.3651 |  |
| CACL | 1.3030 | 103 | 0.7202 | 0.0710 | 0.294★ |
|  | 1.4606 |  | 1.0186 | 0.1004 |  |
| SAGR | 0.1323 | 147 | 0.1412 | 0.0116 | 0.317★ |
|  | 0.1659 |  | 0.1814 | 0.0150 |  |
| NWC | 196.9052 | 103 | 1548.8971 | 152.6174 | 0.576★ |
|  | 112.9585 |  | 1103.8587 | 108.7664 |  |
| LTDEQ | 1.0315 | 169 | 0.8735 | 0.0672 | 0.370★ |
|  | 1.1328 |  | 1.3321 | 0.1025 |  |
| IO | 0.5140 | 87 | 0.2611 | 0.0280 | 0.278★ |
|  | 0.4705 |  | 0.2800 | 0.0300 |  |
| BETA | 0.5166 | 107 | 0.4502 | 0.0435 | 0.435★ |
|  | 0.5777 |  | 0.5258 | 0.0508 |  |

★Significantly different than 0 at the 0.01 level.

When one compares the means of these four variables, one finds that while the DRIP firms have higher figures for both ROE and ROA, the opposite holds for EPS and PE.

Chiang, Frankfurter, and Kosedag are also studying the statistical significance in the differences between DRIP and no-DRIP firms for each one of the 13 variables. They test the null hypothesis, given the number of degrees of freedom, assuming unequal variances for the two types of firms, that the differences between the two means for DRIP and no-DRIP firms is zero [see Mason *et al.* (1999), pp. 329–330].

The details of their findings are not presented here. We only report that they find that the null hypothesis, given this sample, can be rejected only for CASHDIV at the 0.01 (probability 0.003) or less level and for SAGR at the 0.05

(probability 0.035) or less level. With respect to all other variables, the two types of firms are not different whether they have a DRIP (or DPP) or not.

As one can verify from Table 5.3, the differences for CASHDIV are positive, meaning that the average dividend/share is higher for DRIP firms.

At this juncture, about the only statement we can offer regarding the statistical evidence is that perhaps DRIP firms offer higher dividends, *ceteris paribus*, to entice shareholders to subscribe to a DRIP program. Also, with the exception of these two variables that do not support the null hypotheses, there are no statistically significant differences between DRIP and no-DRIP firms. The latter is a negative finding that opens the door for speculation and criticism, as academic research usually is not eager to report ambiguous results. Nevertheless, in some instances, negative findings are more important than the statistical support one can find for one's cherished theories. Let us not also forget that the lack of statistical significance does not mean a lack of economic significance. Unfortunately, it is not easy to uncover the latter if indeed it does exist.

## 5.4 CONCLUSIONS

Paraphrasing Winston Churchill, dividends are an enigma wrapped in mystery inside a puzzle. DRIPs (and, as shown in Chapter 14, firms that do not pay dividends) add an additional layer to the conundrum. Why do some firms (in fact, quite a few) offer DRIPs and others do not? Why are shareholders willing to utilize a DRIP, assuming a tax liability, when the less expensive alternative would have been to leave the "money on the table" (not asking for a dividend)? The DRIP cuts across the grain of almost all supportable academic theories (as shown in the chapters that follow). Then, how is it that academe is persistent in explaining the dividend phenomenon with the rationality of the *homo economicus* and that complex mathematics fail time after time to show the universal validity of such theories/explanations?

Serious DRIP research is far and between. Perhaps this is because of the scarcity of meaningful data and the lack of an explanation that can be squeezed into the frame of a complex statistical model. Also, in finance, as shown later, methods of research common in other social sciences designed to explore motivation, rather than analyzing market and accounting data, are neither common nor accepted. Nevertheless, perhaps solving the riddle of DRIPs would open the gate to the puzzle in which one could find the answer to the enigma.

## REFERENCES

Allen, Grace Casbum. 1991. "Dividend reinvestment plans: the effects on shareholder wealth and equilibrium security returns." Unpublished dissertation, University of South Carolina–Columbia.

Bierman, Harold, Jr. 1997. "The dividend reinvestment plan puzzle." *Applied Financial Economics.* 7:267–271.

Black, Fisher. 1976. "The dividend puzzle." *The Journal of Portfolio Management* 2:5–8.

Black, Fisher. 1990. "Why firms pay dividends." *The Financial Analysts Journal* 46:5.

Carlson, Charles B. 1992. *Buying Stocks without a Broker.* New York: McGraw-Hill, Inc.

Carlson, Charles B. 1995. *No-Load Stocks—How to Buy Your First Share and Every Share Directly from the Company with No Broker's Fee.* New York: McGraw-Hill, Inc.

Carlson, Charles B. 1996. *Buying Stocks Without a Broker.* New York: McGraw-Hill, Inc.

Chang, Otto H., and Donald R. Nichols. 1992. "Tax incentives and capital structures: the case of the dividend reinvestment plan." *Journal of Accounting Research* 30:109–125.

Cherin, Anthony C., and Robert C. Hanson. 1995. "Dividend reinvestment plans: a review of the literature." *Financial Markets, Institutions and Instruments* 4:59–73.

Dubofsky, David A., and Leonard Bierman. 1988. "The effect of discount dividend reinvestment plan announcements on equity value." *Akron Business and Economic Review* 19:58–68.

Eckbo, B. Espen, and Ronald W. Masulis. 1992. "Adverse selection and the rights offer paradox." *Journal of Financial Economics* 32:293–332.

Edwards, Kim. 1994. "A survey of dividend reinvestment plans (DRIP's). Unpublished research paper. Louisiana State University.

Finnerty, John D. 1989. "New issue dividend reinvestment plans and the cost of equity capital." *Journal of Business Research* 18:127–139.

Mason, D. Robert, Douglas A. Lind, and William G. Marchal. 1999. *Statistical Techniques in Business and Economics.* Boston: McGraw-Hill.

Perumpral, Shalini, Arthur J. Keown, and John Pinkerton. 1991. "Market reaction to the formulation of automatic dividend reinvestment plans." *Review of Business and Economic Research* 26:48–58.

Peterson, Pamela P., David R. Peterson, and Normal H. Moore. 1987. "The adoption of new issue dividend reinvestment plans and shareholder wealth." *The Financial Review* 22:221–232.

Saporoschenko, Andy. 1996. "DRIPS, agency and capital structure issues." Working Paper. University of South Carolina.

Smith, Clifford. 1977. "Alternative methods for raising capital: rights versus underwritten offerings." *Journal of Financial Economics* 5:173–207.

Scholes, Myron S., and Mark A. Wolfson. 1989. "Decentralized investment banking: the case of discount dividend-reinvestment and stock-purchase plans." *Journal of Financial Economics* 17:7–35.

Sheets, Ken. 1998. "Who shot DRIPS?" *Kiplinger's Personal Finance Magazine* October:119–124.

Steinbart, Paul John, and Jane Swanson. 1998. "'No-load' dividend reinvestment plans." *Review of Financial Economics* 7:121–141.

# CHAPTER 6

## Preferred Stock and Dividends: A Revealing Divergence

Two stockbrokers are having lunch every market day at a Wall Street eatery. As usual they talk about stocks, bonds, portfolios, in general, the markets. One day one suddenly says to the other: "Look what fools we are. We are having lunch every day for the last 20 years and all we talk about is our work. Why don't we change the subject if only for once?" "You are absolutely right," says the other, "What would you like to talk about?" "Why, women," replies the first. "What kind of women?" asks the second, "common or preferred?"

The adjective "preferred" in preferred stock implies that the holders of such shares are preferred when it comes to the distribution of income. This would mean that before common stock can receive any cash dividend distribution, the preferred stockholder has to be paid. The distribution to the preferred stock-holder is in the form of dividends, paid by and large quarterly, and it is a fixed percent of face value, which is usually $100. For example, if the preferred carries a 6% dividend, then the shareholder gets $1.50 ($6/4) per quarter.

Most preferred stocks are cumulative, meaning that if dividends were not paid in a quarter, it accumulates for the next quarter, and the quarter after, until all accrued dividends are paid. More importantly, common stock cannot receive dividends until all current and past due dividends were paid to the preferred stockholder.

Today, preferred stock is generally considered as never maturing debt, an American variant of the British consoles. When one looks close to what, *de facto*, preferred stocks amount to, one must realize that, indeed, they are just the tail end of the list of claimants in case of liquidation. The facts—that their par value is important, that they "religiously" pay quarterly dividends, that they do not have rights to residual claims, and that, for most, the dividend payment is fixed[1]—lend them the characteristics of debt. MBA schools started conditioning their students on this notion in the mid-1970s. As these finance graduates climbed the corporate ladder, this notion of preferred stocks being *de facto* perpetual debt gained widespread recognition.

The perception of preferred in some minds, however, is still different. Even the official Financial Accounting Standards Board (FASB) treats them as a kind of equity that is preferred over other types of equity, as far as distribution of income is concerned. This perception is rooted in the historical origins of the preferred stock. Accordingly, it will be useful to survey the emergence, evolution, and use of preferred stock as a financial asset.

## 6.1 THE ORIGINS OF PREFERRED STOCK

Transportation firms in 1836 were the first U.S. corporations to use more than one class of stock (Evans, 1929). Railroad firms needed additional infusions of capital, but poor financial conditions precluded raising additional funds from new investors to complete construction projects. At the same time, current investors were not likely to increase their investments in the firms because of the lack of dividends or capital gains on their earlier investments (Baskin, 1988). The idea for preferred stocks can be traced to Europe where shares with dividend priority or preference already existed (Evans, 1929). Transportation, clothing, brewing, and manufacturing corporations in Great Britain and Germany commonly used multiple classes of stock at this time (Evans, 1931).

States were petitioned by transportation firms for aid for both existing project completion and new projects. In 1836, Maryland legislators introduced a bill providing public funds for projects in return for a guaranteed dividend from the stock issue. The bill passed with the semiannual dividend payments starting 3 years after stock issuance. This initial offering was soon followed by preferred stock issue by other corporations in Maryland and in other states. Some of the issues were designed to convert to common shares on a future date, whereas others remained nonparticipating preferred stocks. One issue also allowed the state to have control over the corporation's board of director appointments (Evans, 1929).

The second stage in the development of preferred stock began in the next decade with the sale of shares to private investors. The promise of regular dividends was exchanged for new funds. Because original equity issue investors had received no dividends from their investments, two classes of shares evolved:

---

[1]The exception is, obviously, the participating preferred, a small minority of all preferred stock outstanding.

a class of stock with guaranteed dividends and another with no guarantee of dividends.

Preferred stocks became an accepted vehicle for emergency fund raising by transportation corporations. Several new railroad-preferred issues began trading between 1843 and 1850. Around 1850, nine different preferred issues were available for purchase by investors. These early guaranteed dividend issues were sold only in time of financial need for expansion or reconstruction of existing lines rather than in initial offerings.

The dividend rate and period of payment varied considerably among issues during this period, but dividend rates of 10 to 12% of the original issue price were not unusual. The high rates of returns were required to secure investor interest and to give original issue purchasers the opportunity to earn a fair return on their total investment by increasing their stake in the firm. The board of directors or shareholders determined the duration of the dividend payment and its level. As a rule, the shares were preferred only until a dividend was paid on all shares, after which the stock was converted to common shares. The dividends were cumulative, nonparticipating,[2] and carried the same voting rights as common shares (Evans, 1929).

Until 1850, preferred-stock was used as a temporary mechanism for increasing capital and was employed almost exclusively by the railroad industry. Issuance of preferred stock before 1850 was invariably associated with financial distress. Bond interest was often paid with the proceeds from preferred stock issues. As the number of preferred issues grew, this finance instrument developed a distinct place in corporate structure with more clearly defined rights and privileges. The uses of issue proceeds and characteristics of the issues also began to diverge. The participation feature became customary in preferred stock issues (Evans, 1931). Still, preferred stock issues were, for the most part, nonparticipating in the event of asset distribution (Stevens, 1937).

In 1855, 10 railroad-preferred issues were trading. In the following 20 years the number had increased to 44 issues. Firms began to issue more than one class of preferred stock. At the same time, several corporations began to limit the rights of preferred shareholders (Evans, 1931).

The last 50 years of the 19th century saw railroad stocks in the United States develop into the predominant public market in corporate securities (Baskin, 1988). In 1871 the Pennsylvania Railroad Corporation used preferred stock to fund its merger activity, which made it at the time the world's largest corporation. The firm strengthened the investor's perception of preferred stock— a security without the negative connotation often associated with fixed income securities and less risky than equity issues. Strangely, the attractive dividend rate and the dependability of equity dividends of preferred stock also helped increase

---

[2]Nonparticipating in extra or windfall income, in addition to the regular dividend.

the public's opinion of common stock as a legitimate investment vehicle (Baskin, 1988).

During the late 19th century, the Pennsylvania Railroad Corporation retained a portion of its earnings. This policy, although not uncommon in the United States, prompted investors in Great Britain to send representatives to meet with corporate management and to express their opinion that all corporate earnings should be distributed to shareholders (Baskin, 1988).

Although the power to issue preferred shares was given expressly by statute, exceptions were not uncommon. The legal system of the time viewed preferred issues as a form of mortgage on company assets (Evans, 1929). Around 1852, a change in the legal process of preferred share issuance occurred as a result of the increase in the number of issues. General acts rather than specific acts allowing preferred stock issue became customary (Evans, 1931).

Paying consistent dividends remained of paramount importance for management during the first half of the 19th century. Less than scrupulous corporate managers continued to resort to fraudulent activities to maintain the payment stream. Limited shareholder liability became a standard during the first half of the century and general statutes governing dividend payments began to be enacted. Preferred stock matured from its original use as a simple alternative capital-raising instrument to a security with its own unique set of characteristics.

## 6.2 THE MATURATION AND SPECIALIZATION OF PREFERRED STOCK

Although not traded actively, preferred stock was important in the emergence of industrial corporations (Navin and Sears, 1955). At the end of the 19th century, preferred stock began to be viewed as an investment distinct from common stock. The fixed dividend rate was likened by most investors to bond interest payments (Stevens, 1936a). The issue of preferred stock allowed repatriation of sunk costs without loss of control and was an inexpensive and safe method for raising funds (Navin and Sears, 1955). Preferred shares were customarily viewed as an investment in the firm's tangible assets, whereas common stock was perceived as a representation of the firm's growth potential (Dewing, 1926).

Before 1904, preferred stock had a preference only to dividend payment. In return for this preference, dividends were limited in amount. Later, issues became cumulative and also had prior claim to assets in the event of bankruptcy (Dewing, 1953). Participation in profits by preferred shares began to appear in corporate charters, especially in railroad and utility-preferred issues (Stevens, 1936b).

The investing public was already familiar with preferred issues from the railroads' long use of the security. Industrial and utility corporations began to use preferred stock to raise capital on more liberal terms in the last decade of the 19th century and the first two decades of the 20th century (Dewing, 1926). Between 1890 and 1893, at least 23 investment-grade preferred issues began trading. These issues were offered predominantly in exchange for existing securities and were sold at par without regard to dividend rate. The majority of the industrial preferred issues traded on the New York Stock Exchange had 7 to 8% cumulative dividend rates (Navin and Sears, 1955).

A second type of preferred stock was offered by railroad, utility, industrial, and financial corporations in reorganization. If the firm was unable to extend current liabilities, current debt was often refunded with noncumulative preferred stock. Although yields and other features were unattractive to debt holders, the alternative of default on the debt by the corporation left the creditor with little choice (Dewing, 1953).

Preferred stock dividends averaged over 8% before 1897 and averaged 6.7% between 1897 and 1920. Industrial corporation-preferred stock had the highest yield, as these firms were more disinclined to use debt financing. Utility corporations issued cumulative preferred stock primarily after the depression of 1903 with yields averaging 6 to 7% (Dewing, 1926). Most shares carried voting rights, but investors viewed the right as superfluous as long as dividends were paid (Stevens, 1938). The voting rights were only exercisable under special charter provisions on many of the issues (Bradley et al., 1984).

The issues distributed by firms in reorganization before 1905 were noncumulative and were habitually issued with lower dividend rates (Berle, 1923). The board of directors uniquely determined if dividends were to be paid on the shares (Stevens, 1936c). Of the 51 preferred stocks traded on the exchange, 32 were issued during corporate reorganizations. Despite the precarious economic conditions surrounding origination of the majority of these issues, dividends were paid on these shares 83% of the time (Spal, 1942).

In 1925, 13% of preferred issues had a dividend rate of 6%, 68% paid 7%, and 13% paid 8% (Dewing, 1926). The yield on preferred stocks had fallen to 4.7% by 1929 (Graham et al., 1962).

Widespread use of preferred stock finance was resurrected after World War II with public utilities largely leading the way. This was so because the expanding public energy companies (utilities) used up all their allowable debt that was constrained by the value of their mortgageable property. Because preferred stock was considered equity and not debt by accounting standards, there was no limit imposed by the regulatory and utility rate-fixing agencies.

This resurgence did not last too long, however, because of two reasons:

1. The realization by financial institution and security rating agencies that preferred stock was just another form of debt.
2. The rapid growth of the equity markets, making common stocks a more attractive investment vehicle.

Although the importance of preferred stock has been declining steadily, one must not forget that preferred stocks are still around. As the dividend payout policies trend toward higher payments at the beginning of the 21st century, a marked change vis-à-vis the opposite trend of the 20th century's *fin de siècle*, perhaps preferred stocks will return as an important financing alternative. But like everything else regarding dividend policy and dividends, one must not be hasty to forecast.

# REFERENCES

Baskin, Jonathon Barron. 1988. "The development of corporate financial markets in Britain and the United States, 1600–1914: overcoming asymmetric information." *The Business History Review* 62:199–237.

Berle, Adolf A. 1923. "Non-cumulative preferred stock." *Columbia Law Review* 23:358–367.

Bradley, Michael, Gregg A. Jarrell, and E. Han Kim. 1984. "On the existence of an optimal capital structure: theory and evidence." *The Journal of Finance* 39:857–880.

Dewing, Arthur Stone. 1953. *The Financial of Corporations*, 5th ed. New York: The Ronald Press Company.

Evans, George Herberton Jr. 1931. "Preferred stock in the United States 1850–1870." *The American Economic Review* 21:56–62.

Graham, Benjamin, David L. Dodd, and Sidney Cottle. 1962. *Security Analysis.* 4th ed. New York: McGraw-Hill.

Navin, Thomas R., and Marian V. Sears. 1955. "The rise of a market for industrial securities." *The Business History Review* 29:105–138.

Spal, Sam G. 1942. "The treatment of non-cumulative preferred shareholders with regard to dividends." *The Journal of Business* 15:248–265.

Stevens, W.H.S. 1936a. "Stockholders' participation in profits." *The Journal of Business* 9:114–132.

Stevens, W.H.S. 1936b. "Stockholders' participation in profits (continued)." *The Journal of Business* 9:210–230.

Stevens, W.H.S. 1936c. "The discretion of directors in the distribution of non-cumulative preferred dividends." *Georgetown Law Journal* 24: 371–396.

Stevens, W.H.S. 1937. "Stockholders' Participation in Assets in Dissolution." *The Journal of Business* 10:46–73.

# PART II

# The Evolution of Academic Research on Dividend Policy

# CHAPTER 7

# Early Academic Thinking and Research

Corporate dividend policy has captured the interest of financial economists for almost 100 years and has been the subject of intensive theoretical modeling and empirical examination by financial economists for the last 40. A number of conflicting theoretical models, none with conclusive empirical support, define the current state of attempts to explain the dividend phenomenon.

Common stock theory proponents maintain that the safety and total return from dividends and capital gains of common stock will exceed bond return over the long term. Common stocks are able to sustain purchasing power more effectively than bonds because as commodity prices increase, purchasing power decreases and the bond income and par value returned upon maturity become less valuable (Fisher, 1912). The theory requires only fundamental assumptions: limited investor liability, complete markets, and the ability of investors to diversify their portfolios. A number of elementary empirical studies support this theory.[1]

Initial forays into explaining corporate dividend policy are divided as to their prediction of the dividend payment's effect on share prices. Three ways of thinking seem to be offered: one way is explaining dividends as attractive and a positive influence on stock price, a second way of thought argues that stock prices are negatively correlated with dividend payout levels, and a third avenue of empiricists maintains that the firm's dividend policy is irrelevant in stock price valuation.

[1]See, for example, Norton (1912), Smith (1923), Van Strum (1925), and Harold (1934).

Preinreich (1932) was the first to suggest that dividend policy is merely a residual decision. Dividends are paid to shareholders if and only if revenues remain after all positive investment opportunities have been funded. Another method determines dividend payout by examining and estimating corporate contingencies and financial needs rather than more rudimentary approaches based simply on current funds availability or historical payout patterns (Sage, 1937).

Following the strong language of Graham and Dodd (1934) that the corporation's main objective is to pay the owners of the firms (the shareholders) dividends, a preference for issues that pay regular cash dividends became the prevailing investment strategy in the financial community. A dollar paid as a cash dividend was shown to increase a share's price four times as much as a dollar retained [see, e.g., Auerbach (1979) and Bradford (1979)]. Dividend multiples became the preferred method for share valuation by both amateurs and professional money managers.

Harkavy (1953) showed empirical support for Graham and Dodd's position by estimating a positive correlation between stock price and dividend payout. However, Walter (1956), Gordon (1959), and Solomon (1963) were the first to build a theoretical model for this relationship. The underlying logic of their identical models is the notion that over the long term, share price is the present value of expected dividends. Investors are willing to pay increased price premiums for issues with consistent dividend growth because received cash dividends are less risky than future capital gains or higher expected dividend payments. Accordingly, dividend policy is relevant in firm valuation (Gordon, 1959, 1962). Many refer to these similar models with the generic name of bird in the hand. The reference reflects on the folksy adage propagating the preference for a bird in the hand rather than two in the bush (regardless of what the two in the bush are doing). In other words, it is safer to have something in the hand today (cash) than a risky promise (capital appreciation in the future).

In a private correspondence with one of the authors, Gordon had this to say:

> I have never characterized my theory of dividend policy as the "bird in hand" theory. It may be a good summary statement of the theory. I argue that the value of a share, like any other asset, is the p.v. [present value] of its payment EXPECTATIONS, i.e., its EXPECTED future dividends. Under certain conditions, that EXPECTATION can be represented by the current dividend and its EXPECTED growth rate.
>
> I have argued further that dividend policy can have the objective of (1) adopting a payout and growth rate that maximizes share price given earnings, investment opportunities, etc., and (2) getting investors to arrive at an expectation on the basis of the dividend record and other information that (a) maximizes share price regardless of how accurate the expectation is or (b) helps investors be as informed as possible in arriving at their expectations.
>
> I don't know what if anything you can or should do to incorporate the above in your reference to me. Much of it is in the 1963 you cite [Gordon, 1963] and it is

in Chs. 5 and 6 of my 1994 book [Gordon, 1994], I just want to be sure that you realize it. I believe that the signaling models capture some of it. (Everything in square brackets is our edition to the original text.)

With all the respect due to Myron Gordon for his life-long work in finance, in general and in dividends and dividend policy in particular we have serious problems with the capitalized words in the letter. Even if there were communal expectations of all shareholders, and even if these expectations would exactly appear in the web page of "great_expectations.com" it would be difficult to communicate to all shareholders that indeed that was the basis for the dividend decision. Unfortunately, none of these absurd conditions are given and management not only does not know what the expectations of their shareholders are, they are not even exactly sure who their shareholders are. What management does know is that shareholders like and expect dividends. This knowledge is tattooed in their brains, and the market, ceteris paribus, stands up and cheers the declaration of dividends. This cheering is perceived then as positive reinforcement for the decision.

The "bird-in-the-hand" models work on the implicit assumption that there are two opportunity rates:[2] one for the firm and another one for the investors. If the firm's opportunity rate is higher than that of the investors', the firm should retain 100% of its earnings. If the investors' opportunity rate is higher than the firm's, 100% of earnings should be paid out as dividends. If the two rates are equal, as in the case of perfect capital markets, than the dividend payout ratio is of no consequence.

Lintner (1962) and Gordon (1963) showed a decrease in the investor's required rate of return as dividends increase because the cash received from dividends is more certain than future capital gains. Conversely, Friend and Puckett (1964) claimed that omitted variables, different methods of analysis, and measurement errors are likely to bias early studies' results that show a strong preference for dividends by investors.

The seminal paper of Miller and Modigliani (MM) (1961) is the beginning of contemporary theoretical attempts to explain the role of dividend policy. Their model assumes perfect capital markets, rational investors, full and costless information, competitive markets, no transaction costs, and no taxes. Also, a firm's capital structure is given, there are no bankruptcy costs, and investment policy is exogenous, contingent on the risk class the firm belongs to. Using this partial equilibrium scenario and the arbitrage proof of Modigliani and Miller (1958), MM conclude that the dividend decision does not affect shareholders' wealth nor does it affect the cost of capital, ergo, dividend policy is irrelevant (the second indifference argument of MM).

If investors can buy and sell securities to manufacture their desired dividend payout rate, the expected return required for investors to hold shares is not

---

[2]The marginal rate of investment.

affected by the combination of new issues and gross dividend payments. Because dividend policy does not affect the discount rate of expected future cash flows, the firm's market value is independent of changes in dividend policy. Accordingly, corporations should not have an incentive to follow a systematic dividend policy. Financing decision indifference results in a shareholder indifference to corporate dividend policy.[3] Dividend policy is material only if a change in dividend policy relays information that investors do not have.[3] [Fama (1978) extends the MM model to a general equilibrium.]

MM do not mince words when they discuss the bird-in-the-hand/Graham and Dodd logic (Modigliani and Miller, 1961). They go as far as to call the bird-in-the-hand theory a "fallacy" and to state that if Graham and Dodd's claim regarding the price/earning multiple were true, then "... there would be only one way to account for it; namely, as a result of systematic irrationality on part of the investing public" (Modigliani and Miller, 1961, p. 431).

It is interesting to note that although MM were severely criticized by the "bird-in-the-hand" theorists, the MM model is just a special case of the Walter–Solomon–Gordon models. When the two opportunity rates are equal, the MM irrelevance proposition is the same as the dividend payout indifference of the early models. The two rates under MM must be equal because of their market perfection assumptions. Only under the condition of imperfect capital markets can different opportunity rates exist for the same risky asset.

A serious blow to the bird-in-the-hand logic is the existence of dividend reinvestment plans. Because these plans expose the shareholder to an income tax liability (i.e., double taxation) without receiving the cash, it is tantamount to leaving money on the table. In other words, if as the bird-in-the-hand argument would dictate the share value to be expected cash flows discounted at an opportunity rate, why would an economically rational shareholder not only leave the money in the corporation but also expose himself to an unnecessary tax obligation?

Recall from Chapter 1 the Black (1976, p. 5) mantra: "The harder we look at the dividend picture, the more it seems like a puzzle with pieces that just don't fit together." Black coined the term the "dividend puzzle" as a slighting reflection on the bird-in-the-hand theory (MM's fallacy argument). Later, Black (1990, p. 5) wagered a prophecy in which he foretells the disappearance of dividends: "I think dividends that remain taxable will gradually vanish." Why? Because if shareholders were neutral about dividends then "a firm would apologize to its taxable investors when forced by an accumulated earnings tax to pay dividends"

---

[3]This notion, a mere supposition of MM, gave rise later to the creation of the many dividend-signaling models/scenarios. Recall, also, that Myron Gordon finds common ground between signaling and his bird-in-the-hand model. In addition, MM surmise in this paper the existence of "dividend clienteles," another significant branch of research that followed later.

(Black, 1990). And why are not shareholders neutral? Because investment advisors and institutions treat a high-yield stock as both attractive and safe (Black, 1990).

The roaring *fin de siécle* decade of the 20th century seemed to make Black's prophecy come true. In an article titled "Shares without the Other Bit," subtitled "In Corporate America, Paying Dividends Has Gone out of Fashion," *The Economist* (1999) (also mentioned in Chapter 1) calls the apparent disappearance of dividends the "dividend puzzle." Strange, is it not that the same metaphor fits two exactly opposite phenomena!

Quoting Fama and French, *The Economist* observes that

> In the 1950s, nine out of ten American companies paid dividends. Today only one in five does (see chart). Dividends are disappearing so fast in America that Eugene Fama and Kenneth French, professors of finance at the University of Chicago and the Massachusetts Institute of Technology, respectively, have looked into the phenomenon (The Economist, 1999, p. 93).

Then the article goes on trying to guess the reasons for the disappearance of dividends, dismissing causes such as the tax effects (see Chapter 8) and share buybacks:

> So there must be more to it than tax or buybacks. One possibility, loth though, experts would be to admit it, is mere fashion. Not long ago, bosses were protective of their dividends, because investors saw them as the most potent signal that management could send about the future of its business. To tarry over raising dividends, never mind suspending them, was seen as a confession of failure. Nowadays, the opposite may be true. Mr. French says he has friends in investment banking who "tell their clients that paying dividends is like an admission that you have nothing better to do."

It seems that not just Professors Fama and French of the Chicago school believe in the irrationality of the bird-in-the-hand logic, and in fact in the notion that paying dividends is a *signal* that there is nothing better to do with the money, but also "his friends in investment banking" understand the same. (Birds by their feathers, perhaps?)

The closing two paragraphs of the *Economist*'s article is an example of risk aversion (not willing to commit itself to either side of the fence):

> That does not mean dividends have become completely irrelevant. Mr Escherich [quoted earlier in the article] says that companies that trim their dividend still tend to see their share price drop by an average of 6%; those that suspend dividends altogether see prices drop by 25%.

> But it may mean that they have become less relevant. For most of the century, before the bull market of the 1990s, the dividend yield was one of the most watched measures in the stockmarket. Whenever it dropped to 3% or less, traders assumed the market was overvalued and sold their holdings. Yet today the dividend yield on the S&P 500 shares is 1.2%. Optimists might argue that, since dividends no longer play

the role they once did, this does not, of itself, mean the market is wildly overvalued. But, given the uncertainty over precisely what role dividends now play, to say nothing of the market's heady levels, that is scarcely reassuring.

But what do you know? The ink barely dried on the "Shares without the Other Bit" article and the decline (following the longest streak of a bull market in memory) set in, followed by the crash and burn of the techies and consequently the NASDAQ. To illustrate the verity of the adage "the more things change, the more they remain the same," an article in the August 21, 2001 issue of the *Wall Street Journal* by Jonathon Clements ("Dividends, Not Growth, Is Wave of Future") has this to say:

> If the 1990s were about clocking capital gains, I suspect the current decade will belong to yield investors. The reason: Stocks may return just 8% a year and possibly less, so why not skip some of the uncertainty and claim your reward in cash?
>
> "A little more than a year ago, people laughed at dividends," recalls Jeremy Siegel, a finance professor at the University of Pennsylvania's Wharton School. "In the future, I believe that more attention will be paid to dividends and current earnings and less to growth."
>
> The first three months of 2000 saw a continuation of the late 1990s technology stock frenzy. But since then, pursuing yield has paid off handsomely. Bonds have posted healthy gains. Real-estate investment trusts have been big winners.

Yet, after extolling the virtues of REITs and junk bonds, Mr. Clements is risk averse enough to hedge his bets with the conclusion:

> Moreover, there is a tax cost involved. Because junk bonds and REITs kick off so much immediately taxable income, they are best held in a retirement account. One exception: If you are a retiree who plans to spend your investment income, you might keep your junk bonds and REITs in your taxable account.
>
> "For a long-term investor, I wouldn't do anything radical," says Clifford Asness, managing principal of New York's AQR Capital Management. "But would I have more in higher yielding investments? Yeah, I would. That may sound like market timing. But it's less sinful if you only do it once every decade."

Does this sound like a military always fighting the last war? Or is it a once a decade prudent policy? Most likely both. Sentiments and wisdoms are just as deep as the current business cycle, which might be a good strategy. But then where is the ever-lasting logic of the bird in the hand? Off again on again? The three-card monty?

Empirical evidence is inconclusive as to the irrelevance of dividend policy. The empirical results of Dhrymes and Kurz (1967), Brigham and Gordon (1968), McDonald *et al.* (1975), Bar-Yosef and Kolodny (1976), McCabe (1979), Anderson (1983), Peterson and Benesh (1983), and Jensen *et al.* (1992) all fail to support the MM irrelevance proposition. These studies show the investment and dividend decisions to be interrelated. According to Peterson and

Benesh (1983), market imperfections are the cause of these interdependencies. Nevertheless, the empirical results of these papers are too inadequate to reject the MM irrelevance proposition for three reasons. No statistical test, based on limited data (as all these tests are based on), can be strong enough to reject a proposition that in the confines of its assumptions cannot be rejected. Second, these early works are based on very unsophisticated econometric methods. Finally, there is empirical evidence to the contrary (see later), albeit also subject to same three caveats.

Conversely, Higgins (1972), Fama (1974), Smirlock and Marshall (1983), and Frankfurter and Gong (1993) found empirical support for the MM irrelevance proposition. Fama (1974) postulated that existing market imperfections are not significant enough to invalidate the independence of the two policies. The MM model is generally accepted as valid if its assumptions are not violated. Modification of these assumptions and the introduction of capital market imperfections may cause dividend policy to become relevant. Dividend policy relevancy is possibly a result of market imperfections, inefficiencies, or irrationalities (Brealy and Myers, 1991).

In summary, early thinking about dividends can be lumped into two, diametrically opposing, categories. On one hand, the academic models of the Graham and Dodd school of finance argue that the only source of value for the corporation is the expected discounted cash flow of dividends. On the other hand, the revolutionary argument of irrelevance of a dividend policy to value of MM sees dividends, even in the absence of personal income tax liabilities and transaction costs as not a determining factor of share value. How unfortunate is that the MM theory is inconsistent with an untold number of studies that show a positive empirical connection between a measure of dividends and value. We will see more about the multitude of these studies in the following two chapters.

# REFERENCES

Anderson, G. J. 1983. "The internal financing decisions of the industrial and commercial sector: a reappraisal of the lintner model of dividend disbursements." *Economica* 50:235–248.

Auerbach, Alan J. 1979. "Share valuation and corporate equity policy." *Journal of Public Economics* 11:291–305.

Bar-Yosef, Sasson, and Richard Kolodny. 1976. "Dividend policy and capital market theory." *The Review of Economics and Statistics* 58:181–190.

Black, Fisher. 1976. "The dividend puzzle." *The Journal of Portfolio Management* 2:5–8.

Black, Fisher. 1990. "Why firms pay dividends." *The Financial Analysts Journal* 46:5.

Bradford, David. 1979. "The incidence and the allocation effect of a tax on corporate distributions." Working Paper No. 349, National Bureau of Economics.

Brealy, Richard, and Stewart Myers. 1991. *Principles of Corporate Finance.* 4th ed. New York: McGraw-Hill Book Company.

Brigham, Eugene F., and Myron J. Gordon. 1968. "Leverage, dividend policy, and the cost of capital." *The Journal of Finance* 23:85–103.

Clements, Jonathan. 2001. "Dividends, not growth, is wave of future." *Wall Street Journal* August 21.

Dhrymes, Phoebus J., and Mordecai Kurz. 1964. "On the dividend policy of electric utilities." *The Review of Economics and Statistics* 46:76–81.

Dhrymes, Phoebus J., and Mordecai Kurz. 1967. "Investment, dividend, and external finance behavior of firms." In *Determinants of Investment Behavior: A Conference of the Universities—National Bureau Committee for Economic Research*. Robert Ferber ed. New York: National Bureau of Economic Research.

*The Economist.* 1999. "Shares without the other bit." November 20:93.

Fama, Eugene F. 1974. "The empirical relationships between the dividend and investment decisions of firms." *The American Economic Review* 64:304–318.

Fama, Eugene F. 1978. "The effects of a firm's investment and financing decisions on the welfare of its security holders." *The American Economic Review* 68:272–284.

Fisher, Irving. 1912. *How to Invest When Prices are Rising*. Scranton, PA: G. Lynn Sumner & Co.

Frankfurter, George M., and Jaisik Gong. 1993. "Time-series cross-sectional tests of dividend policy determinants." Louisiana State University: Unpublished working paper.

Friend, Irwin, and Marshall Puckett. 1964. "Dividends and stock prices." *The American Economic Review* 54:656–682.

Gordon, Myron J. 1959. "Dividends, earnings, and stock prices." *The Review of Economics and Statistics* 41:99–105.

Gordon, Myron J. 1962. "The savings, investment and valuation of a corporation." *The Review of Economics and Statistics* 44:37–51.

Gordon, Myron J. 1963. "Optimal investment and financing policy." *The Journal of Finance* 18:264–272.

Gordon, Myron J. 1994. *Finance, Investment and Macroeconomics: The Neoclassical and a Post Keynesian Solution*. Hants, UK: Edward Elgar Publishing Company.

Graham, Benjamin, and David L. Dodd. 1934. *Security Analysis*, New York: Whittlesey House.

Harkavy, Oscar. 1953. "The relation between retained earnings and common stock price for large, listed corporations." *The Journal of Finance* 8:283–297.

Harold, Gilbert. 1934. "A reconsideration of the common-stock theory." *The Journal of Business* 7:42–59.

Higgins, Robert C. 1972. "The corporate dividend-saving decision." *Journal of Financial and Quantitative Analysis* 7:1527–1541.

Jensen, Gerald R., Donald P. Solberg, and Thomas S. Zorn. 1992. "Simultaneous determination of insider ownership, debt, and dividend policies." *Journal of Financial and Quantitative Analysis* 27:247–263.

Lintner, John. 1956. "Optimal dividends and corporate growth under uncertainty." *The Quarterly Journal of Economics* 78:49–95.

McCabe, George M. 1979. "The empirical relationship between investment and financing: a new look." *Journal of Financial and Quantitative Analysis* 14:119–135.

McDonald, John G., Bertrand Jacquillat, and Maurice Nussenbaum. 1975. "Dividend, investment and financing decisions: empirical evidence on french firms." *Journal of Financial and Quantitative Analysis* 10:741–755.

Miller, Merton H., and Franco Modigliani. 1961. "Dividend policy, growth, and the valuation of shares." *The Journal of Business* 34:411–433.

Modigliani, Franco, and Merton H. Miller. 1958. "The cost of capital, corporate finance, and the theory of investment." *The American Economic Review* 48:261–297.

Norton, J. Pease. 1912. "Stocks as an investment when prices are rising." in *How to Invest When Prices are Rising*. ed. Irving Fisher. Scranton, PA: G. Lynn Sumner & Co.

Peterson, Pamela P., and Gary A. Benesh. 1983. "A re-examination of the empirical relationship between investment and financing decisions." *Journal of Financial and Quantitative Analysis* 18:439–453.

Preinreich, Gabriel A. D. 1932. "Stock yields, stock dividends and inflation" *The Accounting Review* 7:273–289.

Sage, George H. 1937. "Dividend policy and business contingencies." *Harvard Business Review* 15:245–252.

Smirlock, Michael, and William Marshall. 1983. "An examination of the empirical relationship between the dividend and investment decisions: a note." *The Journal of Finance* 38:1659–1667.

Smith, Edgar Lawrence. 1923. *Common Stocks as Long Term Investments.* New York: The MacMillan Company.

Solomon, Ezra. 1963. *The Theory of Financial Management.* New York: Columbia University Press.

Van Strum, Kenneth S. 1925. *Investing in Purchasing Power.* New York: Barron's.

Walter, James E. 1956. "Dividend policies and common stock prices." *The Journal of Finance* 11:29–41.

# CHAPTER 8

# Models of Symmetric Information and Empirical Research

The more advanced generation of academic models following "the-bird-in-the-hand" models and Miller and Modigliani (MM) (1961) is conveniently categorized into two model groups: those that assume symmetric information and those that presuppose asymmetric information. At the core of these models are the notion of market imperfection and the tax impetus. The subject of the current chapter is the first group of models.

A large body of theoretical models and empirical research analyzes the effect of the market imperfection of taxes on corporate dividend policy. An early examination of the effect shows that depreciation allowances and individual tax rates substantially influenced dividend payout rates in the United States between 1920 and 1960 (Brittain, 1964). The majority of writers do not question the significance of the effect of the tax code on the determination and implementation of corporate dividend policy. The models developed thus far are therefore not separated into paradigms supporting the contention that taxes do not affect corporate dividend decisions and those modeling the effect of taxes on corporate policy. Rather, the standards can be better classified as tax-adjusted or tax-avoidance dividend models.

## 8.1 THEORETICAL MODELS

Tax-adjusted models surmise that investors require and secure higher expected returns on shares of dividend-paying stocks. The imposition of a tax liability on dividends causes the dividend payment to be grossed up to increase the shareholder's pretax return. Under the capital asset pricing theory, investors offer a lower price for the shares because of the future tax liability of the dividend payment.

One consequence of the tax-adjusted model is the division of investors into dividend tax clienteles. The clientele argument was first proposed in the seminal work of MM (1961). In later work, Modigliani (1982) found that the clientele effect is responsible for only nominal alterations in portfolio composition rather than the major differences predicted by Miller (1977). Masulis and Trueman (1988) modeled cash dividend payments as products of deferred dividend costs. Their model predicts that investors with differing tax liabilities will have diverging preferences as to the optimal firm investment/dividend policy. As the tax liability on dividends increases (decreases), the dividend payment decreases (increases) while earnings reinvestment increases (decreases). Differences can be minimized by the segregation of investors into clienteles.

The model developed by Farrar and Selwyn (1967) assumes that investors maximize after-tax income. In a partial equilibrium framework, investors are presented with two choices. Individuals choose the amount of personal and corporate leverage and also choose whether to receive corporate income distributions either as dividends or as capital gains. If the tax liability of capital gains distributions is less than the liability incurred by dividend distribution, rational investors will prefer capital gains. The preferred payment is the one with the least tax liability. The model contends that no dividends should be paid. Rather, share repurchase should be used to distribute corporate earnings.

Brennan (1970) extended the Farrar and Selwyn (1967) model into a general equilibrium framework. In the Brennan model, investors maximize their expected utility of wealth. Although the model is more robust, the predictions are similar to those of the Farrar and Selwyn model: equilibrium with dividend-paying firms is not consistent with a zero required return per unit of dividend yield.

Auerbach (1979a) developed a discrete time, infinite horizon model in that shareholders maximize their wealth. If a capital gains/dividends tax differential exists, wealth maximization no longer implies firm market value maximization. Subsequently, Auerbach (1979b) posited that dividends are distributed because of the consistent, long-term undervaluation of corporate capital. Undervaluation is the result of a dynamic process encompassing multiple periods of total reinvestment of all firm profits followed by firm returns less than the returns expected by investors. If firms are unable to make distributions to investors except in the form of dividends, shareholders must include the expected tax liabilities of future dividend payments to determine market prices accurately. These liabilities decrease the share price investors are willing to pay so as to increase the expected return from their investment. Stocks with dividend yields higher than the riskless rate are likely to generate positive abnormal returns from the increased risk of these cash flows.[1,2]

Tax-adjusted models are criticized as incompatible with models of rational (economic) behavior. Miller (1986) proposed the strategy of tax sheltering of income by high tax bracket individuals as a behavior more consistent with rationality. Individuals can, of course, refrain from purchasing dividend-paying shares to avoid the tax liability of these payments. Alternatively, using a strategy first advanced by Miller and Scholes (1978), shareholders can purchase dividend-paying stocks and receive the distributions and then simultaneously borrow funds to invest in tax-free senior securities. The interest charges on the loan are used to offset the tax liability of the dividend income while the income from the bonds is free of tax liability and consequently does not increase the investor's taxable income. The firm's value is independent of its dividend policy because of investor indifference between capital gains and dividends.

The use of dividend-specific personal tax shelters (e.g., the existing dividend income exemption) to avoid tax liabilities is advanced by DeAngelo and Masulis (1980b). They contend that the Miller and Scholes (1978) tax shelter strategy is not sufficient to induce positive dividend payment at equilibrium. Fung and Theobald (1984) model tax shelters that are not based on interest charges and apply the theoretical results to the French, German, British, and U.S. tax systems. Dividend tax credits are incapable of inducing a positive dividend equilibrium; noninterest-related tax shelters are required. The dividend payout level depends on the efficiency of the market for tax shelters and country-specific tax law influences.

## 8.2 EMPIRICAL INVESTIGATION OF THE TAX EFFECT ON DIVIDENDS

An examination of the pricing of the tax on dividends has been pursued actively to the extent that the results of these studies should conclusively support either the tax-adjusted model or the tax-avoidance model. The inevitable tax liabilities cause dividends to be grossed up by discounting share prices in the tax-adjusted model. Several studies analyze this issue by adding an additional variable representing the price of the dividend component to the capital asset pricing model (CAPM). If the coefficient on the dividend factor is positive, the results support the tax-adjusted model—returns on dividend-paying shares are

---

[1]The term "abnormal return" is used here as in the context of event studies, a method of analysis that became popular during the early to mid-1970s.

[2]See Bradford (1981) and Fung (1981) for further extensions of this idea.

increased and the tax rate on dividends is greater than zero. If the coefficient of the dividend factor is zero, then dividend-paying shares are valued using the same pricing mechanism as non-dividend paying shares and the results support the tax-avoidance model.

Unfortunately, the results of the empirical studies are diverse. Black and Scholes (1974), Miller and Scholes (1982) and Hess (1982, 1983b) report insignificant or negative dividend coefficients. Christie (1990) finds a negative coefficient for a dummy variable representing zero dividend firms. These zero dividend firms earn abnormal negative returns. Naranjo et al. (1998) state that the dividend yield effect is independent of tax effects. The diverse results raise the question of the appropriate method of analysis (Hess, 1983a). Potential method of analysis inadequacies contributing to conflicting results includes the linear model's suitability (Blume, 1980; Elton et al., 1983), the choice of the market portfolio proxy (Roll, 1977) and the influence of the information effect (Litzenberger and Ramaswamy, 1979; Miller and Scholes, 1982).

Other authors investigate share price changes during the period surrounding the ex-dividend date to determine whether the tax on dividends is priced. This branch of investigation is inspired by an early paper of Campbell and Beranek (1955), who were the first to document the tendency for the share price to decline less on the ex-date than the amount of the dividend payment. Nevertheless, the dividend/price-decline differential is not pronounced. Later work by Durand and May (1960) supported this finding, but the discrepancies between the dividend payment amount and the price decline in this study of American Telephone and Telegraph common stock are also negligible. Marginal shareholders must be indifferent between holding the ex-dividend shares and the after tax dividend or owning the share before the dividend is paid (Elton and Gruber, 1970). This equality allows for indirect estimation of the shareholders' tax rates.

A positive tax rate is implied if the price change/dividend ratio is bounded by 0 and 1. Campbell and Beranek (1955), Elton and Gruber (1970), and Kaplanis (1986) found evidence that supports the tax clientele hypothesis. Other authors, e.g., Brooks and Edwards (1980) and Kalay (1982b), questioned the method's ability to infer tax brackets because of the influence of short-term trading activity and other confounding factors. Gagnon and Suret (1991) showed that the return variance in most empirical study samples precludes tax rate inference and the consequent clientele estimation. Although the full impact of short-term traders on ex-dividend day returns is not known, the effect of these investors has decreased as abnormal returns and transaction costs have decreased following the initiation of a negotiated commission structure (Finnerty, 1981; Eades et al., 1984; Lakonishok and Vermaelen, 1983). Karpoff and Walkling (1988) were unable to demonstrate any correlation between transaction costs and ex-dividend day returns.

The importance of transaction costs to the short-term trader is discussed by Kalay (1982a,b, 1984) and Elton *et al.* (1983). Kalay (1982a,b, 1984) asserted that transaction costs are not a major determinant of trading strategy and do not significantly affect short-term trading activity because floor trader and specialist commission rates are not significant. Traders will exploit the arbitrage opportunities of the share price changes on ex-dividend day if the abnormal returns are large. However, Elton *et al.* (1983) refuted Kalay's findings because of the underestimation of transaction costs. These authors believe that the transaction costs significantly affect trading profits to the extent that abnormal profit capture is not possible and short-term trading activity effects are negated.

A third approach explores the effect a change in the capital gains/dividend tax differential has on the share price of dividend- and nondividend-paying firms. According to the tax-adjusted model, a change in the tax rate should cause a change in the demand curve for dividends and a change in pricing. Alternatively, no change in the pricing of dividends should occur under the tax-avoidance model.

In a study of stock returns before the introduction of federal income taxes in the United States, Barclay (1987) found support for the tax-adjusted model as he could not demonstrate the tax clientele effect. Crockett and Friend (1988) showed that investor dividend preference is little affected by changes in the tax code. Grammatikos (1989) reported that abnormal returns in high-yield stocks have increased following the 1984 Tax Reform Act (1984 TRA). Robin (1991) and Wu and Hsu (1992) found support for the tax clientele hypothesis in the period preceding and following the 1986 TRA. An increase in dividend capture trading activity was documented by Koski (1996) following the 1984 and 1986 TRAs. Conversely, Michaely (1991) and Hearth and Rimbey (1992) found few changes in market activity following the 1986 TRA and little support for the tax clientele theory.

Following a sequence of tax reform acts in Canada, Khoury and Smith (1977), Morgan (1980), Amoako-Adu (1983), Booth and Johnston (1984), and McKenzie and Thompson (1995) found support for the tax-adjusted model using Canadian stock market data from the period preceding and following the changes in the tax law. Similarly, Bond *et al.* (1996) found the same pattern in United Kingdom dividend streams. These findings notwithstanding, Lakonishok and Vermaelen's (1983) findings support the short-term trading hypothesis. The tax-adjusted model is also supported in studies using British data by Feldstein (1970), Poterba and Summers (1984), Ang *et al.* (1991), and Bond *et al.* (1996) and in a study using German data (Amihud and Murgia, 1997).

Another approach uses direct examination of investor portfolios to test the tax clientele hypothesis. The tax-adjusted model predicts that certain subgroups of taxable investors will hold dividend-paying stocks, whereas the tax-avoidance model posits that only tax-exempt investors and shareholders who are able to shelter the dividend income will hold dividend-paying shares.

Blume *et al.* (1974) found an inverse relationship between the portfolio dividend yield and the investors' tax bracket. Although high-income investors hold lower dividend-paying stocks in their portfolios, yield differences between high-income investor portfolios and low-income investor portfolios are less than the tax bracket differential. In a following study of individual brokerage accounts, Pettit (1972) found that the large dividend/capital gains tax differential induces high tax bracket individuals to hold low-yield issues. Portfolio dividend yields also increase as age and liquidity needs increase. A subsequent reexamination of the Pettit (1972) investor portfolios by Lewellen *et al.* (1978) found little evidence of the tax clientele effect. Rather, dividend-paying shares are found in the portfolios of investors with differing tax liabilities.

A further group of studies attempted to determine if shareholders pay taxes on dividends. The tax-adjusted model predicts that tax payments will be made because pretax returns are grossed up as a result of potential investor awareness of the tax liability; the tax-avoidance model predicts that no taxes will be paid because nontax-exempt investors will shelter the income. Feenberg (1981) found that only 2.5% of dividends are paid to individuals eligible to take the interest deduction proposed by Miller and Scholes (1978). Also, Peterson *et al.* (1985) reported that shareholders pay considerable taxes on dividends and that they do not shelter their income. Other research showed that an increase (decrease) in the tax liability of dividends versus capital gains leads to a decrease (increase) in aggregate dividends in the United States (Lent, 1948; Brittain, 1964), Canada (Khoury and Smith, 1977) and Great Britain (Feldstein, 1970).

Consistent with Lintner (1962), transaction costs, tax differentials, and heterogeneous shareholder expectations should induce a capital gain preference if firms are following an optimal investment strategy. Stiglitz (1981) and Modigliani (1982) asserted that corporations acting in the shareholder's best interest should pay zero dividends if capital gains tax liability is less than dividend tax liability. However, corporations continue to pay dividends despite their apparent liabilities. This is not completely unexpected. The general equilibrium of standard finance models demands that prices adjust upward to induce firms to make taxable distributions (DeAngelo, 1991).

The underlying tax structure significantly affects corporate dividend policy. Empirical analysis of these effects better support the tax-adjusted model than the alternative tax-avoidance model. Under the tax-adjusted model, high dividend yield stocks with high tax liabilities are priced to increase the pretax expected returns. The theory that rational shareholders require a higher return from dividend-paying shares is logically consistent.

Haugen and Senbet (1986) showed evidence supportive of the dividend clientele hypothesis, documenting the differences in the ex-dividend day return performance of high-yield and low-yield stocks. However, the proportion of nondividend-paying stocks is much smaller than expected if the majority of investors are subject to the tax liabilities associated with dividends.

A paper in the tax effect genre is by Kalay and Michaely (2000). On reading the Kalay and Michaely paper, titled "Dividends and Taxes: A Re-Examination," three things come to mind.

- The quote from Dostoyevsky's *Idiot* that "Zeal overcomes all."
- The definition of a fanatic as "someone who doubles his efforts when he has lost sight of the objective."
- Sam Kinnison, the late stand-up comic, who was responding to the plight of the sub-Sahara people facing their perennial drought (and as a consequence: starvation) by screaming that "THERE IS NO FOOD THERE, GO LIVE SOMEWHERE WHERE THERE IS FOOD!" (Expletives deleted.)

Kalay and Michaely (2000), after spending 21 journal pages and an untold number of weekly (?) regressions with the "usual" variables, concluded

> Our empirical evidence—time-series return variations and no cross-sectional return variations—is not explained by known tax models. It could very well be that these empirical findings are somehow related to a *more complex* [our italics] theory of tax effects, yet to be developed (p. 73).

This is so because their study, as many others' before them, failed to link the changes in tax laws to changes of dividend policies of firms. The tax effect on dividends, perhaps the most economically rational exogenous effect, yet again could not be shown as a significant determinant of corporate dividend policy. The conclusion, therefore, that must have been drawn from the results of this, and many other studies we mentioned already, is not to ratchet the complexity up one notch or more, but to ponder the possible logical reasons why dividend policies do not follow the rationality exclusively assumed in financial economics.

In essence, the final conclusion one can reach from these models and tests is that one cannot reach a final conclusion. There is ample evidence, supported equally well by the same data that is both supportive of as well as contradictory, to all the hypotheses discussed in this chapter. That avenue of research that is contrary to the explicit or implicit assumption made thus far by presupposing asymmetric information is the subject of the next chapter.

# REFERENCES

Amihud, Yakov, and Maurizio Murgia. 1997. "Dividends, taxes, and signaling: evidence from Germany." *The Journal of Finance* 52:397–408.

Amoako-Adu, Ben. 1983. "The Canadian tax reform and its effect on stock prices: a note." *The Journal of Finance* 38:1669–1675.

Ang, James S., David W. Blackwell, and William L. Megginson. 1991. "The effect of taxes on the relative valuation of dividends and capital gains: evidence from dual-class British investment trusts." *The Journal of Finance* 46:383–399.

Auerbach, Alan J. 1979a. "Share valuation and corporate equity policy." *Journal of Public Economics* 11:291–305.

Auerbach, Alan J. 1979b. "Wealth maximization and the cost of capital." *The Quarterly Journal of Economics* 93:433–446.

Barclay, Michael J. 1987. "Dividends, taxes, and common stock prices." *Journal of Financial Economics* 19:31–44.

Black, Fisher, and Myron Scholes. 1974. "The effects of dividend yield and dividend policy on common stock prices and returns." *Journal of Financial Economics* 1:1–22.

Blume, Marshall E. 1980. "Stock returns and dividend yields: some more evidence." *The Review of Economics and Statistics* 62:567–577.

Blume, Marshall, Jean Crockett, and Irwin Friend. 1974. "Stock ownership in the United States: characteristics and trends." *Survey of Current Business* 54:16–40.

Bond, Stephen R., Lucy Chennells, and Michael P. Devereux. 1996. "Taxes and company dividends: a microeconometric investigation exploiting cross-section variation in taxes." *The Economic Journal* 106:320–333.

Booth, L. D., and D. J. Johnston. 1984. "The ex-dividend day behavior of Canadian stock prices: tax changes and clientele effects." *The Journal of Finance* 39:457–476.

Bradford, David F. 1981. "The incidence and allocation effects of a tax on corporate distributions." *Journal of Public Economics* 15:1–22.

Brennan, Michael J. 1970. "Taxes, market valuation, and corporation financial policy." *National Tax Journal* 23:417–427.

Brittain, John A. 1964. "The tax structure and corporate dividend policy." *The American Economic Review* 54:272–287.

Brooks, LeRoy D., and Charles E. Edwards. 1980. "Marginal stockholders and implied tax rates." *The Review of Economics and Statistics* 62:616–619.

Campbell, James A., and William Beranek. 1955. "Stock price behavior on ex-dividend dates." *The Journal of Finance* 10:425–429.

Christie, William G. 1990. "Dividend yield and expected returns." *Journal of Financial Economics* 28:95–125.

Crockett, Jean, and Irwin Friend. 1988. "Dividend policy in perspective: can theory explain behavior?" *The Review of Economics and Statistics* 70:603–613.

DeAngelo, Harry. 1991. "Payout policy and tax deferral." *The Journal of Finance* 46:357–368.

DeAngelo, Harry, and Ronald W. Masulis. 1980a. "Leverage and dividend irrelevancy under corporate and personal taxation." *The Journal of Finance* 35:453–464.

DeAngelo, Harry, and Ronald W. Masulis. 1980b. "Optimal capital structure under corporate and personal taxation." *Journal of Financial Economics* 8:90–118.

Durand, David, and Alan M. May. 1960. "The ex-dividend behavior of American telephone and telegraph stock." *The Journal of Finance* 15:19–31.

Eades, Kenneth M., Patrick J. Hess, and E. Han Kim. 1984. "On interpreting security returns during the ex-dividend period." *Journal of Financial Economics* 13:3–34.

Elton, Edward J., and Martin J. Gruber. 1970. "Marginal stockholder tax rates and the clientele effect." *The Review of Economics and Statistics* 52:68–74.

Elton, Edward J., Martin J. Gruber, and Joel Rentzler. 1983. "A simple examination of the empirical relationship between dividend yields and deviations from the CAPM." *Journal of Banking and Finance* 7:135–146.

Farrar, Donald E., and Lee L. Selwyn. 1967. "Taxes, corporate financial policy and return to investors." *National Tax Journal* 20:444–462.

Feenberg, Daniel. 1981. "Does the investment interest limitation explain the existence of dividends?" *Journal of Financial Economics* 9:265–269.

Feldstein, Martin S. 1970. "Corporate taxation and dividend behavior." *Review of Economic Studies* 37:57–72.

Finnerty, John D. 1981. "The behavior of electric utility common stock prices near the ex-dividend date." *Financial Management* 10:59–69.

Fung, William K. H. 1981. "Taxes, clientele effect of dividend and risk, return linearity." *Journal of Banking and Finance* 5:405–424.

Fung, William K. H., and Michael F. Theobald. 1984. "Dividends and debt under alternative tax systems." *Journal of Financial and Quantitative Analysis* 19:59–72.

Gagnon, Jean-Marie, and Jean-Marc Suret. 1991. "Ex-dividend day price changes and implied tax rates: an evaluation." *The Journal of Financial Research* 14:255–262.

Grammatikos, Theoharry. 1989. "Dividend stripping, risk exposure, and the effect of the 1984 TRA on the ex-dividend day behavior." *The Journal of Business* 62:157–173.

Haugen, Robert A., and Lemma W. Senbet. 1986. "Corporate finance and taxes: a review." *Financial Management*, 15, Autumn, 5–21.

Hearth, Douglas, and James H. Rimbey. 1992. "The dividend-clientele controversy and the Tax Reform Act of 1986." Unpublished working paper.

Hess, Patrick. 1982. "The ex-dividend day behavior of stock returns: further evidence on tax effects." *The Journal of Finance* 37:445–456.

Hess, Patrick. 1983a. "The dividend debate: 20 years of discussion." in *Issues in Corporate Finance*. New York: Stern Stewart and Co.

Hess, Patrick. 1983b. "Test for tax effects in the pricing of financial assets." *Journal of Business* 56:537–554.

Kalay, Avner. 1982a. "The ex-dividend day behavior of stock prices." *The Journal of Finance* 37:1059–1070.

Kalay, Avner. 1982b. "Stockholder-bondholder conflict and dividend constraints." *Journal of Financial Economics* 10:211–233.

Kalay, Avner. 1984. "The ex-dividend day behavior of stock prices; a re-examination of the clientele effect: a reply." *The Journal of Finance* 37:557–561.

Kalay, Avner, and Roni Michaely. 2000. "Dividends and taxes: a re-examination." *Financial Management* 29:55–75.

Karpoff, Jonathon M., and Ralph A. Walkling. 1988. "Short-term trading around ex-dividend days." *Journal of Financial Economics* 21:291–298.

Khoury, N. T., and K. V. Smith. 1977. "Dividend policy and the capital gains tax in Canada." *Journal of Business Administration* 8:19–37.

Koski, Jennifer Lynch. 1996. "A microstructure analysis of ex-dividend stock price behavior before and after the 1984 and 1986 Tax Reform Acts." *Journal of Business* 69:313–338.

Lakonishok, Josef, and Theo Vermaelen. 1983. "Tax reform and ex-dividend day behavior." *The Journal of Finance* 38:1157–1179.

Lent, George E. 1948. *The Impact of the Undistributed Profits Tax 1936–1937*. New York: Columbia University Press.

Lewellen, Wilbur G., Kenneth L. Stanley, Ronald C. Lease, and Gary G. Schlarbaum. 1978. "Some direct evidence on the dividend clientele phenomenon." *The Journal of Finance* 33:1385–1399.

Lintner, John. 1962. "Dividends, earnings, leverage, stock prices, and the supply of capital to corporations." *The Review of Economics and Statistics* 44:243–469.

Litzenberger, Robert H., and Krishna Ramaswamy. 1979. "The effect of personal taxes and dividends on capital asset prices: theory and empirical evidence." *Journal of Financial Economics* 7:163–195.

Kaplanis, Costas P. 1986. "Options, taxes, and ex-dividend day behavior." *The Journal of Finance* 41:411–424.

Masulis, Ronald W., and Brett Trueman. 1988. "Corporate investment and dividend decisions under differential personal taxation." *Journal of Financial and Quantitative Analysis* 23:369–386.

McKenzie, Kenneth J., and Aileen J. Thompson. 1995. "Dividend taxation and equity value: the canadian tax changes of 1986." *Canadian Journal of Economics* 28:463–472.

Michaely, Roni. 1991. "Ex-dividend day stock price behavior: the case of the 1986 Tax Reform Act." *The Journal of Finance* 46:845–859.

Miller, Merton H. 1977. "Debt and taxes." *The Journal of Finance* 32:261–275.

Miller, Merton H. 1986. "Behavior rationality in finance: the case of dividends." *The Journal of Business* 59:S451–S468.

Miller, Merton H., and Franco Modigliani. 1961. "Dividend policy, growth, and the valuation of shares." *The Journal of Business* 34:411–433.

Miller, Merton H., and Myron S. Scholes. 1978. "Dividends and taxes." *Journal of Financial Economics* 6:333–364.

Miller, Merton H., and Myron S. Scholes. 1982. "Dividends and taxes: some empirical evidence." *Journal of Political Economy* 90:1118–1141.

Modigliani, Franco. 1982. "Debt, dividend policy, inflation and market valuation." *The Journal of Finance* 37:255–273.

Morgan, I. G. 1980. "Dividend and stock price behavior in Canada." *Journal of Business Administration* 12:91–107.

Naranjo, Andy, M. Nimalendran, and Mike Ryngaert. 1998. "Stock returns, dividend yields, and taxes." *The Journal of Finance* 53:2029–2057.

Peterson, Pamela P., David R. Peterson, and James S. Ang. 1985. "Direct evidence on the marginal rate of taxation on dividend income." *Journal of Financial Economics* 14:267–282.

Pettit, R. Richardson. 1972. "Dividend announcements, security performance, and capital market efficiency." *The Journal of Finance* 27:993–1007.

Poterba, James M., and Lawrence H. Summers. 1984. "Dividend taxes, corporate investment, and 'Q'." *Journal of Public Economics* 22:135–167.

Robin, Ashok J. 1991. "The impact of the 1986 Tax Reform Act on ex-dividend day returns." *Financial Management* 20:60–70.

Roll, Richard. 1977. "A critique of the asset price theory's test; Part I: On past and potential testability of theory." *Journal of Financial Economics* 4:129–176.

Stiglitz, Joseph E. 1981. "Ownership, control, and efficient markets: some paradoxes in the theory of capital markets." In *Economic Regulation: Essays in Honor of James R. Nelson*. Kenneth D. Boyer and William G. Shepherd. eds. Lansing, MI: Michigan State University Press.

Wu, Chunchi, and Junming Hsu. 1992. "The impact of the 1986 tax reform on ex-dividend day volume and price behavior." Unpublished working paper.

# CHAPTER 9

## Models of Asymmetric Information and Empirical Research

The market imperfection of asymmetric information is the basis for three distinct efforts to explain corporate dividend policy. Mitigation of the informational asymmetries between managers and owners via unexpected changes in dividend policy is the cornerstone of dividend-signaling models. Agency cost theory uses dividend policy to better align the interests of shareholders and corporate managers. The free cash flow hypothesis combines attributes of both signaling and agency costs paradigms, where the payment of dividends can decrease the level of funds available for perquisite consumption by corporate managers. In this chapter the results of research in these three distinct hypotheses are discussed.

## 9.1 SIGNALING AND "THE INFORMATION CONTENT OF DIVIDEND" HYPOTHESIS

In their seminal work, Miller and Modigliani (MM) (1961) argued that the share price is independent of dividend policy—the value of a share reflects both the future cash flow stream and future growth opportunities. MM acknowledged that dividend changes influence stock prices and attributed this phenomenon to the "information content of dividends." A stock price change resulting from a change in dividend payout because of the informational content of dividends represents differences in the private information known by corporate managers and the information available to the public. Only unexpected changes in dividend levels and the release of new information should affect stock prices under perfect market assumptions.

Corporate managers hold private information concerning the firm's future value. Managers are motivated to release this information to investors but must do so indirectly to prevent competing firms from profiting from the release. The signal of this information must be credible, i.e., costly, to prevent false signaling by other firms in the marketplace. If managers have information that is not known by the public and an incentive to release this information indirectly, they can relay this information to shareholders through unexpected changes in dividend policy (Myers and Majluf, 1984).

As explained by Myers (1987), the price reaction to the announcement of changes in dividend policy is rational. The dividend information message of unobservable true earnings foreshadows expected future earnings. The market price of the shares should increase (decrease) from the raised (lowered) expectations. Communication of managerial expectations using dividends is less ambiguous than earnings announcements, as dividend policy is solely at the discretion of management and represents a costly cash outflow to shareholders. Reluctance on the part of managers to reduce dividends is a necessary condition for dividend use as a credible signal (Kalay, 1980).

The results of early empirical attempts to support the information content of dividends hypothesis are ambiguous. Separate studies by Fama *et al.* (1969), Pettit (1972, 1976), Griffen (1976), and Laub (1976) showed positive (negative) excess returns accruing following unexpected dividend increases (decreases). Work by Ang (1975) and Gonedes (1978) failed to support the premise, whereas Watts (1973) found that transaction costs preclude excess return capture by market participants. Charest (1978) reported that earnings announcement and dividend announcement effects are confounded. Inconsistencies in the results can be traced to differences in data, sample period, methods of analysis, and model misspecification.

## 9.2 FORMAL SIGNALING MODELS AND THEIR EMPIRICAL TESTS

Akerlof's (1970) model of the used car industry as a pooling equilibrium in the absence of signaling activities serves as a primer to signaling models in financial economics considering the costs of informational asymmetries. The generalization of Akerlof's model by Spence (1974) became the prototype for all financial models of signaling.[1] The model defines a unique and specific signaling equilibrium in that market participants seeking employment in a world of

---

[1]This, despite Spence's explicit caveat that his model fits only very specific situations without any ambivalence as to the signaler, signalee, and the signal.

uncertainty and asymmetric information rely on signals of their quality rather than reputation acquisition to find positions. Although formulated in the job market, Spence believes that findings can be extended to a limited number of other settings (admissions procedures, promotions, and credit application). A necessary condition for signaling to be successful is an inverse relation between a signal's costs and true productivity because costs are relatively higher for inferior workers to signal. The signaling mechanisms must be controlled, must be able to be modified by the signaler, and must be costly. Because managers cannot determine a worker's quality through observation, a high-quality worker signals his value through additional education, resulting in higher pay. A similar model is formulated for the insurance market (Rothschild and Stiglitz, 1976). The general sufficient conditions for a signaling equilibrium to exist are formalized by Riley (1979).

Numerous theoretical models of signaling have been formulated to explain how managerial activities attempt to reduce the information asymmetries between corporate shareholders and managers. These include share repurchases (Stewart, 1976; Vermaelen, 1981; Barclay and Smith, 1988), ownership equity proportion (Leland and Pyle, 1977), capital structure (Ross, 1977), convertible bond conversion (Harris and Raviv, 1985), insider trading (Damodaran and Liu, 1993), and models with dual signals of the insider trading activity occurring around other corporate signaling activities (John and Mishra, 1990; John and Lang, 1991).

Signaling models of corporate dividend policy are formalized by Bhattacharya (1979, 1980), Talmor (1981), Hakansson (1982), John and Williams (1985), Miller and Rock (1985), Bar-Yosef and Huffman (1986), Makhija and Thompson (1986), Ambarish *et al.* (1987), Ofer and Thakor (1987), Kumar (1988), Kale and Noe (1990), and Rodriguez (1992).

The majority of these theorists presuppose (albeit never verify) that signaling via corporate dividend policy has a lower cost than alternatives (e.g., advertising or public relations campaigns) that would accomplish the same result. If less costly alternatives are available, prudent corporate managers would choose these alternatives rather than dividend policy to signal their inside information (Ambarish *et al.*, 1987; Ofer and Thakor, 1987). The use of dividends as signals implies that alternative methods of signaling are not perfect substitutes (Asquith and Mullins, 1986).

The dividend-signaling model developed by Bhattacharya (1979) descended from Ross (1977). In this model of an all equity firm, a higher dividend payment per share implies a higher firm value. Unexpected increases in dividends are favorable signals relaying unique information of managements' expectations of future cash flows. The costs associated with dividend payments—the opportunity costs of the use of internal funds or the transaction costs associated with external financing—make the signal costly for firms lacking positive information to imitate. Unlike Spence (1974), the costs of signaling occur in the future while the firm benefits from the strategy during the current period. The increase in share value associated with the signal offsets the shareholders' tax liability from dividend income. In this environment, closely held firms are likely to pay higher dividends to communicate their value to outside shareholders because information availability is constrained in such firms. If the least profitable firms pay zero dividends, the dividend and earnings relation will be linear. [The model's predictions are supported by earlier empirical evidence by Brittain (1966).]

Bhattacharya (1980) extended the model to a two-period intertemporal setting, whereas Talmor (1981) expanded it to a multivariate model with several valuation parameters and signaling mechanisms. In Talmor's model, managers make several financing decisions simultaneously. The firm's management considers all financial decisions as a single operation, even if the individual activities are not explicitly recognized by the shareholders as signaling vehicles.

In their extension of the model, Makhija and Thompson (1986) defined the least profitable firm differently than Bhattacharya (1979). If all firms have nonzero earnings, the dividend/earnings relation will be nonlinear. To ensure equilibrium existence, the dividend policy of the most profitable firms must be constrained and additional limiting conditions likely have to be imposed.

A signaling equilibrium will exist only if firm quality dispersion is limited in the extension of the Bhattacharya (1979) model developed by Rodriguez (1992). If a cash flow range is specified for each firm, an upper bound on firm quality distribution exists. Then, equilibrium is not feasible beyond this upper bound. If the lowest quality firms have zero cash flows, dividends in equilibrium will increase linearly with firm quality. If some firms pay excess dividends because of the wide distribution in firm quality, equilibrium is not likely. Dividend-signaling levels in equilibrium are an increasing function of the firms' differences in quality, a contention that is consistent with Ofer and Thakor (1987).

Equilibrium with homogeneous shareholder beliefs and efficient markets precludes the use of dividend policy to signal (Hakansson, 1982). Increased market efficiency via private information dissemination through corporate dividend policy will occur provided one of three sufficient conditions are met: (1) shareholders have heterogeneous probability assessments, (2) markets are incomplete, or (3) investors have different consumption allocations over time.

These three conditions are not mutually exclusive. In this model, the information content of a change in dividend policy is significant, but the signaling function alone cannot explain dividend persistence. Unexpected changes in dividends convey private information of expected future payoff patterns. The release of information through dividend policy changes proxies for additional financial markets. The model only discusses gains in shareholder welfare from dividend payments. It does not explain how investors induce managers to pay dividends or the preference for cash dividends.

John and Williams (1985) developed a signaling model with multiple equilibria using the assumption that firms with unique private information will receive varied marginal benefits following changes in dividend policy. The model is developed in an adverse environment where only dividends are taxed. Managers' expectations of future returns are signaled. An increase in dividends increases the share price—consistent with the goal of shareholder value maximization, which is different from the goal in Bhattacharya (1979). Information dissemination causes a premium to be offered by investors for dividend-paying shares that offsets the costs of the signaling—increased shareholder tax liabilities and constrained firm liquidity.

In equilibrium, firms with more favorable information pay higher dividends and are consequently valued more highly by investors. Firms with lower cash flow levels pay dividends no greater than firms with higher expected cash flows. Dividend clienteles exist in the John and Williams (1985) model. Although modeled in a world with unfavorable market conditions, equilibrium exists with dissipative dividends. The firm's optimal equilibrium is determined by internalizing the investment decision.

Miller and Rock (1985) modeled a net dividend concept—the unexpected net dividend is determined by subtracting external financing from the total dividend paid—to signal expected current earnings information that implies future earnings levels. The model combines dividends and external financing that are stylized as different sides of the same coin. The signal of current earnings differs from the models of Bhattacharya (1979) and John and Williams (1985). The cost of the signal in the model is a nonoptimal investment policy—the payment of dividends uses cash that could otherwise be used for investment opportunities. Earnings, dividends, and financing announcements are closely related, and dividends and earnings announcements are perfect substitutes by the model's assumptions. Unexpected increases in dividends provide increases in shareholder wealth.

The assumption of a managerial incentive reward/penalty policy underlies the signaling model developed by Bar-Yosef and Huffman (1986). In this equilibrium, dividends increase as managerial expectations of cash flows increase, but the marginal effect of cash flows on dividends gets smaller and smaller as cash flows increase. Consistent with Leland and Pyle (1977), higher levels of uncertainty are associated with firms with lower dividend payout ratios. Unlike the Bhattacharya (1979) model, interest rate effects on dividend payment levels are indeterminate.

Ambarish et al. (1987) generalized the models of Myers and Majluf (1984), John and Williams (1985), and Miller and Rock (1985). In this model, dividends are less efficient than other methods (investment policy, share repurchase, and equity issues) of releasing insider's information to the market. The private information known to managers is communicated through combinations of changes in dividend and investment policies or changes in dividend policy and new equity issue or share repurchase announcements. If all private information can be conveyed via an alternative signaling venue, relaying information through changes in dividend policy is redundant. Dividends exist in this equilibrium only if the cost of using multiple signaling mechanisms is less than using individual vehicles. The tax liability of dividend payment is the cost of signaling. The use of two corporate policy decisions minimizes the costs associated with signaling.

In Ofer and Thakor (1987), both dividends and stock repurchases are used as signals. The difference in costs of the two approaches precludes their substitutability. In addition to the financing costs associated with dividend payments, share repurchases have the additional cost of increasing managerial risk because of the proportional increase in managerial ownership following a repurchase. It follows that share repurchases disseminate more information because of their higher cost. Dividends are used to signal small market underpricings of the firm, whereas repurchase is reserved for periods when the stock is significantly underpriced because of the cost differential between the two methods.

The ability to use a multivariate signal does not preclude the use of a single signal. In a model developed by Hausch and Seward (1993), cash distributions are assumed to signal changes in managerial expectations of firm potential. Two types of distribution policies exist: a deterministic policy with known, declared amounts of cash payments (dividends) and a stochastic policy characterized by the firm's precommitment to pay an unspecified amount of cash (share repurchases). Each alternative has distinct signaling properties, and the distribution's size and the announcement effect's magnitude are uncorrelated. If firms have identical production possibilities but dissimilar cash levels, firms with decreasing absolute risk aversion are more likely to hold higher levels of cash and have a lower relative cost of stochastic disbursement. High-quality firms can distinguish themselves from low-quality firms by their choice of distribution policy.

A corporation's prospects can only be partially revealed using dividend policy because managers routinely smooth the payment stream; changes in dividend policy are only a rough signal of future expected earnings.

Kumar (1988) modeled a rational expectations signaling equilibrium in that dividends convey only broad information of changes in a firm's prospects. The model implies that although dividend increases (decreases) signal important positive (negative) information about the firm's prospects, dividends are a poor predictor of corporate earnings because of the smoothing process applied by managers.

In a two-period model developed by Kale and Noe (1990), dividend increases signal increased future cash flow stability and decreased riskiness of the cash flows. In this model, dividends are positively correlated with share price returns and are inversely related to expected cash flow variance and underwriting costs.

## 9.3 EMPIRICAL TESTS OF THE INFORMATIONAL CONTENT OF THE DIVIDEND HYPOTHESIS

Empirical tests of the information content of the dividend hypothesis are largely supportive of the theory. A large number of studies using diverse sample periods find that unexpected changes in dividend policy relay information and that the information released by a change in dividend policy is not trivial. The magnitude of the price change associated with unexpected decreases in dividend payouts is greater than the change following unexpected increases and is positively related to the excess returns and trading volume associated with the change. Earnings and dividend announcements are not perfect substitutes; each convey unique information. Changes in regular dividends provide more information than special dividends. A size effect (more pronounced reactions following dividend changes by smaller firms) because of the decreased level of small firm information available to the market is shown. Results can be confounded by ex-dividend/announcement effects, wealth transfers, and decreases in profitable investment opportunities.

Several studies show results that contrast with the previous findings and that are inconsistent with the information content of dividend hypothesis/signaling models. The impact of an unexpected and substantial change in dividend policy is more diverse and of greater complexity than signaling models predict. Although dividend changes and stock price movements show contemporaneous causality, the relationship is stronger over a long-term horizon due to the effects of extraneous factors (Sung and Urrutia, 1995).

Managerial subjectivity and ignorance in the estimation of earnings likely cause inaccuracies in future earning prognostications and severely limit the usefulness of the private information released through changes in corporate dividend payout levels (DeAngelo et al., 1996). The decrease in the earnings growth rate of firms following the announcement of the change in policy is also inconsistent with theory predictions. Further, the wide variance in excess return distributions associated with changes in policy is not compatible with the models' predictions.

An interesting empirical study by DeAngelo et al. (1992) finds increased earnings following dividend decreases. Dividend cuts most often occur at the low point of a firm's financial health. Corporate restructuring and a rebound in the firm's operations soon follow (Jensen and Johnson, 1995).

A major drawback of testing signaling models is that the variables specified in the theoretical framework are not directly observable. Frankfurter and Gong (1992) provided a direct test of a signaling model by examining the model developed by John and Williams (1985), who specified an empirically testable form of their model. Frankfurter and Gong (1992) showed that liquidity demands

and dividend payments are negatively correlated. This result is diametrically opposite to the model's predictions. Shareholder liquidity requirements partially determine firm dividend policy. Share prices increase (decrease) and trading volumes
decrease (increase) following dividend increases (decreases). Although a caveat for
the presence of misspecified variables is in order, this empirical test puts into
question empirical support of the John and Williams (1985) model. In the
opinion of the authors of this monograph, this is a common encumbrance of all
testable dividend-signaling models. Of course, for models that are not testable,
either the Popperian criteria of lack of scientific value or Friedman's positivism
apply. Accounting to the former such models lack scientific value. According to
the latter models sans predictive ability are useless.

Crockett and Friend (1988) concluded that the John and Williams (1985)
model prediction that zero-dividend firms have little investment capital and cash
flows instead of capital constraints is improbable. Managerial imposition of costs
on remaining shareholders to benefit sellers of the shares is irrational. In the
model developed by Miller and Rock (1985), increased dividends can release
misinformation that benefits selling shareholders. This is a conclusion in direct
contradiction with behavior rationality. In addition, consistent underinvestment
by management would make the firm a target for takeovers. Brennan and Thakor
(1990) asserted that the choice of cash distribution method cannot depend solely
on information asymmetries because share price is not an absolute composite of
private information because of the costs involved with information collection.

However, the majority of empirical tests on the information content on
dividend support the hypothesis—unexpected changes in dividend policy result
in excess returns. The results are not without possible inadequacies, however,
because they are partially driven by other events. The methods of analysis used
in these tests are likely to be less than appropriate. The arbitrary assignment of
a dividend change as unexpected (defining unexpected by the magnitude of the
change) and the length of the event window used in excess return determination are likely to bias the results. The expansive application of the event study
method of analysis, a method of questionable scientific validity (see Frankfurter
and McGoun 1993, 1995), also calls into question these findings.

Miller (1987) reviewed Riley's (1979) sufficient conditions for a signaling
equilibrium concentrating on their application in a financial setting.[2] Miller concluded that the adaptation of the Riley condition to financial modeling is difficult if not impossible. The costs associated with signaling in finance are, for the

---

[2] It is interesting to note, that since 1961, Miller had changed his position on the dividend
issue six times, each stance being mutually exclusive of any one of the others. This, by itself, is not
disturbing. What is disturbing is the fact that he had been wrong each time since 1961. We sincerely
hope that this remark will not be construed as derogatory to his memory, or to the great contribution he made while working with Franco Modigliani.

most part, opportunity costs—departures from optimal investment strategies under full information conditions.

The existence of benefits from signaling are obvious—what the benefits specifically are and whom they benefit are not. Financial researchers differ in their opinions of what is being signaled. Whether it is the permanence of past earnings, as in Lintner (1956), Fama and Babiak (1964), and Benartzi *et al.* (1997), a more precise measure of current earnings (Watts, 1973; Gonedes, 1978; Miller and Rock 1985), or future earnings expectations (Marsh and Merton, 1986). Grundy (1991) showed that the models developed by John and Williams (1985) and Miller and Rock (1985) fail to satisfy Riley's (1979) conditions if negative investments, prices, or quantities are possible.

The ability of changes in dividend policy to serve as signals of insiders' information will likely never be fully understood because of misapplications of the model. Spence (1973) wrote that his signaling model is not likely to be representative of many markets because of the different informational structures in those markets. The leap from the specific model developed by Spence to the theoretical financial signaling models of the last decade is likely to have been inappropriate given the original model's assumptions that pertain to a very narrowly defined situation (e.g., a job interview).

The questions of what dividends signal, how they signal, and why less expensive methods are less successful in communicating private information have not been answered conclusively. Signals are "self-verifying"—the mechanism is believable only if the message is reasonable and accurate (Leftwich and Zmijewski, 1996). Messages relayed through changes in dividend policy are often ambiguous—insolvent firms are liquidated via dividends following changes in dividend policy (Easterbrook, 1984).

Signaling cannot totally explain the continued existence of dividends. The assumption that dividend payments in excess of optimal levels are partially explained by signaling is simple; proving this assumption is far more difficult, as other factors determine policy (Miller, 1987). The price reaction is evidence of the capacity for signaling. If dividends are changed solely for the purpose of signaling firm-specific information, then fluctuations in aggregate dividends should be stochastic and insignificant in magnitude. If altered for any other reason, then the lack of information makes dividends useful in measuring the firm's information content in dividend announcements (Marsh and Merton, 1987). Managers' preference of using cash dividend policy to signal rather than less expensive alternatives lacks a reasonable explanation (Feldstein and Green, 1983; Thakor, 1989; Noe and Robello, 1996). If managers are not attempting to relay information through dividend policy, other dissipative methods of cash disbursement are available and should be used to ensure shareholder wealth maximization (Myers, 1987). Future research efforts will likely be more successful in explaining why dividends cannot be used as signals rather than why they can (Miller, 1987).

# 9.4  AGENCY  COST  THEORY

The recognition of potential agency costs associated with the separation of management and ownership is not new; differences in managerial and shareholder priorities have been recognized for over three centuries. Adam Smith (1937) found the management of early joint stock companies to be negligent in many of their activities

> The trade of a joint stock company is always managed by a court of directors. This court, indeed, is frequently subject, in many respects, to the control of a general court of proprietors. But the greater part of those proprietors seldom pretend to understand anything of the business of the company, and when the spirit of faction happens not to prevail among them, give themselves no trouble about it, but receive contentedly such half-yearly or yearly dividend as the directors think proper to make to them. The directors of such companies, however, being the managers of other people's money rather than of their own, it cannot well be expected that they should watch over it with the same anxious vigilance with which the partners in a private copartnery frequently watch over their own. Like the stewards of a rich man, they are apt to consider attention to small matters as not for their master's honor, and very easily give themselves a dispensation from having it. Negligence and profusion, therefore, must always prevail, more or less, in the management of the affairs of such a company. It is upon this account that joint stock companies for foreign trade have seldom been able to maintain competition against private adventurers (pp. 264–265).

These problems were especially prevalent in the British East Indies Company, and attempts to monitor managers were largely unsuccessful because of inefficiencies and costs associated with shareholder monitoring (Kindleberger, 1984). Scott (1912) and Carlos (1992) questioned these assertions—while control and organization were less than ideal, the continued success and long life of the corporation imply general sound managerial practices. Although some fraud no doubt existed, the majority of managerial activities coincided with shareholder desires.

Modern financial agency theory (Jensen and Meckling, 1976) seeks to explain corporate capital structure as the result of attempts to minimize the costs associated with the separation of corporate ownership and control. Agency costs are lower in firms with high managerial ownership stakes because of the better alignment of shareholder and manager goals and in firms with large block shareholders that are better able to monitor managerial activities (Shleifer and Vishney, 1986). Agency problems result from informational asymmetries, potential wealth transfers from bondholders to stockholders through the acceptance of high risk and high return projects by managers, and failure to accept positive net present value projects and perquisite consumption in excess of the level consumed by prudent corporate managers.

Dividend policy influences these relations in two ways. Fama and Jensen (1983a,b) espoused that potential shareholder and bondholder conflicts can be mitigated by covenants governing claim priority. These orderings can be circumvented by large dividend payments to stockholders. The payment of large dividends to shareholders can also result in the rejection of positive net present value projects and misuse of low-cost capital (Myers, 1977). Debt covenants to minimize dividend payments are necessary to prevent bondholder wealth transfers to shareholders (John and Kalay, 1982). Although potentially substantial in their precipitation of agency costs, dividend policy is not a major source of bondholder wealth expropriation. In firms where dividend payouts are limited by bondholder covenants, dividend payout levels are still below the maximum level allowed by the constraints (Kalay, 1982b).

The second way dividend policy affects agency costs is the reduction of these costs through increased monitoring by capital markets. Large dividend payments reduce funds available for perquisite consumption and investment opportunities and require managers to seek financing in capital markets. As Easterbrook (1984) contended, the efficient monitoring of capital markets curbs the less than optimal investment activity and excess perquisite consumption and hence reduces the costs associated with ownership and control separation. We are sure, however, that Post-Enron, -Tyco, -Worldcom, -Global crossing Adelphia era would have changed Professor Easterbrook's contention, perhaps just a tad.

In an empirical examination, Rozeff (1982) found three common trends in corporate dividend policy.

1. Lower dividend payment levels are found in high growth firms— investment requirements reduce the funds available for dividend payment.
2. Corporations with higher firm-specific risks or leverage ratios pay smaller dividends.
3. Higher payouts are found in firms with little insider ownership and a large number of outside shareholders.

These results imply that dividend policy mitigates agency costs because of the partial monitoring activity provided by dividend payments. A late study by Johnson (1995) supported these findings; increased dividend payments require regular capital market visits and the concurrent increases in monitoring. Other research generally supports the agency costs hypothesis.

## 9.5 THE FREE CASH FLOW HYPOTHESIS

The "free cash flow" hypothesis (Jensen, 1986) is just a minor variant of the agency argument discussed in the previous section. Prudent corporate managers working in the shareholders' best interests should invest in all profitable opportunities. However, management and owner separation affords corporate managers the temptation to consume or otherwise waste surplus funds.

Berle and Means (1932) were the first to recognize the inefficient use of funds by management in excess of profitable investment opportunities. Berle and Means' work served as the intellectual basis for the Jensen and Meckling (1976) agency paradigm. Jensen's (1986) free cash flow hypothesis updated this assertion, combining market information asymmetries with agency theory. The funds remaining after financing all positive net present value projects cause conflicts of interest between managers and shareholders. Dividend and debt interest payments decrease the free cash flow available to managers for use in investment in marginal net present value projects and manager perquisite consumption. This combination of agency and signaling theory should better explain dividend policy than either theory alone, but the free cash flow hypothesis better explains the corporate takeover frenzy of the 1980s (Myers, 1987, 1990) than anything else.

An alternate information hypothesis that changes in dividend policy signal changes in management's expected investment policy is formulated by Lang and Litzenberger (1989). The model's inferences support the free cash flow and over-investment hypotheses better than the signaling hypothesis.

Although both the signaling and the free cash flow hypotheses find some support, empirical research results better support the free cash flow hypothesis. Barber and Castanias (1992) viewed the two paradigms as complementary rather than competing.

Although MM's informational content of dividend hypothesis is supported by the majority of empirical studies, a direct test of a signaling model (Frankfurter and Gong, 1992) fails to support the model. Empirical research generally lines up on the side up the agency costs hypothesis and the partial mitigation of these costs through dividend payments. However, neither information relay nor agency cost mitigation is sufficient to explain the existence and persistence of corporate dividend policy. The consensus is that Jensen's (1986) free cash flow hypothesis, a slight variant of agency theory, explains corporate dividend policy more adequately than either of these theories individually. Nevertheless, it is hard to contend that either management is forced to behave according to this rationale or that it does so on its own volition. Of course, the pecking order hypothesis posited by Myers and Majluf (1984) is a direct contradiction of the free cash flow hypothesis.

One also must consider the fact that academic research is cleverly funneled into supporting hypotheses in vogue. It is safe to say that a multitude of studies "proving" the signaling, free cash flow and agency hypotheses would show entirely contradictory results if 2000–2002 data were used. One also cannot consider research with contradictory evidence when such work was rejected by the academic journals and never surfaced in the public domain.

# REFERENCES

Akerlof, George. 1970. "The market for 'lemons': quality uncertainty and the market mechanism." *The Quarterly Journal of Economics* 84:488–500.

Ambarish, Ramasastry, Kose John, and Joseph Williams. 1987. "Efficient signalling with dividends and investments." *The Journal of Finance* 42:321–343.

Ang, James S. 1975. "Dividend policy: informational content or partial adjustment." *The Review of Economics and Statistics* 57:65–70.

Asquith, Paul, and David W. Mullins, Jr. 1983. "The impact of initiating dividend payments on shareholders' wealth." *The Journal of Business* 56:77–96.

Barber, Brad M., and Richard C. Castanias. 1992. "why do firms initiate dividends?" Unpublished working paper.

Barclay, Michael J., and Clifford W. Smith, Jr. 1988. "Corporate payout policy: cash dividends versus open-market repurchases." *Journal of Financial Economics* 22:61–82.

Bar-Yosef, Sasson, and Lucy Huffman. 1986. "The information content of dividends: a signalling approach." *Journal of Financial and Quantitative Analysis* 21:47–58.

Benartzi, Shlomo, Roni Michaely, and Richard Thaler. 1997. "Do changes in dividends signal the future or the past?" *The Journal of Finance* 52:1007–1034.

Berle, Adolf A., and Gardiner C. Means. 1932. *The Modern Corporation and Private Property.* New York: The MacMillan Company.

Bhattacharya, Sudipto. 1979. "Imperfect information, dividend policy, and 'the bird in the hand' fallacy." *Bell Journal of Economics* 10:259–270.

Bhattacharya, Sudipto. 1980. "Nondissipative signaling structures and dividend policy." *The Quarterly Journal of Economics* 95:1–24.

Brennan, Michael J., and Anjan V. Thakor. 1990. "Shareholder preferences and dividend policy." *The Journal of Finance* 45:993–1018.

Brittain, John A. 1966. *Corporate Dividend Policy.* Washington: The Brookings Institution.

Carlos, Ann M. 1992. "Principal-agent problems in early trading companies: a tale of two firms." *The American Economic Review* 82:140–145.

Charest, Guy. 1978. "Dividend information, stock returns, and market efficiency—II." *Journal of Financial Economics* 6:297–330.

Crockett, Jean, and Irwin Friend. 1988. "Dividend policy in perspective: can theory explain behavior?" *The Review of Economics and Statistics* 70:603–613.

Damodaran, Aswath, and Crocker H. Liu. 1993. "Insider trading as a signal of private information." *The Review of Financial Studies* 6:79–119.

DeAngelo, Harry, Linda DeAngelo, and Douglas J. Skinner. 1992. "Dividends and losses." *Journal of Finance* 47:1837–1864.

DeAngelo, Harry, Linda DeAngelo, and Douglas J. Skinner. 1996. "Reversal of fortune: dividend signaling and the disappearance of sustained earnings growth." *Journal of Financial Economics* 40:341–371.

Easterbrook, Frank H. 1984. "Two agency-cost explanations of dividends." *The American Economic Review* 74:650–659.

Fama, Eugene F., and Harvey Babiak. 1968. "Dividend policy: an empirical analysis." *Journal of American Statistical Association* 63:1132–1161.

Fama, Eugene F., Lawrence Fisher, Michael C. Jensen, and Richard Roll. 1969. "The adjustment of stock prices to new information." *International Economic Review* 10:1–21.

Fama, Eugene F., and Michael C. Jensen. 1983a. "Separation of ownership and control." *Journal of Law and Economics* 26:301–325.

Fama, Eugene F., and Michael C. Jensen. 1983b. "Agency problems and residual claims." *Journal of Law and Economics* 26:327–349.

Feldstein, Martin S., and Jerry Green. 1983. "Why do companies pay dividends?" *The American Economic Review* 73:17–30.

Frankfurter, George M., and Jaisik Gong. 1992. "Empirical tests of a dividend signaling equilibrium model." Louisana State University, Unpublished working paper.

Frankfurter, George M., and Elton G. McGoun. 1993. "The event study: an industrial strength method." *The International Review of Financial Analysis* 2:121–142

Frankfurter, George M., and Elton G. McGoun. 1995. "The event study: is it either?" *The Journal of Investing* 4:8–16.

Gonedes, Nicholas J. 1978. "Corporate signaling, external accounting, and capital market equilibrium: evidence on dividends, income, and extraordinary items." *Journal of Accounting Research* 16:26–79.

Griffen, Paul A. 1976. "Competitive information in the stock market: an empirical study of earnings, dividends, and analysts' forecasts." *The Journal of Finance* 31:631–650.

Grundy, Bruce D. 1989. "The viability of dividend signalling." Unpublished working paper.

Hakansson, Nils H. 1982. "To pay or not to pay dividend." *The Journal of Finance* 37:415–428.

Harris, Milton, and Arthur Raviv. 1985. "A sequential signalling model of convertible debt call policy." *The Journal of Finance* 40:1263–1281.

Hausch, Donald B., and James K. Seward. 1993. "Signaling with dividends and share repurchases: a choice between deterministic and stochastic cash disbursements." *The Review of Financial Studies* 6:121–154.

Jensen, Gerald R., and James M. Johnson. 1995. "The dynamics of corporate dividend reductions." *Financial Management* 24:31–51.

Jensen, Michael C. 1986. "Agency costs of free cash flow, corporate finance, and takeovers." *The American Economic Review* 76:323–329.

Jensen, Michael C., and William H. Meckling. 1976. "Theory of the firm: managerial behavior, agency costs and ownership structure." *Journal of Financial Economics* 3:305–360.

John, Kose, and Avner Kalay. 1982. "Costly contracting and optimal payout constraints." *The Journal of Finance* 37:457–470.

John, Kose, and Larry H. P. Lang. 1991. "Insider trading around dividend announcements: theory and evidence." *The Journal of Finance* 46:1361–1389.

John, Kose, and Banikanta Mishra. 1990. "Information content of insider trading around corporate announcements: the case of capital expenditures." *The Journal of Finance* 45:835–855.

John, Kose, and Joseph Williams. 1985. "Dividends, dilution, and taxes: a signalling equilibrium." *The Journal of Finance* 40:1053–1070.

Johnson, Shane A. 1995. "Dividend payout and the valuation effects of bond announcements." *Journal of Financial and Quantitative Analysis* 30:407–423.

Kalay, Avner. 1980. "Signaling, information content, and the reluctance to cut dividends." *Journal of Financial and Quantitative Analysis* 15:855–869.

Kalay, Avner. 1982a. "The ex-dividend day behavior of stock prices." *The Journal of Finance* 37:1059–1070.

Kalay, Avner. 1982b. "Stockholder-bondholder conflict and dividend constraints." *Journal of Financial Economics* 10:211–233.

Kale, Jayant R., and Thomas H. Noe. 1990. "Dividends, uncertainty, and underwriting costs under asymmetric information." *The Journal of Finance* 13:265–277.

Kindleberger, Charles P. 1978. *Manias, Panics, and Crashes (A History of Financial Crises)*. New York: Basic Books, Inc.

Kindleberger, Charles P. 1984. *A Financial History of Western Europe*. London: George Allen & Unwin.

Kumar, Praveen. 1988. "Shareholder-manager conflict and the information content of dividends." *The Review of Financial Studies* 1:111–136.

Lang, Larry H. P., and Robert H. Litzenberger. 1989. "Dividend announcements: cash flow signalling vs. free cash flow hypothesis?" *Journal of Financial Economics* 24:181–191.

Laub, P. Michael. 1976, "On the informational content of dividends." *The Journal of Business* 49:73–80.

Leland, Hayne E., and David H. Pyle. 1977. "Informational asymmetries, financial structure, and financial intermediation." *The Journal of Finance* 32:371–388.

Lintner, John. 1956. "Optimal dividends and corporate growth under uncertainty." *The Quarterly Journal of Economics* 78:49–95.

Makhija, Anil K., and Howard E. Thompson. 1986. "Some aspects of equilibrium for a cross-section of firms signaling profitability with dividends: a note." *The Journal of Finance* 41:249–253.

Marsh, Terry A., and Robert C. Merton. 1986. "Dividend variability and variance bounds tests for the rationality of stock market prices." *The American Economic Review* 76:483–498.

Miller, Merton H. 1987. "The informational content of dividends." In *Macroeconomics: Essays in Honor of Franco Modigliani.* John Bosons, Rudiger Dornbusch, and Stanley Fischer, eds. Cambridge, MA: MIT Press.

Miller, Merton H., and Franco Modigliani. 1961. "Dividend policy, growth, and the valuation of shares." *The Journal of Business* 34:411–433.

Miller, Merton H., and Kevin Rock. 1985. "Dividend policy under asymmetric information." *The Journal of Finance* 40:1031–1051.

Myers, Stewart C. 1977. "Determinants of corporate borrowing." *Journal of Financial Economics* 4:147–175.

Myers, Stewart C. 1987. "Comments on "The informational content of dividends." In *Macroeconomics: Essays in Honor of Franco Modigliani.* John Bosons, Rudiger Dornbusch, and Stanley Fischer, eds. Cambridge, MA: MIT Press.

Myers, Stewart C. 1990. "Still searching for capital structure." Keynote address delivered at the HEC International Conference.

Myers, Stewart C., and Nicholas S. Majluf. 1984. "Corporate financing and investment decisions when firms have information that investors do not have." *Journal of Financial Economics* 13:187–221.

Noe, Thomas H., and Michael J. Robello. 1996. "Asymmetric information, managerial opportunism, financing, and payout policies." *The Journal of Finance* 51:637–660.

Ofer, Aharon R., and Anjan V. Thakor. 1987. "A theory of stock price responses to alternative corporate cash disbursement methods: stock repurchases and dividends." *The Journal of Finance* 42:365–394

Pettit, R. Richardson. 1972. "Dividend announcements, security performance, and capital market efficiency." *The Journal of Finance* 27:993–1007.

Pettit, R. Richardson. 1976. "The impact of dividend and earnings announcements: a reconciliation." *The Journal of Business* 49:86–96.

Riley, John G. 1979. "Informational equilibrium." *Econometrica* 47:331–359.

Rodriguez, Ricardo J. 1992. "Quality dispersion and the feasibility of dividends as signals." *The Journal of Financial Research* 15:307–315.

Ross, Stephen A. 1977. "The determination of financial structure: the incentive-signalling approach." *Bell Journal of Economics* 8:23–40.

Rothschild, Michael, and Joseph Stiglitz. 1976. "Equilibrium in competitive insurance markets: an essay on the economics of imperfect information." *The Quarterly Journal of Economics* 90:629–649.

Rozeff, Michael S. 1982. "Growth, beta and agency costs as determinants of dividend payout ratios." *The Journal of Financial Research* 5:249–259.

Scott, William Robert. 1912. *The Constitution and Finance of English, Scottish, and Irish Joint Stock Companies to 1720.* Cambridge, MA: Cambridge University Press.

Shleifer, Andrei, and Robert W. Vishney. 1986. "Large shareholders and corporate control." *Journal of Political Economy* 94:461–488.

Smith, Adam. 1937. *The Wealth of Nations.* New York: Random House, Inc.

Spence, Michael. 1973. "Job market signaling." *The Quarterly Journal of Economics* 87:355–374.

Spence, Michael. 1974. "Competitive and Optimal Responses to Signals: An Analysis of Efficiency and Distribution." *Journal of Economic Theory* 7:296–332.

Stewart, Samuel S., Jr. 1976. "Should a corporation repurchase its own stock." *The Journal of Finance* 31:911–921.

Sung, Hyun Mo, and Jorge L. Urrutia. 1995. "Long-term and short-term causal relations between dividends and stock prices: a test of Lintner's dividend model and the present value model of stock prices." *The Journal of Financial Research* 18:171–188.

Talmor, Eli. 1981. "Asymmetric information, signaling, and optimal corporate financial decisions." *Journal of Financial and Quantitative Analysis* 16:413–435.

Thakor, Anjan V. 1989. "Strategic issues in financial contracting: an overview." *Financial Management* 18:39–58.

Vermaelen, Theo. 1981. "Common stock repurchases and market signaling." *Journal of Financial Economics* 9:139–183.

Watts, Ross. 1973. "The information content of dividends." *The Journal of Business* 46:191–211.

# CHAPTER 10

# Determinants of Dividend Policies

The subject of this chapter is an empirical investigation of the determining factors of dividend policies.[1] A structural model, based on determinants of earlier dividend theories, is designed and tested.

The body of literature dealing with dividend determinants can be grouped into two distinct categories: (1) those based on the implicit assumption of symmetric information and (2) those based on the explicit assumption of asymmetric information.

In the symmetric information milieu, the seminal work is that of Lintner (1956). According to Lintner's model, current dividends are predicated upon past dividends and current profits. Lintner's "two-variable" model is supported by the empirical evidence of Fama and Babiak (1968).[2]

Theories based on the supposition of asymmetric information include agency, pecking order, and, most profoundly, dividend-signaling theories. Agency

---

[1]This chapter contains material representing Dr. Jasik Gong's work performed as the graduate assistant of the first author of this book and an unpublished paper, Frankfurter and Gong (1993). The bulk of the data presented here is also included in Dr. Gong's dissertation, titled "Three Essays in Dividend Policy."

[2]A somewhat different work is that of Marsh and Merton (1987), who developed a dynamic aggregate dividend behavior model based on both accounting data and stock market data. In contrast to Marsh and Merton, the present study treats the dividend policy problem endogenous to the firm. In addition, there are marked differences between the two studies, both in method of analysis and in data used. Nevertheless, the conclusions of this study and the Marsh and Merton study concerning the validity of signaling models are surprisingly similar.

theory explanations of dividend policy build on the works of Easterbrook (1984) and Jensen (1986). The pecking order theory (the complete opposite of the agency theory explanation[3]) is espoused by Myers (1984) and Myers and Majluf (1984).

Signaling theory, first proposed by Bhattacharya (1979, 1980), asserts that "good" firms are able to signal their expected fortunes via the disbursement of dividends, the tax costs of which are fully recovered by ensuing stock price increases. Further, dividend payments as signals result in a separating equilibrium between the signaling firms (the "good guys" and "bad" ones that are unable to signal).

The work described in this chapter differs from preceding studies in three ways. First, this study explicitly tests the free-cash-flow concept of both agency theory and pecking order theory, thus filling an obvious void in the literature. Second, time-series cross-sectional tests are performed using individual firm data, while the vector autoregression (VAR) method is applied to aggregate data. In previous studies, important information explaining differences in dividend policy over time was lost because of the application of cross-sectional analysis to either firm-specific or aggregate data. Last, but not least, a wide scope of dividend determinants is considered in the present work.

## 10.1  METHOD OF ANALYSIS

Data, sample and variable selection, and variable definitions are presented in Appendix A.

### 10.1.1  TIME–SERIES CROSS-SECTIONAL ANALYSIS

A time-series cross-sectional model is applied to individual firm data. A generalized linear model is considered, where observations are taken $T$ time periods for each of $N$ firms. The model at time $t$ for each firm $i$ is then

$$DIV_{it} = \Theta_0 + \Theta_1 INV_{it} + \Theta_2 EARN_t + \Theta_3 DEBT_{it} + \Theta_4 FCASH_{it} + u_{it},$$
$$i = 1, \ldots, N \quad t = 1, \ldots, T \tag{10.1}$$

where $\Theta$ are coefficients and $u_{it}$ is an error term.

---

[3]In a nutshell, agency theory argues for paying out all free cash flows as dividends. In contrast, the pecking order hypothesis contends that management will select from the least expensive sources of funds to the most expensive source to finance its planned activities. While both theories are ad hoc, the latter is consistent with observable behavior, whereas the former is not.

To estimate $\Theta_{0-4}$, the error components model (ECM) of Fuller and Battese (1974) is followed. In the ECM, the regression error, $u_{it}$, is assumed to be the sum of three independent components:

$$u_{it} = \gamma_i + \delta_i + \varepsilon_{it}, \tag{10.2}$$

where $\gamma_i \sim (0, \sigma_\gamma^2)$ is a unique cross-sectional effect, $\delta_i \sim (0, \sigma_\delta^2)$ is a unique time effect, and $\varepsilon_{it} \sim (0, \sigma_\varepsilon^2)$ is an error term.

Under these assumptions, the covariance matrix of the regression error term $u_{it}$ is

$$E(u'u) = \sigma_\gamma^2 (\mathbf{I}_N \otimes \mathbf{j}_T \mathbf{j}_T') + \sigma_\delta^2 (\mathbf{j}_N \mathbf{j}_N' \otimes \mathbf{I}_T) + \sigma_\varepsilon^2 \mathbf{I}_{NT}, \tag{10.3}$$

where $\mathbf{I}_N$ is an $N \times N$ identity matrix, $\otimes$ is the Kronecker product matrix, and $\mathbf{j}_T$ is a $T \times T$ matrix of ones.

Fuller and Battese (1974) showed that transformation through premultiplying Eq. (10.1) by the covariance matrix yields uncorrelated errors with variance $\sigma_\varepsilon^2$.

Because the procedure transforms the variables by the covariance matrix of residuals, it corrects for heteroscedasticity in a less restrictive way than a simple division of the variables by firm size (or some other variable). Concurrently, the procedure also adjusts time-series data for serial correlation. Thus, unbiased and efficient generalized least-squares (GLS) estimates are obtained by an OLS regression applied to these transformed data.

The estimated $\Theta_{0-4}$ values and $t$ statistics for $H_0$: $\Theta_0 = \Theta_1, \ldots, \Theta_4 = 0$ are used to test the relationship between dividends and the explanatory variables.

## 10.1.2 Vector Autoregression Model (VAR)

A VAR model is used to analyze aggregate data.[4] Under the VAR model, a system of dynamic linear equations is constructed such that a vector of dependent variables is related to lagged vectors of all variables in the system. For example, the dividend equation takes the form

$$DIV_t = \alpha_0 + \sum_{k=1}^{m} \alpha_k DIV_{t-k} + \sum_{k=1}^{m} \xi_k INV_{t-k} + \sum_{k=1}^{m} \vartheta_k EARN_{t-k}$$

$$+ \sum_{k=1}^{m} \chi_k DEBT_{t-k} + \sum_{k=1}^{m} \omega_k FCASH_{t-k} + \varepsilon_t, \tag{10.4}$$

where $\alpha$, $\xi$, $\vartheta$, $\chi$, and $\omega$ are the coefficients; $m$ is the lag length; and $\varepsilon_t$ is white noise.

[4]See, for example, Sims (1980).

The structural VAR model—a system of five equations—has the form:

$$\underset{(5x1)}{\mathbf{X}} = \underset{(5x1)}{\mathbf{A}(L)} \ \underset{(5x1)}{\mathbf{X}} + \underset{(5x1)}{\mathbf{C}} + \underset{(5x1)}{\mathbf{E}},$$

(10.5)

where $\mathbf{X}$ is the vector of variables (i.e., DIV, INV, EARN, DEBT, and FCASH); $A(L)$ is a matrix polynomial in the lag operator L (i.e., $A(L) = A_1L + A_2L^2 + \ldots + A_mL^m$); $\mathbf{C}$ is a vector of constant terms; and $\mathbf{E}$ is a vector of error terms (i.e., $\varepsilon_{DIV}$, $\varepsilon_{INV}$, $\varepsilon_{EARN}$, $\varepsilon_{DEBT}$, and $\varepsilon_{FCASH}$).

Equation (10.5) can be rewritten compactly as

$$\mathbf{B}(L)\mathbf{X} = [\mathbf{I} - \mathbf{A}(L)]\mathbf{X} = \mathbf{C} + \mathbf{E},$$

(10.6)

where $\mathbf{B}(L)$ is a matrix polynomial in the lag operator L [i.e., $\mathbf{B}(L) = \mathbf{I} - \mathbf{A}_1L - \mathbf{A}_2L^2 - \ldots - \mathbf{A}_mL^m$] and $\mathbf{I}$ is the identity matrix.

If $\mathbf{X}$ is stationary and the roots of $\mathbf{B}(L)$ lie outside the unit circle, Eq. (10.6) is inverted to form

$$\mathbf{X} = \mathbf{B}(L)^{-1}\mathbf{C} + \mathbf{B}(L)^{-1}\mathbf{E}.$$

(10.7)

According to Wold's decomposition theorem, the vector process of Eq. (10.7) consists of a deterministic and an indeterministic component that can be represented as a vector moving average:

$$X_t = \bar{x}_t + \sum_{i=0}^{\infty} \mathbf{\Phi}_i \varepsilon_{t-i},$$

(10.8)

where $\bar{x}_t$ is a constant, $\mathbf{\Phi}_i$ is the coefficient matrix, and $\varepsilon_t$ is the vector of white noise.

Following Sims (1980), the VAR method generally uses two statistics derived from the coefficient matrix $\mathbf{\Phi}$ of Eq. (10.8). The first VAR statistic is the variance decomposition of forecast errors for $X_t$. Constructed to show the dynamic relationship between the system variables, it measures the proportion of each variable's contribution to the forecast error variance in the $h$-step ahead forecast of $X_t$ (where $h$ is a positive integer). Because the $h$-step ahead forecast of $X_t$ is

$$F_{t,h} = \bar{x}_{t+h} + \sum_{i=h}^{\infty} \mathbf{\Phi}_i \varepsilon_{t+h-i},$$

(10.9)

the forecast error and its variance matrix are calculated as

$$X_{t+h} - F_{t,h} = \sum_{i=0}^{h-1} \mathbf{\Phi}_i \varepsilon_{t+h-i} \quad \text{and} \quad Var(X_{t+h} - F_{t,h})$$

$$= \sum_{i=0}^{h-1} \mathbf{\Phi}_i Var(\varepsilon_{t+h-i})\mathbf{\Phi}_i' = \sum_{i=0}^{h-1} \mathbf{\Phi}_i \mathbf{\Phi}_i'$$

(10.10)

The $h$-step forecast error variance of the $k$th variable, $X_k$, is expressed as the sum of the $k$th diagonal elements of each $\Phi_i\Phi_i'$ in Eq. (10.10), where the $k$th diagonal elements of $\Phi_i\Phi_i'$ is defined as the sum of the squares of elements in the $k$th row of $\Phi_i$.

$$\sum_{i=0}^{h-1}(\Phi_i\Phi_i')_{kk} = \sum_{i=0}^{h-1}\left(\sum_{m=1}^{n}\phi_{km,i}^2\right), \tag{10.11}$$

where $\phi_{km,i}$ is the $km$th element of $\Phi_i$ and $n$ is the number of variables. The contribution of the $j$th variable, $X_j$, to the $h$-step forecast error variance of $X_k$ is

$$\sum_{i=0}^{h-1}\phi_{kj,i}^2, \tag{10.12}$$

where $\phi_{kj,i}$ is the $kj$th element of $\Phi_i$.

Then, the relative proportion of the $j$th variable, $X_j$, to the $h$-step forecast error variance of $X_k$ is measured by

$$\frac{\displaystyle\sum_{i=0}^{h-1}\phi_{kj,i}^2}{\displaystyle\sum_{i=0}^{h-1}\left(\sum_{m-1}^{n}\phi_{km,i}^2\right)}. \tag{10.13}$$

This decomposes the $h$-step forecast error variance for each variable into (1) the components accounted for by its own surprise movement and (2) the shocks to other variables in the system.

Because the error variance of a variable is identified as the sum of contributions by all variables in the system, this decomposition method is useful for exploring the influence of one variable on another variable. For example, if investments make significant contributions to the forecast error variance of dividends, the ramification is that investments are a major influence on dividends.

The second test statistic in the VAR technique is the impulse response function (IRF), conceived to trace out the response path of the system variables to an unexpected unit shock in a variable.[5] Because the impulse response of $X_t$ to the shock $\varepsilon_t$ is measured as $\partial F_{t,h}/\partial\varepsilon_t$, the $h$th moving average coefficient of $X_t$ is obtained from Eq. (10.9):

$$\frac{\partial F_{t,h}}{\partial\varepsilon_t} = \Phi_h. \tag{10.14}$$

---

[5]The normalized unit shock to a variable is given by a one standard deviation surprise movement in that variable. This is often called innovation accounting because it traces out the system's reaction to a shock (innovation) in a variable (see Sims, 1980).

Consequently, the IRF can be regarded as a dynamic multiplier that indicates the size and direction of the response of system variables to a unit shock in a variable (McMillin and Parker, 1990). For example, if the impulse response of dividends to a unit shock in investments is significant and negative, then Miller and Modigliani's (1961) proposition of irrelevance cannot hold. This is so, because dividends and investments would be substitutes for the firm's funds.

Before VAR estimation can commence, the error terms $\varepsilon_t$ in Eq. (10.8) must be orthogonalized in order to eliminate any contemporaneous correlation. To obtain the orthogonalized errors, the Choleski decomposition transforms Eq. (10.8) by using the lower triangular matrix, **P**, from the covariance matrix, **E**:

$$X_t = \overline{x}_t + \sum_{i=0}^{\infty} \Phi_i \mathbf{P}\mathbf{P}^{-1}\varepsilon_{t-i} = \overline{x}_t + \sum_{i=0}^{\infty} \Phi_i^* \varepsilon_{t-i}^* \tag{10.15}$$

where $\Phi_i^* = \Phi_i\mathbf{P}$ is the transformed coefficient matrix and $\varepsilon_t^* = \mathbf{P}^{-1}\varepsilon_t$ is the transformed vector white noise.

This VAR model has much appeal over earlier models. In the VAR model, all variables are represented jointly to reflect their dynamic relationship without imposing any *a priori* restrictions. Also, VAR has no risk of misspecification (such as serially correlated and heteroscedastic errors), a problem vexing many who have studied the subject before.

## 10.2  EMPIRICAL RESULTS

### 10.2.1  SAMPLE CHARACTERISTICS

Table 10.1 presents sample characteristics for the 446 firms included in this study. The cross-sectional medians, means, and standard deviations for each variable's averages from the second quarter of 1979 to the fourth quarter of 1990 are shown in Table 10.1A.

It is interesting to note from the means column that the sum of DIV and INV representing outflows of corporate funds approximates the sum of EARN, DEBT, and FCASH representing inflows of corporate funds. This seems to be consistent with Dhrymes and Kurz's (1967) suggestion that one of the firm's long-term objectives is to grow while keeping the stream of cash flows on an even keel. Another conspicuous number is the standard deviation of SIZE. This figure is quite large compared to the other variables' standard deviation, pointing toward the possible presence of heteroscedasticity.

The correlation matrix between the variables is shown in Table 10.1B.[6] There are several interesting points to note in Table 10.1B. First, the correlations

---

[6] Accounting variables are standardized on SIZE in order to adjust for potential heteroscedasticity.

Table 10.1

Sample Characteristics

A: Cross-sectional mean and standard deviation of each variable averaged from 1979:II to 1990:IV

| Variable | Variable description | Median | Mean | Standard deviation |
|---|---|---|---|---|
| DIV | Common stock dividends paid (in millions) | $5.658 | $21.709 | $56.717 |
| INV | Change in investment (in millions) | $7.359 | $31.830 | $81.490 |
| EARN | Earnings available to common stockholders (in millions) | $12.145 | $40.996 | $111.645 |
| DEBT | Change in long-term debt (in millions) | $3.854 | $22.744 | $87.316 |
| FCASH | Estimated free cash flow (in millions) | $6.748 | −$6.158 | $306.313 |
| SIZE | Book value of assets (in millions) | $1,155.400 | $5,735.038 | $15,049.108 |
| BETA | Beta coefficient | 0.894 | 0.845 | 0.358 |

B: Cross-sectional correlations between each variable averaged from 1979:II to 1990:IV

| Variable[a] | DIV | INV | EARN | DEBT | FCASH |
|---|---|---|---|---|---|
| INV | 0.0230 (0.627) | | | | |
| EARN | 0.6831 (0.0001)[b] | 0.2452 (0.0001)[b] | | | |
| DEBT | 0.0300 (0.527) | 0.5078 (0.0001)[b] | 0.0133 (0.778) | | |
| FCASH | −0.1270 (0.007)[b] | 0.4158 (0.0001)[b] | 0.1023 (0.030)[c] | 0.0875 (0.064) | |
| BETA | −0.2696 (0.0001)[b] | −0.1444 (0.002)[b] | −0.1304 (0.005)[b] | −0.0107 (0.820) | −0.0942 (0.046)[c] |

C: Sample by industry

| Industry | SIC code | Sample frequency | Distribution of firm sizes (in millions) | | |
|---|---|---|---|---|---|
| | | | Median | Mean | Standard deviation |
| Mining and construction | 1000–1999 | 28 (6.28%) | $633.118 | $2,710.202 | $7,028.921 |
| Nondurable manufacturing | 2000–2999 | 93 (20.85%) | $1,053.903 | $4,195.658 | $9,405.505 |
| Durable manufacturing | 3000–3999 | 127 (28.48%) | $361.115 | $3,441.985 | $10,648.941 |
| Transportation and utilities | 4000–4999 | 124 (27.80%) | $2,112.433 | $3,318.134 | $3,593.406 |
| Wholesale and retail trade | 5000–5999 | 11 (2.47%) | $330.290 | $1,262.387 | $1,847.221 |
| Finance, insurance, and real estate | 6000–6999 | 52 (11.65%) | $10,240.014 | $23,533.952 | $33,293.750 |
| Services | 7000–8999 | 11 (2.47%) | $384.695 | $501.159 | $491.321 |
| | | 446 (100%) | | | |

[a] Accounting variables, including DIV, INV, EARN, DEBT, and FCASH, are standardized on SIZE.
[b] Significant at the 0.01 level.
[c] Significant at the 0.05 level.

between DIV and other explanatory variables provide a preliminary picture of the subsequent tests. The correlations with INV and DEBT are not significant. The correlation with EARN is positive and significant, whereas the correlations with FCASH and BETA are negative and significant.

Second, although some correlations between the explanatory variables are significant, the risk of serious multicollinearity is, nevertheless, not excessive.[7] The correlations of INV with EARN, DEBT, FCASH, and BETA are significant. The correlation between EARN and BETA is negative and significant. Because these correlations are low, the implication is that controlling for heteroscedasticity results in the reduction of multicollinearity, also.

Table 10.1C displays the sample by industry classification. The firms in each industry are grouped by firm size. Cross-industry variations in firm size are evident. The finance, insurance, and real estate industries have the largest mean firm size, while the smallest mean firm size is services, wholesale, and retail trade industries.

## 10.2.2 TIME-SERIES CROSS-SECTIONAL REGRESSION RESULTS

Time-series, cross-sectional regressions are estimated, as discussed earlier, using the error components model of Fuller and Battese (1974). Table 10.2, divided into four sections, presents the estimates of the time-series, cross-sectional regressions. Table 10.2A shows the estimates for the full sample. The most striking result is the verification of Miller and Modigliani's (1961) dividend irrelevance proposition: the coefficient estimates on INV and DEBT are insignificant. Equally surprising is the negative (and significant) coefficient estimate of FCASH. This gives credence to the pecking order hypothesis.[8] The coefficient of EARN is positive and significant, consistent with Lintner's (1956) prediction.

Tables 10.2B–10.2D present the estimates for subsamples classified by size, beta, and industry, respectively. Coefficient estimates on EARN and FCASH are quite consistent with the findings for the full sample. However, the signs and significance of the INV and DEBT estimates reveal mixed results. The intercept estimates are interesting, too, because they provide some insight into tests that follow.

---

[7]Multicollinearity is not a profound problem in this study for several reasons. First, the coefficients of the simple correlations are not high. Second, this kind of multicollinearity can be remedied when time-series cross-sectional regressions follow the estimated generalized least-squares (GLS) procedure with more than 20,000 observations. Third, the VAR analysis focuses on forecast error variance decompositions and impulse response functions, both unaffected by multicollinearity.

[8]As shown earlier, the effect of FCASH should be explored in the context of its dynamic interaction with DIV.

Coefficient estimates of the intercept in the subsamples sorted by size are significant and positively related to firm size. In contrast, for the subsamples sorted by beta, the intercept estimates are inversely related to beta. Coefficient estimates of the intercept in the industrial subsamples vary both in significance and magnitude. This suggests that missing variables may cause model misspecification collapsing into the intercept term.

Time-series cross-sectional regression estimates using six different model specifications are reported in Table 10.3. Model 1 is the regression in which the variable BETA is included. The coefficient estimate on BETA is negative and significant. In model 2, four size variables are included. Of these, two, $S_4$ and $S_5$, representing large firm sizes, show positive and significant estimates. When BETA and the size variables are entered simultaneously into model 3, the effects of beta and firm size are the same as those in models 1 and 2.

Model 4 includes industry variables. Results show that none of the industry variables are statistically significant at the 0.01 level. When BETA is added to model 4 (to form model 5), BETA has a negative and significant coefficient estimate. Regardless, even in model 5 the industry variables do not have significant estimates.

Also shown are the regression results of model 6 in which four size variables are added to model 4. Two large size variables have positive and significant coefficient estimates, whereas the sixth industry variable representing finance, insurance, and real estate has a negative (and significant) coefficient estimate. Finally, in model 7, all the variables are included in the regression. The sets of coefficient estimates on BETA and size variables are consistent with the estimate results in other models of Table 10.3. Although other industry variables are insignificant at the 0.01 level, the industry variable for finance, insurance, and real estate is significant, similar to those of model 6.

These results are sufficient to cast doubt on an "industry effect" in dividend policy. As noted in Table 10.1, the finance, insurance, and real estate industries have the largest mean firm size. Also, this industry variable has a significant coefficient only when size variables enter the model. This (along with the insignificant estimates of other industry variables) suggests that industrial variations in dividend policy, as documented in Michel (1979), might be only a reflection of the size effect.

The estimates of INV, EARN, DEBT, and FCASH in model 7 are entirely consistent with the findings for the full sample in Table 10.2, as well as those for other models in Table 10.3. The coefficient estimates of INV and DEBT are insignificant. The EARN coefficient estimate is positive, large, and has highly significant $t$ statistics, whereas the FCASH coefficient estimate is negative and significant.

## Table 10.2

### Time-Series Cross-Sectional Estimates from Regressing Fuller and Battese Model for 446 Firms in the Sample from 1979:II to 1990:IV

$$DIV_{it} = \Theta_0 + \Theta_1\, INV_{it} + \Theta_2\, EARN_{it} + \Theta_3\, DEBT_{it} + \Theta_4\, FCASH_{it} + u_{it}$$
$$i = 1, \ldots, N \quad t = 1, \ldots, T$$

| | No. of Firms | INTERCEPT ($\Theta_0$) | INV ($\Theta_1$) | EARN ($\Theta_2$) | DEBT ($\Theta_3$) | FCASH ($\Theta_4$) | Adjusted $R^2$ | Probability of $F$ |
|---|---|---|---|---|---|---|---|---|
| A: Full Sample | | | | | | | | |
| | 446 | 19.5665 (10.494)[a] | 0.00035 (0.582) | 0.0509 (18.433)[a] | 0.00032 (1.574) | −0.0060 (−8.854)[a] | 0.2059 | <0.0001 |
| B: Classification by size | | | | | | | | |
| <$161.21 million | 89 | 0.3336 (6.014)[a] | −0.00013 (−0.094) | 0.0836 (17.220)[a] | 0.0036 (1.975) | −0.0403 (−11.952)[a] | 0.3256 | <0.0001 |
| <$687.74 million | 90 | 2.1373 (8.742)[a] | 0.0109 (3.267)[a] | 0.0882 (10.576)[a] | −0.0036 (−1.342) | −0.0806 (−17.316)[a] | 0.3177 | <0.0001 |
| <$2,004.02 million | 89 | 8.8031 (7.090)[a] | −0.0107 (−1.579) | 0.2594 (13.451)[a] | 0.1032 (18.051)[a] | −0.3904 (−49.089)[a] | 0.4365 | <0.0001 |
| <$5,265.82 million | 88 | 19.6253 (6.432)[a] | 0.0203 (13.611)[a] | 0.1448 (9.690)[a] | 0.1485 (19.819)[a] | −0.1279 (−22.175)[a] | 0.2805 | <0.0001 |
| <$162,742.87 million | 90 | 67.2550 (8.686)[a] | 0.0033 (3.115)[a] | 0.0371 (13.711)[a] | −0.00009 (−0.516) | 0.00091 (1.414) | 0.3895 | <0.0001 |
| C: Classification by beta | | | | | | | | |
| <0.48219 | 89 | 22.9196 (11.098)[a] | 0.0031 (2.101)[b] | 0.1187 (21.435)[a] | 0.0016 (2.806)[a] | 0.0032 (2.378)[b] | 0.5654 | <0.0001 |
| <0.80477 | 90 | 45.6883 (6.650)[a] | −0.00057 (−0.473) | 0.0548 (7.745)[a] | 0.00044 (0.882) | −0.0042 (−3.046)[a] | 0.2498 | <0.0001 |

|  |  |  |  |  |  |  |  |  |
|---|---|---|---|---|---|---|---|---|
| <0.96376 | 89 | 12.5335 (5.719)ᵃ | 0.0052 (5.142)ᵃ | 0.0551 (19.513)ᵃ | -0.00047 (-3.142)ᵃ | 0.0058 (4.081)ᵃ | 0.3525 | <0.0001 |
| <1.13844 | 89 | 8.7077 (5.862)ᵃ | 0.0086 (6.615)ᵃ | 0.0197 (10.643)ᵃ | -0.0025 (-4.969)ᵃ | -0.0171 (-22.841)ᵃ | 0.4333 | <0.0001 |
| <1.78289 | 89 | 5.9218 (4.203)ᵃ | 0.0310 (8.446)ᵃ | 0.1561 (19.432)ᵃ | 0.0195 (9.835)ᵃ | -0.3256 (-42.072)ᵃ | 0.2511 | <0.0001 |
| **D: Classification by industry** |  |  |  |  |  |  |  |  |
| Mining and construction | 28 | 20.0135 (2.509)ᵇ | 0.0121 (5.807)ᵃ | 0.0503 (2.172)ᵇ | -0.0191 (-1.597) | -0.0791 (-9.132)ᵃ | 0.0404 | <0.0001 |
| Nondurable manufacturing | 93 | 28.0192 (5.945)ᵃ | -0.0027 (-1.456) | 0.0606 (10.371)ᵃ | 0.0076 (3.666)ᵃ | -0.00080 (-0.951) | 0.2578 | <0.0001 |
| Durable manufacturing | 127 | 15.0960 (4.501)ᵃ | 0.0135 (10.778)ᵃ | 0.0505 (23.100)ᵃ | -0.00035 (-3.437)ᵃ | 0.0223 (17.363)ᵃ | 0.2762 | <0.0001 |
| Transportation and utilities | 124 | 19.2413 (10.518)ᵃ | -0.00076 (-0.809) | 0.0698 (17.641)ᵃ | 0.0119 (8.063)ᵃ | -0.0017 (-1.443) | 0.4508 | <0.0001 |
| Wholesale and retail trade | 11 | 9.1465 (1.524) | -0.2089 (-9.164)ᵃ | 0.1527 (2.009)ᵇ | 0.4074 (24.805)ᵃ | -0.4749 (-23.700)ᵃ | 0.3278 | <0.0001 |
| Finance, insurance, and real estate | 52 | 13.4203 (3.344)ᵃ | 0.0022 (1.594) | 0.0089 (4.232)ᵇ | -0.00086 (-2.016)ᵇ | -0.0200 (-21.231)ᵃ | 0.2738 | <0.0001 |
| Services | 11 | 1.9735 (2.538)ᵇ | 0.0012 (1.139) | 0.0204 (5.216)ᵃ | -0.00093 (-1.329) | 0.0022 (1.854) | 0.3549 | <0.0001 |

[1]The Fuller and Battese model corrects for heteroscedasticity and autocorrelation considerably. When the model is regressed after transforming data by firm size, the coefficient estimate results are almost the same, but the adjusted $R^2$ decreases. This indicates that some information shown in predictive power is lost.

[2]$t$ statistics are given in parentheses.

ᵃSignificant at the 0.01 level.

ᵇSignificant at the 0.05 level.

# Table 10.3

## Time-Series Cross-Sectional Regression Analysis Using Alternative Model Specifications

Model 1: $DIV_{it} = \Theta_0 + \Theta_1\,INV_{it} + \Theta_2\,EARN_{it} + \Theta_3\,DEBT_{it} + \Theta_4\,FCASH_{it} + \Theta_5\,BETA_{it} + u_{it}$

Model 2: $DIV_{it} = \Theta_0 + \Theta_1\,INV_{it} + \Theta_2\,EARN_{it} + \Theta_3\,DEBT_{it} + \Theta_4\,FCASH_{it} + \Theta_{t+5}\,S_{jit}(j = 1, 2) + \Theta_{t+4}\,S_{jit}(j = 4, 5) + u_{it}$

Model 3: $DIV_{it} = \Theta_0 + \Theta_1\,INV_{it} + \Theta_2\,EARN_{it} + \Theta_3\,DEBT_{it} + \Theta_4\,FCASH_{it} + \Theta_5\,BETA_{it} + \Theta_{t+5}\,S_{jit}(j = 1, 2) + \Theta_{t+4}\,S_{jit}(j = 4, 5) + u_{it}$

Model 4: $DIV_{it} = \Theta_0 + \Theta_1\,INV_{it} + \Theta_2\,EARN_{it} + \Theta_3\,DEBT_{it} + \Theta_4\,FCASH_{it} + \Theta_{k+9}\,I_{kit}(k = 1, \ldots, 6) + u_{it}$

Model 5: $DIV_{it} = \Theta_0 + \Theta_1\,INV_{it} + \Theta_2\,EARN_{it} + \Theta_3\,DEBT_{it} + \Theta_4\,FCASH_{it} + \Theta_5\,BETA_{it} + \Theta_{k+9}\,I_{kit}(k = 1, \ldots, 6) + u_{it}$

Model 6: $DIV_{it} = \Theta_0 + \Theta_1\,INV_{it} + \Theta_2\,EARN_{it} + \Theta_3\,DEBT_{it} + \Theta_4\,FCASH_{it} + \Theta_5\,BETA_{it} + \Theta_{t+5}\,S_{jit}(j = 1, 2) + \Theta_{t+4}\,S_{jit}(j = 4, 5) + \Theta_{k+9}\,I_{kit}$

$(k = 1, \ldots, 6) + u_{it}$

| Independent variable | Coefficient estimate | 1 | 2 | 3 | 4 | 5 | 6 | 7 |
|---|---|---|---|---|---|---|---|---|
| INTERCEPT | $\hat{\Theta}_0$ | 46.6110 | 7.6296 | 23.3976 | 1.8107 | 60.3861 | 6.8805 | 50.0191 |
| | | $(10.723)^a$ | $(2.095)^b$ | $(4.543)^a$ | (0.166) | $(4.820)^a$ | (0.650) | $(4.157)^a$ |
| INV | $\hat{\Theta}_1$ | 0.00034 | 0.00025 | 0.00025 | 0.00035 | 0.00034 | 0.00026 | 0.00026 |
| | | (0.577) | (0.417) | (0.421) | (0.582) | (0.573) | (0.439) | (0.439) |
| EARN | $\hat{\Theta}_2$ | 0.0508 | 0.0491 | 0.0492 | 0.0506 | 0.0501 | 0.0486 | 0.0483 |
| | | $(18.433)^a$ | $(17.830)^a$ | $(17.867)^a$ | $(18.345)^a$ | $(18.154)^a$ | $(17.621)^a$ | $(17.525)^a$ |
| DEBT | $\hat{\Theta}_3$ | 0.00032 | 0.00033 | 0.00033 | 0.00033 | 0.00033 | 0.00034 | 0.00034 |
| | | (1.579) | (1.608) | (1.607) | (1.588) | (1.614) | (1.641) | (1.657) |
| FCASH | $\hat{\Theta}_4$ | -0.0060 | -0.0057 | -0.0057 | -0.0060 | -0.0060 | -0.0059 | -0.0059 |
| | | $(-8.898)^a$ | $(-8.462)^a$ | $(-8.499)^a$ | $(-8.889)^a$ | $(-8.941)^a$ | $(-8.752)^a$ | $(-8.795)^a$ |
| BETA | $\hat{\Theta}_5$ | -31.9883 | | -19.9181 | | -56.5140 | | -43.2736 |
| | | $(-6.871)^a$ | | $(-4.294)^a$ | | $(-8.819)^a$ | | $(-7.101)^a$ |
| $S_1$ | $\hat{\Theta}_6$ | | -7.2680 | -3.5108 | | | -7.7714 | -7.0710 |
| | | | (-1.443) | (-0.693) | | | (-1.498) | (-1.388) |
| $S_2$ | $\hat{\Theta}_7$ | | -5.5299 | -1.7639 | | | -6.1317 | -2.1227 |
| | | | (-1.101) | (-0.349) | | | (-1.216) | (-0.426) |
| $S_4$ | $\hat{\Theta}_8$ | | 14.8332 | 13.4302 | | | 15.6219 | 13.4800 |
| | | | $(2.937)^a$ | $(2.679)^a$ | | | $(3.103)^a$ | $(2.721)^a$ |

| | | | | | | | | |
|---|---|---|---|---|---|---|---|---|
| $\hat{\Theta}_9$ | $S_5$ | | 57.7390 (11.474)[a] | 56.9181 (11.411)[a] | | | 69.1401 (13.044)[a] | 66.1989 (12.678)[a] |
| $\hat{\Theta}_{10}$ | $I_1$ | | | | 15.5316 (1.216) | 16.4847 (1.318) | 8.7472 (0.736) | 10.4958 (0.899) |
| $\hat{\Theta}_{11}$ | $I_2$ | | | | 27.1574 (2.373)[b] | 20.0540 (1.785) | 10.7804 (1.008) | 6.9523 (0.661) |
| $\hat{\Theta}_{12}$ | $I_3$ | | | | 14.4793 (1.283) | 16.9568 (1.535) | 2.8580 (0.272) | 5.9167 (0.573) |
| $\hat{\Theta}_{13}$ | $I_4$ | | | | 18.3050 (1.621) | −13.9025 (−1.194) | −5.1035 (−0.478) | −27.4248 (−2.509)[b] |
| $\hat{\Theta}_{14}$ | $I_5$ | | | | 7.8816 (0.515) | −2.4196 (−0.161) | 3.7958 (0.266) | −3.2087 (−0.228) |
| $\hat{\Theta}_{15}$ | $I_6$ | | | | 14.7584 (1.238) | 7.4650 (0.638) | −32.1528 (−2.818)[a] | −34.5493 (−3.082)[a] |
| Adjusted $R^2$ | | 0.2318 | 0.3193 | 0.3285 | 0.2117 | 0.2533 | 0.3448 | 0.3683 |
| Probability of $F$ | | <0.0001 | <0.0001 | <0.0001 | <0.0001 | <0.0001 | <0.0001 | <0.0001 |

[1] The size dummy variables, $S_j$s, are defined as follows: $S_1 = 1$ if SIZE < \$161.21 million, $S_1 = 0$ otherwise; $S_2 = 1$ if \$161.21 million ≤ SIZE < \$687.74 million, $S_2 = 0$ otherwise; $S_3 = 1$ if \$687.74 million ≤ SIZE < \$2,004.02 million, $S_3 = 0$ otherwise; $S_4 = 1$ if \$2,004.02 million ≤ SIZE < \$5,265.82 million, $S_4 = 0$ otherwise; $S_5 = 1$ if \$5,265.82 million ≤ SIZE, $S_5 = 0$ otherwise.

[2] The industry dummy variables, $I_j$s, are defined as follows: $I_1 = 1$ if mining and construction industry, $I_1 = 0$ otherwise; $I_2 = 1$ if nondurable manufacturing industry, $I_2 = 0$ otherwise; $I_3 = 1$ if durable manufacturing industry, $I_3 = 0$ otherwise; $I_4 = 1$ if transportation and utility industry, $I_4 = 0$ otherwise; $I_5 = 1$ if wholesale and retail trade industry, $I_5 = 0$ otherwise; $I_6 = 1$ if finance, insurance, and real estate industry, $I_6 = 0$ otherwise; $I_7 = 1$ if service industry, $I_7 = 0$ otherwise.

[3] For the purpose of estimation, dummy variables not represented here are $S_5$ for SIZE variable and $I_7$ for INDUSTRY variable.

[4] t statistics are given in parentheses.

[a] Significant at the 0.01 level.

[b] Significant at the 0.05 level.

## 10.2.3 VAR Results

The assumption of VAR is that the regression variables are stationary over time. Because statistical inference based on nonstationary variables results in incorrect conclusions, it is imperative to examine this assumption. The tests of stationarity applied here are the well-known unit root and cointegration tests. Results of these tests are shown in Table 10.4.

In Table 10.4A, results of the unit root tests using the augmented Dickey–Fuller (ADF) model are displayed. The existence of a unit root implies nonstationarity. Thus, the null hypothesis of a single unit root ($H_0: \rho = 0$) is tested against the alternative of $H_A: \rho < 0$ (that the variable is stationary). Because the $t$ statistic does not have Student's $t$ distribution under the null hypothesis of non-stationarity, critical values for the $t$ statistic on $\rho$, $Z(t_\rho)$, are simulated by Fuller (1976).

The single-unit root test in Table 10.4, with the exception of DEBT, does not reject the null hypothesis of a unit root at the 10% significance.[9] For the two-unit root test, the procedure is repeated for first difference data. The null hypothesis of a unit root in the differenced variables is rejected at the 10% level for all variables. Overall, results suggest that the variables become stationary only after first differencing. This is to be interpreted that the variables follow an I(1) process.

Table 10.4B presents results of the cointegration tests. Cointegration means that the difference between two variables becomes stationary when these variables move closely over time. If the variables are cointegrated, tests for stationarity may not be reliable. Furthermore, Engle and Granger (1987) suggest that VAR, using differenced data, is misspecified because of omitted constraints for variables that are cointegrated.

Cointegration tests are performed by repeating unit root tests on the cointegrating residuals. The null hypothesis of no cointegration is that the cointegrating residuals have a unit root. As can be seen from Table 10.4B, no ADF statistic is significant at the 10% level. Therefore, the null hypothesis that the variables are not cointegrated cannot be rejected.

Accordingly, first-order differences are used in the VAR analysis. The variance decompositions from VAR are presented in Table 10.5. The ordering of the variables is INV, DIV, EARN, FCASH, and DEBT.[10]

Confidence intervals of 99% for the point estimates are computed by a Monte Carlo simulation[11] with 1000 replications. This confidence interval is

---

[9]It is customary to apply a 10% critical value in stationarity tests.
[10]Results reported here appear to be quite robust to ordering. We experimented with several different orderings obtaining imperceptibly different outcomes.
[11]This method constructs the posterior distributions of the estimate.

**Table 10.4**

**Tests of Stationarity**

Augmented Dickey–Fuller (ADF) statistic:
  $Z(t_\rho)$ for $H_0$: $\rho = 0$ vs. $H_A$: $\rho < 0$

A: Unit root tests
  (1) Single unit root test

$$\Delta X_t = \lambda + \rho X_{t-1} + \sum_{i=1}^{4} \varphi_i \Delta X_{t-i} + u_t,$$

where $X_t$ is DIV, INV, EARN, DEBT, and FCASH, respectively

|          | DIV      | INV     | EARN    | DEBT       | FCASH   |
|----------|----------|---------|---------|------------|---------|
| $Z(t_\rho)$ | −0.2195 | −2.2447 | −1.8646 | −2.6520[b] | −1.3142 |

  (2) Two-unit root test

$$\Delta^2 X_t = \lambda + \rho \Delta X_{t-1} + \sum_{i=1}^{4} \varphi_i \Delta^2 X_{t-i} + u_t,$$

where $X_t$ is DIV, INV, EARN, DEBT, and FCASH, respectively

|          | DIV        | INV        | EARN       | DEBT       | FCASH      |
|----------|------------|------------|------------|------------|------------|
| $Z(t_\rho)$ | −4.0436[a] | −4.2361[a] | −2.7356[b] | −3.7148[a] | −2.6296[b] |

B: Cointegration tests

$$Y_t = C + \psi X_t + u_t$$

$$\Delta u_t = \rho u_{t-1} + \sum_{i=1}^{4} \varphi_i \Delta u_{t-i} + \varepsilon_t,$$

where $X_t$ and $Y_t$ are DIV, INV, EARN, DEBT, and FCASH, respectively, but $X_t \neq Y_t$

|       | DIV | INV     | EARN    | DEBT    | FCASH   |
|-------|-----|---------|---------|---------|---------|
| DIV   | —   | −0.1066 | −0.6306 | −0.3728 | −0.4036 |
| INV   | —   | —       | −2.4782 | −2.5240 | −1.9256 |
| EARN  | —   | —       | —       | −2.1185 | −1.8504 |
| DEBT  | —   | —       | —       | —       | −1.9434 |

[1]The augmented Dickey–Fuller test is recommended for testing the series stationarity in Engle and Granger (1987), as it has as good power properties as alternative test statistics.
[2]Significance levels without trend for a time series of 50 are 10%, −2.60; 5%, −2.93; and 1%, −3.58 (see Fuller, 1976).
[a]Significant at the 0.01 level.
[b]Significant at the 0.10 level.

bounded by 0 and 100%. If the confidence interval includes 0, the null hypothesis of no impact cannot be rejected.

  Point estimates in Table 10.5 measure the degree of exogeneity for a given variable in the sense that the "$h$-quarter ahead" forecast error variance in a variable is allocated to each source and that a strictly exogenous variable explains all

## Table 10.5

### Decompositions of Forecast Error Variance

A: Relative percentage of dividend (DIV) forecast variance $h$ quarter ahead explained by each shock to

| QUARTER ($h$) | DIV | INV | EARN | DEBT | FCASH |
|---|---|---|---|---|---|
| 2 | 96.1585 | 1.1059 | 0.9422 | 1.6988 | 0.0944 |
|  | $(73.4; 100)^a$ | $(0; 18.6)$ | $(0; 7.5)$ | $(0; 8.3)$ | $(0; 5.1)$ |
| 4 | 80.1501 | 6.1841 | 3.8958 | 6.2031 | 3.5666 |
|  | $(46.0; 98.6)^a$ | $(0; 35.7)$ | $(0; 15.2)$ | $(0; 14.7)$ | $(0; 12.8)$ |
| 8 | 73.0453 | 4.4445 | 12.0853 | 5.3206 | 5.1041 |
|  | $(35.3; 91.1)^a$ | $(0; 34.5)$ | $(0; 27.9)$ | $(0; 14.5)$ | $(0; 15.2)$ |
| 12 | 71.2991 | 4.8714 | 12.1061 | 5.6114 | 6.1118 |
|  | $(29.8; 89.6)^a$ | $(0; 37.2)$ | $(0; 29.3)$ | $(0; 15.5)$ | $(0; 16.8)$ |

B: Relative percentage of investment (INV) forecast variance $h$ quarter ahead explained by each shock to

| QUARTER ($h$) | DIV | INV | EARN | DEBT | FCASH |
|---|---|---|---|---|---|
| 2 | 2.2569 | 87.2037 | 3.1358 | 0.6559 | 6.7475 |
|  | $(0; 13.7)$ | $(65.3; 100)^a$ | $(0; 12.2)$ | $(0; 5.1)$ | $(0; 18.2)$ |
| 4 | 8.0445 | 77.6004 | 4.6429 | 0.8877 | 8.8242 |
|  | $(0; 35.6)$ | $(40.4; 100)^a$ | $(0; 19.1)$ | $(0; 6.9)$ | $(0; 22.5)$ |
| 8 | 7.7374 | 76.3027 | 4.7048 | 1.6020 | 9.6528 |
|  | $(0; 42.7)$ | $(31.1; 98.9)^a$ | $(0; 21.2)$ | $(0; 10.1)$ | $(0; 23.3)$ |
| 12 | 7.7901 | 75.3135 | 5.1110 | 2.0212 | 9.7640 |
|  | $(0; 44.7)$ | $(26.3; 95.7)^a$ | $(0; 23.7)$ | $(0; 12.0)$ | $(0; 23.2)$ |

C: Relative percentage of earnings (EARN) forecast variance $h$ quarter ahead explained by each shock to

| QUARTER ($h$) | DIV | INV | EARN | DEBT | FCASH |
|---|---|---|---|---|---|
| 2 | 15.7961 | 2.7635 | 45.9658 | 18.4599 | 17.0145 |
|  | $(0; 43.2)$ | $(0; 22.3)$ | $(18.1; 69.7)^a$ | $(0; 35.1)$ | $(0; 35.7)$ |
| 4 | 20.5698 | 6.2978 | 38.9069 | 17.8462 | 16.3790 |
|  | $(0; 50.4)$ | $(0; 36.0)$ | $(9.9; 60.5)^a$ | $(0; 33.4)$ | $(0; 34.5)$ |
| 8 | 22.9841 | 12.4979 | 34.9319 | 16.6153 | 12.9705 |
|  | $(0; 52.3)$ | $(0; 46.0)$ | $(6.8; 52.9)^a$ | $(0; 29.1)$ | $(0; 27.6)$ |
| 12 | 28.1824 | 11.3649 | 34.1938 | 14.9142 | 11.3445 |
|  | $(1.2; 56.7)^a$ | $(0; 46.7)$ | $(5.8; 51.1)^a$ | $(0; 26.9)$ | $(0; 25.4)$ |

D: Relative percentage of debt (DEBT) forecast variance $h$ quarter ahead explained by each shock to

| QUARTER ($h$) | DIV | INV | EARN | DEBT | FCASH |
|---|---|---|---|---|---|
| 2 | 36.3906 | 4.5996 | 8.6597 | 47.9804 | 2.3694 |
|  | $(5.0; 65.9)^a$ | $(0; 25.3)$ | $(0; 25.9)$ | $(16.3; 68.5)^a$ | $(0; 13.5)$ |
| 4 | 55.9334 | 1.9179 | 20.2229 | 20.6968 | 1.2288 |
|  | $(27.7; 76.4)^a$ | $(0; 18.2)$ | $(0; 39.4)$ | $(4.0; 33.8)^a$ | $(0; 9.3)$ |

**Table 10.5** (*continued*)

D: Relative percentage of debt (DEBT) forecast variance $h$ quarter ahead explained by each shock to

| QUARTER ($h$) | DIV | INV | EARN | DEBT | FCASH |
|---|---|---|---|---|---|
| 8 | 46.4060 | 7.1753 | 29.5955 | 13.0490 | 3.7739 |
|  | (15.7; 69.4)[a] | (0; 36.6) | (1.6; 50.2)[a] | (0.3; 24.0)[a] | (0; 13.9) |
| 12 | 38.1480 | 12.5902 | 30.4431 | 9.8142 | 5.0042 |
|  | (7.0; 65.3)[a] | (0; 55.6) | (0; 53.1) | (0; 20.4) | (0; 16.4) |

E: Relative percentage of free cash flow (FCASH) forecast variance $h$ quarter ahead explained by each shock to

| QUARTER ($h$) | DIV | INV | EARN | DEBT | FCASH |
|---|---|---|---|---|---|
| 2 | 16.3005 | 4.0063 | 1.2025 | 4.0588 | 74.4317 |
|  | (0; 44.2) | (0; 23.8) | (0; 13.7) | (0; 13.5) | (38.4; 94.7)[a] |
| 4 | 18.7732 | 4.6180 | 2.6570 | 6.6930 | 67.2585 |
|  | (0; 48.7) | (0; 27.8) | (0; 16.9) | (0; 17.0) | (29.0; 82.3)[a] |
| 8 | 11.1667 | 14.6336 | 5.2756 | 6.4788 | 62.4451 |
|  | (0; 38.4) | (0; 47.5) | (0; 21.0) | (0; 16.8) | (21.0; 74.5)[a] |
| 12 | 8.9709 | 20.9885 | 6.6926 | 6.8339 | 56.5139 |
|  | (0; 38.9) | (0; 58.9) | (0; 25.0) | (0; 17.5) | (11.7; 71.5)[a] |

[1]The 99% confidence intervals are presented in parentheses.
[a]Significant at the 0.01 level.

its forecast error variance. If the forecast error variance in a variable is largely due to unexpected shocks to itself in the last $h$ quarters, then the implication is that there are no strong interactions with other variables.

Table 10.5A exhibits variance decompositions for DIV for horizons of 2, 4, 8, and 12 quarters. For the 2-quarter horizon, 96.15% of the variance in DIV is explained by its own disturbance, whereas only 1.10% of the variance is accounted for by INV. Other variables as well (such as EARN, DEBT, and FCASH) have little or no impact on DIV. At the 12-quarter horizon, DIV explains 71.29% of its own variance, whereas INV, EARN, DEBT, and FCASH account for 4.87, 12.10, 5.61, and 6.11%, respectively. This suggests that nearly all the variation in DIV is attributable to the shocks to DIV itself and that DIV has no dynamic interaction with other variables. This of course shows the effect of "smoothing" dividends, as a policy.

Variance decompositions for INV are shown in Table 10.5B. At the 2-quarter horizon, 87.20% of the variance in INV is attributed to its own shocks. The percentage of the variance in INV explained by other variables ranges from 0.65 to 6.74%. At the 12-quarter horizon, the percentage of INV variance due to its own shocks is still a dominating 75.31%. DIV explains only 7.79% of the variance in INV, which is insignificant at the 0.01 level. The contribution of

EARN, DEBT, and FCASH to the variance in INV is 5.11, 2.02, and 9.76%, respectively, also insignificant at the 0.01 level. These results imply that the variance in INV is fully explained by its own shocks and thus INV appears to be exogenous.

Table 10.5C presents variance decomposition for EARN. At the two-quarter horizon, less than half (45.97%) the variance in EARN is accounted for by its own shocks. At this short horizon, INV explains only 2.76% of the variance in EARN, whereas DIV, DEBT, and FCASH account for 15.79, 18.45, and 17.01%, respectively.

At the longer horizon of 12 quarters, EARN has 34.19% of its variance accounted for by its own shock, whereas INV gradually becomes more important, explaining 11.36% of the variance. DIV accounts for 28.18% of the variance, significant at the 0.01 level. This may indicate that dividends possibly signal future earnings. DEBT and FCASH explain 14.91 and 11.34% of the variance, respectively, suggesting strong interactions among the variables.

The variance decomposition for DEBT is presented in Table 10.5D. Of the variance in DEBT, 47.98% is attributable to its own shocks. Interestingly, however, for the two-quarter horizon, DIV explains 36.39% of the variance, which is significant. The contribution to variability in DEBT by EARN, INV, and FCASH is 8.65, 4.59, and 2.36%, respectively, all *de facto*, inconsequential.

For the 12-quarter horizon, the proportion of the variance in DEBT explained by DIV is 38.14%, which is still significant. However, the proportion of the variance in DEBT attributable to its own shocks decreases to an insignificant 9.81%. EARN, INV, and FCASH contribute to the variance in DEBT 30.44, 12.59, and 5.00%, respectively. This suggests that DEBT is a residual of all other corporate decisions. Clearly, the implication is that firms borrow in order to finance dividend payments (because DIV has a significant effect on DEBT).

Table 10.5E shows variance decomposition for FCASH. Of the variance in FCASH, 74.43% is accounted for by its own shocks. For the two-quarter horizon, DIV explains 16.30% of the variance, implying that free cash flows may be restricted by dividend payments. The proportion of the variance in FCASH explained by INV, EARN, and DEBT ranges between 1.20 and 4.05%.

For the 12-quarter horizon, the proportion of the FCASH variance explained by its own shocks declines to 56.51%, slightly more than half the variability. The contribution of DIV to the variance in FCASH decreases to 8.97%. In contrast, INV (explaining 20.98% of the variance) becomes more important, whereas EARN and DEBT still account for only 6.69 and 6.83%, respectively.

In order to test for sample sensitivity of the VAR results, two subsamples of 100 firms and 300 firms each are selected randomly. Variance decompositions are calculated for each subsample.[12] Table 10.6 reports the results of this sensitivity analysis for dividend variance decompositions.

---

[12]This procedure is also helpful in mitigating potential selection bias due to sample screening.

**Table 10.6**

**Sensitivity Analysis for Dividend Variance Decompositions Using Randomly Selected Samples**

A: Dividend variance decompositions for a randomly selected sample of 100 firms

| QUARTER (h) | DIV | INV | EARN | DEBT | FCASH |
|---|---|---|---|---|---|
| 2 | 95.3325 | 3.3542 | 0.6830 | 0.6298 | 0.0003 |
| | (68.7; 100)[a] | (0; 24.8) | (0; 8.1) | (0; 5.5) | (0; 4.7) |
| 4 | 91.4485 | 3.1638 | 3.1169 | 0.7545 | 1.5160 |
| | (54.8; 100)[a] | (0; 31.2) | (0; 15.5) | (0; 5.8) | (0; 11.3) |
| 8 | 85.5553 | 5.1670 | 3.4936 | 2.1685 | 3.6153 |
| | (37.3; 96.1)[a] | (0; 42.7) | (0; 18.8) | (0; 8.7) | (0; 16.5) |
| 12 | 79.2105 | 8.1190 | 5.1158 | 2.3727 | 5.1817 |
| | (27.4; 89.8)[a] | (0; 48.0) | (0; 22.2) | (0; 9.2) | (0; 19.8) |

B: Dividend variance decompositions for a randomly selected sample of 300 firms

| QUARTER (h) | DIV | INV | EARN | DEBT | FCASH |
|---|---|---|---|---|---|
| 2 | 97.8047 | 0.2666 | 0.7764 | 0.4970 | 0.6550 |
| | (77.4; 100)[a] | (0; 15.8) | (0; 6.5) | (0; 4.5) | (0; 6.5) |
| 4 | 82.3413 | 6.9480 | 3.2055 | 5.0657 | 2.4392 |
| | (49.4; 99.2)[a] | (0; 33.1) | (0; 14.4) | (0; 13.5) | (0; 10.3) |
| 8 | 75.2359 | 5.8914 | 10.4133 | 5.6000 | 2.8592 |
| | (38.2; 92.4)[a] | (0; 33.3) | (0; 26.7) | (0; 15.3) | (0; 10.6) |
| 12 | 74.0143 | 6.9195 | 10.2091 | 5.7214 | 3.1354 |
| | (33.4; 90.9)[a] | (0; 37.0) | (0; 27.4) | (0; 16.1) | (0; 11.4) |

[1]The 99% confidence intervals are presented in parentheses.
[a]Significant at the 0.01 level.

Tables 10.6A and 10.6B shows dividend variance decompositions for a randomly selected sample of 100 and 300 firms, respectively. At all horizons, the proportion of the variance in DIV explained by its own shocks is more than 70%, whereas other variables explain less than 8% of the variance in DIV. These figures reinforce the findings reported in Table 10.5A. Overall, it can be concluded that variance decomposition results are quite robust.

## 10.2.4 THE LAGGED DIVIDEND MODEL

The previous results suggest contemporary relationships among dividends, earnings, free cash flows, beta, and firm size. It is found that dividend policy has a short memory of its own past, whereas any given shock in other decision variables under study does not precipitate significant deviations in dividends. This suggests that stronger lag specifications might be useful in investigating determinants of dividend policy. This is done herein for several additional specifications of the time-series cross-sectional regression model, including lagged dividend variables and tests for their robustness.

Since the early work of Lintner (1956), empirical tests of lagged dividend models have been scarce.[13] These studies have also failed to explain the reason for the inclusion of lagged dividends. Likewise, serious econometric problems resulting from the application of lagged-dependent variable models or the use of time-series cross-sectional data have not been addressed effectively.

Estimating lagged-dependent variables in the regression causes severe econometric problems. If the disturbances are serially correlated in the lagged-dependent variable model, OLS estimates are inconsistent. Even if the disturbances are "well behaved," OLS estimation produces biased coefficients in finite samples. In order to adjust for these problems in the context of time-series cross-sectional regressions, the method of instrumental variables is suggested. The lagged dividend variable is first regressed on all other explanatory variables. The resulting predicted values are then used in an ECM (error correction mode) to obtain time-series cross-sectional regression estimates.

Table 10.7 reports time-series cross-sectional regression results using lagged dividend variables. Model 1 is Lintner's (1956) model in which current dividends are determined by previous dividends and current earnings. The coefficient estimates on $DIV_{-1}$ and EARN are positive and significant. The adjusted $R^2$ is 51.89%, and the $F$ test rejects the null hypothesis at the less than 0.01 level.

Model 2 includes additional lagged variables of dividends in the model of EARN and FCASH, which are significant as per data in Table 10.2. As predicted, the coefficient estimates are positive significant for EARN and negative significant for FCASH. With the introduction of more lagged dividend variables, the first, second, and fourth lags show significant estimates, and the adjusted $R^2$ increases to 65.74%. This implies some persistence of dividend policy, as current dividends seem to be affected by the dividends paid one quarter, two quarters, or four quarters before.

Similarly, models 3 and 4 introduce BETA and size dummy variables, which are shown as significant earlier. The coefficient estimate of BETA is negative significant at the 0.01 level, whereas the coefficient estimates on the two largest size variables are positive significant at the same level of significance. The positive impacts of the first, second, and fourth lagged dividend variables are the same as in model 2.

In model 5, all variables used in models 1–4 are added. The estimates are essentially the same as in other models, indicating robustness. The adjusted $R^2$ is 66.10%.

The findings in Table 10.7 have several interesting implications. First, contrary to what Lintner argues, added lags in dividends are important determinants

---

[13]The exception is Fama and Babiak (1968) and Fama (1974).

Table 10.7

## Time-Series Cross-Sectional Regressions with Lagged-Dependent Variables

Model 1: $DIV_{it} = \Psi_0 + \Psi_1 DIV_{-1,it} + \Psi_5 EARN_{it} + u_{it}$

Model 2: $DIV_{it} = \Psi_0 + \Psi_1 DIV_{-1,it} + \Psi_2 DIV_{-2,it} + \Psi_3 DIV_{-3,it} + \Psi_4 DIV_{-4,it} + \Psi_5 EARN_{it}$
$\qquad + \Psi_6 FCASH_{it} + u_{it}$

Model 3: $DIV_{it} = \Psi_0 + \Psi_1 DIV_{-1,it} + \Psi_2 DIV_{-2,it} + \Psi_3 DIV_{-3,it} + \Psi_4 DIV_{-4,it} + \Psi_5 EARN_{it}$
$\qquad + \Psi_6 FCASH_{it} + \Psi_7 BETA_{it} + u_{it}$

Model 4: $DIV_{it} = \Psi_0 + \Psi_1 DIV_{-1,it} + \Psi_2 DIV_{-2,it} + \Psi_3 DIV_{-3,it} + \Psi_4 DIV_{-4,it} + \Psi_5 EARN_{it}$
$\qquad + \Psi_6 FCASH_{it} + \Psi_{j+7} S_{j,it}(j = 1,2) + \Psi_{j+6} S_{j,it}(j = 4,5) + u_{it}$

Model 5: $DIV_{it} = \Psi_0 + \Psi_1 DIV_{-1,it} + \Psi_2 DIV_{-2,it} + \Psi_3 DIV_{-3,it} + \Psi_4 DIV_{-4,it} + \Psi_5 EARN_{it}$
$\qquad + \Psi_6 FCASH_{it} + \Psi_7 BETA_{it} + \Psi_{j+7} S_{j,it}(j = 1,2) + \Psi_{j+6} S_{j,it}(j = 4,5) + u_{it}$

| Independent variable | Coefficient estimate | 1 | 2 | 3 | 4 | 5 |
|---|---|---|---|---|---|---|
| INTERCEPT | $\Theta_0$ | 13.4902 | 8.9897 | 22.7459 | 1.7407 | 9.5618 |
|  |  | $(9.538)^a$ | $(7.291)^a$ | $(8.148)^a$ | $(0.738)$ | $(2.847)^a$ |
| $DIV_{-1}$ | $\Theta_1$ | 0.3829 | 0.2149 | 0.2116 | 0.2043 | 0.2029 |
|  |  | $(34.277)^a$ | $(12.255)^a$ | $(12.069)^a$ | $(11.690)^a$ | $(11.606)^a$ |
| $DIV_{-2}$ | $\Theta_2$ |  | 0.1692 | 0.1676 | 0.1602 | 0.1597 |
|  |  |  | $(7.349)^a$ | $(7.288)^a$ | $(6.988)^a$ | $(6.966)^a$ |
| $DIV_{-3}$ | $\Theta_3$ |  | $-0.0361$ | $-0.0375$ | $-0.0392$ | $-0.0398$ |
|  |  |  | $(-1.521)$ | $(-1.580)$ | $(-1.656)$ | $(-1.684)$ |
| $DIV_{-4}$ | $\Theta_4$ |  | 0.2642 | 0.2607 | 0.2510 | 0.2495 |
|  |  |  | $(14.982)^a$ | $(14.790)^a$ | $(14.273)^a$ | $(14.191)^a$ |
| EARN | $\Theta_5$ | 0.0293 | 0.0257 | 0.0257 | 0.0238 | 0.0240 |
|  |  | $(9.684)^a$ | $(8.252)^a$ | $(8.279)^a$ | $(7.693)^a$ | $(7.730)^a$ |
| FCASH | $\Theta_6$ |  | $-0.0054$ | $-0.0055$ | $-0.0050$ | $-0.0051$ |
|  |  |  | $(-7.921)^a$ | $(-8.006)^a$ | $(-7.360)^a$ | $(-7.425)^a$ |
| BETA | $\Theta_7$ |  |  | $-16.0414$ |  | $-9.8201$ |
|  |  |  |  | $(-5.491)^a$ |  | $(-3.272)^a$ |
| $S_1$ | $\Theta_8$ |  |  |  | $-2.7386$ | $-0.9233$ |
|  |  |  |  |  | $(-0.852)$ | $(-0.282)$ |
| $S_2$ | $\Theta_9$ |  |  |  | $-2.3470$ | $-0.5164$ |
|  |  |  |  |  | $(-0.732)$ | $(-0.158)$ |
| $S_4$ | $\Theta_{10}$ |  |  |  | 8.5426 | 7.9051 |
|  |  |  |  |  | $(2.648)^a$ | $(2.444)^b$ |
| $S_5$ | $\Theta_{11}$ |  |  |  | 36.6389 | 36.4119 |
|  |  |  |  |  | $(11.238)^a$ | $(11.159)^a$ |
| Adjusted $R^2$ |  | 0.5189 | 0.6574 | 0.6580 | 0.6604 | 0.6610 |
| Probability of $F$ |  | <0.0001 | <0.0001 | <0.0001 | <0.0001 | <0.0001 |

[1] The size dummy variables, $S_j$s, are defined as follows: $S_1 = 1$ if SIZE < \$161.21 million, $S_1 = 0$ otherwise; $S_2 = 1$ if \$161.21 million $\leq$ SIZE < \$687.74 million, $S_2 = 0$ otherwise; $S_3 = 1$ if \$687.74 million $\leq$ SIZE < \$2004.02 million, $S_3 = 0$ otherwise; $S_4 = 1$ if \$2004.02 million $\leq$ SIZE < \$5265.82 million, $S_4 = 0$ otherwise; $S_5 = 1$ if \$5265.82 million $\leq$ SIZE, $S_5 = 0$ otherwise.

[2] For the purpose of estimation, one dummy variable is lost. The dummy variable not represented in the table is $S_3$ for SIZE variable.

[3] $t$ statistics are given in parentheses.

[a] Significant at the 0.01 level.

[b] Significant at the 0.05 level.

of dividend policy. More lags, reflecting past memory of dividends, increase the explanatory power of the model. Second, as shown earlier, current earnings have a positive impact on dividends, whereas free cash flows and beta have negative effects. Also, firm size appears to play an important role in dividend policy.

Since the sensitivity of the estimates to alternative model specifications has been established in previous sections, a sample sensitivity analysis of the time-series cross-sectional model 7 is conducted for selected subsamples and sub-periods. In order to test for robustness of the model, the full sample is first split into three randomly selected subsamples of 100, 200, and 300 firms. Then, the time-series cross-sectional model 7 is estimated for each subsample. These estimates are shown in Table 10.8.

The sets of coefficient estimates on $DIV_{-1}$, $DIV_{-4}$, EARN, $S_4$, and $S_5$ are the same as in Table 10.7. However, the coefficient estimates on $DIV_{-2}$ and $DIV_{-3}$ show mixed results for each subsample. The coefficient estimate of BETA is insignificant in the subsample of 100 firms, whereas it is significant in the subsamples of 200 and 300 firms.

To test for coefficient stability over time, the time-series and cross-sectional model is estimated for two subperiods: 1979:II–1984:IV and 1985:I–1990:IV. The coefficient estimates of explanatory variables for the two subperiods shown in Table 10.8 are consistent with those in Table 10.7, except for the third lagged dividend variable for the first subperiod. This is an additional confirmation of the model's robustness.

To summarize the results thus far:

1. Contemporaneously, dividends are not affected by investments and long-term debt.
2. Dynamically, dividends are not influenced by any other past variable except lagged dividends.[14]
3. There are no significant industry effects.
4. Dividends are positively related to current earnings (as in Lintner 1956) and to firm size.
5. Dividends are negatively related to current free cash flows and beta.

## 10.2.5 INTERPRETATION

This study is concerned with the relationship between the firm's investment and financing decisions and their relation, if any, to dividend policy. According to Miller and Modigliani, investment decisions are independent of financing decisions such as new debt or dividends because, in perfect capital markets, the

---

[14]Moreover, investments and free cash flows are not affected dynamically by any other past variables, whereas long-term debts are influenced by past dividends and earnings.

value of a firm is affected only by its investment decision. And both the financing decision and dividend policy are irrelevant in the process of determining the firm's value.

A stronger formulation of this proposition is that investment and financing variables also should not affect each other dynamically. For instance, current investment decisions should be determined independently of the previous debt and dividend decisions. Based on the dynamic and the contemporaneous tests, the results here support the Miller–Modigliani propositions.

Dhrymes and Kurz (1964, 1967), in contrast, claimed that a total separation of investments and financing decisions is implausible because, in imperfect capital markets, financing should be considered as part of the firm's investment decision. The empirical literature associated with the Miller–Modigliani proposition shows mixed results. Dhrymes and Kurz (1967) and McCabe (1979) found that the firm's investment decision is linked to its financing decision. Higgins (1972), Fama (1974), and Smirlock and Marshall (1983) documented no interdependence between investments and dividends. It is argued here that these tests seem to be misspecified or inappropriate because they have omitted important explanatory variables and/or lagged variables.

The results of this study also showed that dividends and new debt are contemporaneously independent, but that current dividend decisions affect future debt decisions. This is an indication that new debt decisions are subordinated to the dividend decision. At the same time, it is shown [as Lintner (1956) argued] that current earnings and first lagged dividends predict current dividends well.

This study also demonstrates a strong persistence in dividend policy. It is found that current dividend decisions are affected by dividends paid two or four quarters before, in addition to immediately preceding dividends.

The results relating to free cash flows have some fascinating interpretations. Although the contemporaneous relationship between dividends and free cash flows is negative, dividends, regardless, are dynamically unaffected by free cash flows. The agency theory explanation of dividend payments is that the firm should pay dividends to reduce agency costs associated with excess cash flows. Easterbrook (1984) further argued that paying dividends can reduce agency costs because it forces managers to return to the market for cash, thus keeping them under constant monitoring.

In contrast, the pecking order hypothesis of Myers and Majluf (1984) states that dividend payments are negatively influenced by free cash flows. Myers and Majluf (1984) claim that "firms can build up financial slack by restricting dividends when investment requirements are modest" (p. 220). In this study, it is shown that current dividends are affected by preceding free cash flows. Consequently, the dynamic results here are inconsistent with either the agency theory argument or the pecking order hypothesis.

## Table 10.8

### Robustness Tests of the Lagged Dividend Model

$$DIV_{it} = \Psi_0 + \Psi_1 DIV_{-1,it} + \Psi_2 DIV_{-2,it} + \Psi_3 DIV_{-3,it} + \Psi_4 DIV_{-4,it} + \Psi_5 EARN_{it} + \Psi_6 FCASH_{it} + \Psi_7 BETA_{it} + \Psi_{7+6}S_{jit}(j=1,2) + \Psi_{t+7}S_{jit}(j=4,5) + u_{it}$$

| Independent variable | Coefficient estimate | Randomly selected samples (1979:II–1990:IV) | | | Total samples | |
|---|---|---|---|---|---|---|
| | | 100 firms | 200 firms | 300 firms | 446 firms (1979:II–1984:IV) | 446 firms (1985:I–1990:IV) |
| INTERCEPT | $\Theta_0$ | 13.4331 | 7.1513 | 11.2924 | 8.9091 | 9.7421 |
| | | (1.567) | (1.772) | (2.556)[b] | (3.254)[a] | (2.269)[b] |
| $DIV_{-1}$ | $\Theta_1$ | 0.3196 | 0.5247 | 0.2447 | 0.1522 | 0.2345 |
| | | (11.431)[a] | (12.536)[a] | (10.613)[a] | (8.030)[a] | (9.980)[a] |
| $DIV_{-2}$ | $\Theta_2$ | 0.0455 | 0.0456 | 0.1455 | 0.1786 | 0.1830 |
| | | (1.444) | (0.856) | (4.882)[a] | (6.714)[a] | (6.008)[a] |
| $DIV_{-3}$ | $\Theta_3$ | 0.1077 | −0.4002 | −0.0594 | −0.1085 | −0.0208 |
| | | (3.321)[a] | (−7.134)[a] | (−1.941) | (−3.885)[a] | (−0.667) |
| $DIV_{-4}$ | $\Theta_4$ | 0.1478 | 0.5519 | 0.2491 | 0.2198 | 0.2804 |
| | | (5.318)[a] | (12.263)[a] | (10.758)[a] | (11.660)[a] | (11.642)[a] |
| EARN | $\Theta_5$ | 0.0218 | 0.0304 | 0.0381 | 0.0151 | 0.0296 |
| | | (4.562)[a] | (3.948)[a] | (8.472)[a] | (4.636)[a] | (7.084)[a] |
| FCASH | $\Theta_6$ | −0.0304 | −0.0271 | −0.0056 | −0.0016 | −0.0061 |
| | | (−11.370)[a] | (−12.434)[a] | (−6.545)[a] | (−3.702)[a] | (−5.921)[a] |

| | | | | | |
|---|---|---|---|---|---|
| BETA | $\Theta_7$ | -13.3591 | -7.5758 | -11.2783 | -9.3450 | -10.0923 |
| | | (-1.733) | (-2.038)[b] | (-2.834)[a] | (-3.793)[a] | (-2.616)[a] |
| $S_1$ | $\Theta_8$ | -1.3309 | -0.5976 | -1.0523 | -0.4959 | -1.0510 |
| | | (-0.143) | (-0.155) | (-0.244) | (-0.185) | (-0.251) |
| $S_2$ | $\Theta_9$ | -2.0229 | 0.1095 | -0.7056 | -0.1524 | -0.6896 |
| | | (-0.272) | (0.028) | (-0.171) | (-0.057) | (-0.165) |
| $S_4$ | $\Theta_{10}$ | 2.2909 | 6.6538 | 8.7361 | 6.9132 | 8.0647 |
| | | (0.284) | (1.757) | (2.001)[b] | (2.606)[a] | (1.941) |
| $S_5$ | $\Theta_{11}$ | 36.9703 | 22.5234 | 29.3538 | 34.9107 | 36.4566 |
| | | (5.032)[a] | (5.447)[a] | (6.961)[a] | (13.106)[a] | (8.576)[a] |
| Adjusted $R^2$ | | 0.7427 | 0.4990 | 0.5754 | 0.6664 | 0.5530 |
| Probability of $F$ | | <0.0001 | <0.0001 | <0.0001 | <0.0001 | <0.0001 |

[1]The size dummy variables, $S_i$s, are defined as follows: $S_1 = 1$ if SIZE < $161.21 million, $S_1 = 0$ otherwise; $S_2 = 1$ if $161.21 million ≤ SIZE < $687.74 million, $S_2 = 0$ otherwise; $S_3 = 1$ if $687.74 million ≤ SIZE < $2,004.02 million, $S_3 = 0$ otherwise; $S_4 = 1$ if $2,004.02 million ≤ SIZE < $5,265.82 million, $S_4 = 0$ otherwise; $S_5 = 1$ if $5,265.82 million ≤ SIZE, $S_5 = 0$ otherwise.

[2]For the purpose of estimation, one dummy variable is lost. The dummy variable not represented in the table is $S_3$ for SIZE variable.

[3]$t$ statistics are given in parentheses.

[a]Significant at the 0.01 level.
[b]Significant at the 0.05 level.

The last point concerns beta, size, and industry effects. The negative correlation between dividends and beta indicates that firms with higher betas pay lower dividends to reduce the costs of external financing, either because higher betas are associated with higher leverage (Rozeff, 1982) or because firms distribute dividends to affect the systematic risk of their stocks (Dyl and Hoffmeister, 1986). Because the variables related to firm size are adjusted explicitly, it should be noted that the differences in dividend policy between small and large firms are substantial. The evidence here seems to indicate that larger firms choose to increase dividend payments rather than retain earnings to finance faster growth.

Also, in contrast to Michel (1979), we find no evidence of a systematic relationship between dividend policy and industrial classification.[15] This suggests that variations in dividend policy by industry might be the sole effect of firm size. This is so, because in certain industries firm size is a function of economies of scale, or other determining factors.

## 10.3  SUMMARY AND CONCLUSIONS

The purpose of this study has been the empirical analysis of a wide range of dividend determinants, including investments, earnings, debt, free cash flows, firm size, beta, and industry classification. It was found that the firm's dividend payments are significantly related to earnings, free cash flows, beta, and firm size. More importantly, perhaps, it was shown that dividends are not influenced by investments and debt, consistent with the irrelevance proposition of Miller and Modigliani (1961). It was also found that industry effects might not exist or might be only the manifestation of a size effect.

Next, it was demonstrated that dividends have significant short-run effects on themselves, whereas other variables have no dynamic effects on dividends. It also appears that dividends have short memory of their own past and that other variables have no dynamic interactions with dividends.

Finally, the evidence herein suggests that current dividend payments are very much influenced by the consistency of past dividend payments and by contemporaneous factors, such as earnings and free cash flows. Even though some of the models here might be exploratory in nature, they nevertheless shed some light on the dividend puzzle. One possible avenue for future research might be the application of a model that simultaneously incorporates both contemporaneous variables and dynamic factors.

It would be perhaps worthwhile to mention here a survey-based study of financial decision makers (mostly, CEOs and CFOs) that Baker and Powell (2000)

---

[15]Higgins (1972) also found no pervasive industry effects, whereas Dhrymes and Kurz (1967) documented significant interindustry differences.

conducted in 1997. Baker and Powell (2000) rehashed the responses to a survey they reported first in an earlier paper (Baker and Powell, 1999). In the more recent paper, their concern is with determinants of dividend policy as reflected by the views of corporate decision makers. That is, this type of research is perhaps a check of the purely econometric research that has been the brunt, indeed, the sole purpose, of this chapter.

Baker and Powell (2000) found that the "factors" influencing dividend decisions are consistent with Lintner's (1956) findings. That is, the level of current and expected future earnings and a pattern of continuity are the most important determinants of dividend policy. Also, they report that industry effects they found earlier seem to "diminish." These results are quite consistent with the statistical results of market and firm data we use here, perhaps hinting that executives put their money where their mouth is. Neither the study we discussed in this chapter nor the Baker and Powell (2000) study, however, can answer the question why do firms do what they do.

# REFERENCES

Baker, H. Kent, and Garry E. Powell. 1999. "How corporate managers view dividend policy." *Quarterly Journal of Economics and Business* 38:17–35.

Baker, H. Kent, and Garry E. Powell. 2000. "Determinants of corporate dividend policy: a survey of NYSE firms." *Financial Practice and Education* 9:29–40.

Bhattacharya, Sudipto. 1979. "Imperfect information, dividend policy and the bird in the hand fallacy." *Bell Journal of Economics* 10:259–270.

Bhattacharya, Sudipto. 1980. "Nondissipative signaling structures and dividend policy." *Quarterly Journal of Economics* 95:1–24.

Dhrymes, P. J., and Kurz, M. 1964. "On the dividend policy of electric utilities." *Review of Economics and Statistics* 76–81.

Dhrymes, P. J., and Kurz. M. 1967. "Investment, dividend, and external finance behavior of firms." In R. Ferber, ed., *Determinants of Investment Behavior*, New York, 427–467.

Dyl, Edward A., and Hoffmeister, J. R. 1986. "A note on dividend policy and beta." *Journal of Business Finance and Accounting* 13:107–115.

Easterbrook, F. 1984. "Two agency cost explanations for dividend payments." *American Economic Review* 74:680–689.

Engle, R. F., and Granger, C. W. J. 1987. "Cointegration and error correction: representation, estimation, and testing." *Econometrica* 55:251–276.

Fama, Eugene F. 1974. "The empirical relationships between the dividend and investment decisions of firms." *American Economic Review* 64:304–318.

Fama, Eugene F., and Babiak, H. 1968. "Dividend policy: an empirical analysis." *Journal of American Statistical Association* 63:1132–1161.

Frankfurter, George M., and Jasik Gong. 1993. "Time-series cross-sectional tests of dividend policy determinants." Unpublished working paper. Louisiana State University.

Friend, I., and Hasbrouck, J. 1988. "Determinants of capital structure." *Research in Finance* 7:1–19.

Fuller, W.A. 1976. *Introduction to Statistical Time Series*. New York: John Wiley.

Fuller, W.A., and Battese, G.E. 1974. "Estimation of linear models with crossed-error structure." *Journal of Econometrics* 2:67–78.

Higgins, R. C. 1972. "The corporate dividend-saving decision." *Journal of Financial and Quantitative Analysis* 7:1527–1541.

Jensen, M. C. 1986. "Agency costs of free cash flow, corporate finance and takeovers." *American Economic Review* 76:323–339.

Lehn, K., and Poulsen, A. 1989. "Free cash flow and stockholder gains in going private transactions." *Journal of Finance* 44:771–787.

Lintner, John. 1956. "Distribution of incomes of corporations among dividends, retained earnings and taxes." *American Economic Review* 46:97–113.

Marsh, T. A., and Merton, R. C. 1987. "Dividend behavior for the aggregate stock market." *Journal of Business* 60:1–40.

McCabe, G. M. 1979. "The empirical relationship between investment and financing: a new look." *Journal of Financial and Quantitative Analysis* 14:119–135.

McMillin, W. D., and Parker, R. E. 1990. "Federal debt, tax-adjusted q, and macroeconomic activity." *Journal of Money, Credit, and Banking* 22:100–109.

Michel, A. 1979. "Industry influence on dividend policy." *Financial Management* (Autumn) 22–26.

Miller, M. H., and Franco Modigliani. 1961. "Dividend policy, growth, and the valuation of shares." *Journal of Business* 34:411–433.

Myers, Stuart C. 1984. "The capital structure puzzle." *Journal of Finance* 39:575–592.

Myers, Stuart C., and Majluf, N. S. 1984. "Corporate financing and investment decisions when firms have information that investors do not have." *Journal of Financial Economics* 13:187–221.

Rozeff, Michael S. 1982. "Growth, beta and agency costs as determinants of dividend payout ratios." *Journal of Financial Research* 5:249–259.

Sharpe, W.F. 1963. "A simplified model for portfolio analysis." *Management Science* 9:277–293.

Sims, C. 1980. "Macroeconomics and reality." *Econometrica* 48:1–49.

Smirlock, M., and Marshall, W. 1983. "An examination of the empirical relationship between the dividend and investment decisions: a note." *Journal of Finance* 38:1659–1667.

Wansley, James W., and William R. Lane. 1987. "A financial profile of the dividend initiating firm." *Journal of Business Finance and Accounting* 14:425–436.

# APPENDIX A

## DATA

Five firm-specific accounting variables—dividends, earnings, investments, long-term debt, and free cash flows—are analyzed over the period 1979–1990 using quarterly data. Aggregate data are obtained by cumulating individual firms' data.[16] The data sources are the Quarterly COMPUSTAT and the Monthly Center for Research in Stock Prices (CRSP) files.

For a firm to be included in the sample, it must meet three criteria. First, data must be available for the entire sample period. Second, the fiscal year-end must be December.[17] Third, it must be included in both the quarterly COMPUSTAT and the monthly CRSP files. Application of these criteria results in a final sample of 446 firms.

## VARIABLE DEFINITIONS

All accounting variables are seasonally unadjusted quarterly data. It is assumed that because of budget constraints, firms are more concerned with the levels of accounting variables than with the percentage changes of these levels. Accordingly, flow variables for each quarter are measured for dividends, earnings, investments, long-term debt, and free cash flows.

Investment and long-term debt are stock data obtained from each firm's balance sheet, whereas earnings and free cash flows are flow data calculated from the firm's income statement.

## DIVIDENDS (DIV)

Three different proxies of dividend are usually used in financial economics research.

---

[16]Tests of aggregate data may be affected by an aggregation bias because some variables are not strictly nonnegative. This aggregation problem is explored later by testing for sensitivity to sample size.

[17]This requirement is necessary for matching quarterly data items across firms.

1. Amount of common stock dividend paid (Lintner, 1956; Dhrymes and Kurz, 1967; Higgins, 1972; McCabe, 1979; Smirlock and Marshall, 1983).
2. Change in dividends (Fama and Babiak, 1968; Fama, 1974).
3. Dividend payout ratio (Rozeff, 1982).

The dividend proxy used in this study is the amount of common stock dividends paid. This measure is calculated by COMPUSTAT data item #15 (common shares used to calculate earnings per share) times data item #16 (dividends per share).

## INVESTMENTS (INV)

Proxies of investments include: (1) change in net plant and equipment (Higgins, 1972; Fama, 1974) and (2) investment in fixed assets (Dhrymes and Kurz, 1967).

The proxy for investments used in this study is the difference: property plus plant plus equipment less depreciation. This difference is calculated from COMPUSTAT data item #42 (total property, plant, and equipment) less lagged data item #42.

## EARNINGS (EARN)

Available earnings after taxes for common stockholders are defined as net income[18]–preferred dividends (Lintner, 1956; Higgins, 1972; Fama, 1974).

## DEBT (DEBT)

Long-term debt, including new debt (McCabe, 1979), is calculated from COMPUSTAT data item #51.

## Free Cash Flow (FCASH)

This is defined as in Lehn and Poulsen (1989) as[19]

$$CF = INC - TAX - INTEXP - PFDDIV - COMDIV,$$

---

[18]Net income (available for common) is obtained from COMPUSTAT data item #25.

[19]Even though accounting numbers are interdependent, simultaneous estimation methods and structural models can still produce superior results even under such conditions (see Appendix B).

where INC is operating income before depreciation; TAX is total income taxes, minus change in deferred taxes from the previous year to the current year; INTEXP is gross interest expense on short- and long-term debt; PFDDIV is total amount of preferred dividend requirement on cumulative stock and dividends paid on noncumulative preferred stock; and COMDIV is total dollar amount of dividends declared on common stock (Lehn and Poulsen, 1989, p. 777).

The quarterly measure of free cash flows is calculated from COMPUSTAT data items #6, #15, #16, #21, #22, #24, and #52.

## FIRM SIZE (SIZE)

The logarithm of book assets (Wansley and Lane, 1987; Friend and Hasbrouck, 1988) is given by COMPUSTAT data item #44 (total assets).

## INDUSTRY (INDUSTRY)

Two–digit SIC industry classification.

## BETA (BETA)

Sharpe's (1963) market model is used to estimate beta coefficients.

# APPENDIX B

# The Relationship Between DIV and FCASH

In order to examine the contemporaneous relationship between free cash flows and dividend payments, first a simple regression is assumed:[20]

$$Y = X_1\beta_1 + X_2\beta_2 + \varepsilon, \tag{B.1}$$

where $Y$ is DIV, $X_1$ is EARN, $X_2$ is FCASH, and $\varepsilon \sim N\,(0,\,\sigma^2)$.

A two-step procedure is followed to estimate the coefficient of $X_2$. The first step is to regress $X_2$ on $X_1$. The estimated residual terms from this step is

$$\begin{aligned}
\hat{u} &= X_2 - X_1\psi \\
&= X_2 - X_1(X_1'X_1)^{-1}X_1'X_2 \\
&= \left[I - X_1(X_1'X_1)^{-1}X_1'\right]X_2 \\
&= M_1X_2, \tag{B.2}
\end{aligned}$$

where $\psi$ is $(X_1'X_1)^{-1}X_1'X_2$ and $M_1 = [I - X_1(X_1'X_1)^{-1}X_1']$.

The second step is to regress $Y$ on the residual terms of the first step. The resulting coefficient estimate of $\hat{u}$ from the second step is equal to the coefficient estimate of $X_2$ in Eq. (B.1).

$$\begin{aligned}
\hat{\beta}_2 &= (\hat{u}'\hat{u})^{-1}\hat{u}'Y \\
&= \left[(M_1X_2)'(M_1X_2)\right]^{-1}(M_1X_2)'Y \\
&= \left[X_2'M_1M_1X_2\right]^{-1}(X_2'M_1)Y. \tag{B.3}
\end{aligned}$$

Substituting $X_2 = X_1 - Y$ into Eq. (B.3),

$$\begin{aligned}
\hat{\beta}_2 &= \left[X_2'M_1M_1X_2\right]^{-1}(X_1 - Y)'M_1Y \\
&= \left[X_2'M_1M_1X_2\right]^{-1}X_1'M_1Y - \left[X_2'M_1M_1X_2\right]^{-1}Y'M_1Y. \tag{B.4}
\end{aligned}$$

Because $M_1$ is idempotent,

---

[20]The measure of free cash flows is estimated as operating income minus income taxes, minus interest expenses, minus total amounts of dividends paid.

$$M_1^2 = M_1; \text{ and}$$
$$X_1'M_1 = X_1'\left[I - X_1(X_1'X_1)^{-1}X_1'\right]$$
$$= X_1' - X_1'X_1(X_1'X_1)^{-1}X_1'$$
$$= X_1' - X_1'$$
$$= 0.$$

Thus,

$$\beta_2 = -[X_2'M_1X_2]^{-1}Y'M_1Y < 0. \qquad (B.5)$$

Let $X_2 = X_1 - Y - X_3$ (where $X_3$ may be interest expense). Substituting this constraint into Eq. (B.3) yields

$$\beta_2 = [X_2'M_1M_1X_2]^{-1}(X_1 - Y - X_3)'M_1Y$$
$$= [X_2'M_1M_1X_2]^{-1}X_1'M_1Y - [X_2'M_1M_1X_2]^{-1}Y'M_1Y$$
$$- [X_2'M_1M_1X_2]^{-1}X_3'M_1Y.$$
$$= -[X_2'M_1M_1X_2]^{-1}Y'M_1Y - [X_2'M_1M_1X_2]^{-1}X_3'M_1Y. \qquad (B.6)$$

The sign of the first term in Eq. (B.6) is always negative, but the sign of the second term depends on the correlation between $X_3$ and $Y$. As a consequence, it is not easy to predict the sign of $\beta_2$. As more terms (e.g., taxes) are added to the constraint, the sign of $\beta_2$ will be affected by the complex correlations between the dependent variable and the elements in the constraint.

# PART III

# What Academic Research Proves and What It Does Not Prove

# CHAPTER 11

## The "Balance Sheet" of Academic Research: What It Does/Does Not Prove

The inconsistent and often contradictory results of empirical analyses of dividends and dividend policy are commonly blamed on differences in modeling, method of analysis, data type, and sample period. The choice of variables included in, or omitted from, a model (Watts, 1976b; McCabe, 1979; Frankfurter and Gong, 1993) and the definition used in the estimation of important factors (Miller and Scholes, 1982) can also significantly influence a study's results. Roll (1977) asserted that the lack of an adequate proxy can make a theoretical model untestable.[1] The use of different method of analyses across studies can limit the comparability of the results as well (Morgan, 1982).

As shown by Baker and Farrelly (1988), attempts to empirically validate theoretical dividend models are thus far inconclusive or, in some cases, even contradictory. Numerous rationales have been offered as explanations for these divergent results. The model and empirical method of analysis applied (Watts, 1973; Morgan, 1982), the frequency of sample observation (Watts, 1976a; Laub, 1976), and the sample period (Watts, 1973) are identified as potential causes of the inconsistencies.

This chapter is an empirical test in a rigorous statistical framework what the preponderance of models that attempt to explain empirically the dividend puzzle show or do not show. Models considered and reviewed in Chapters 7–9

---

[1] Taking Roll's statement at face value and applying strict Popperian criteria to determine the scientific value of empirically untestable theories would be tantamount to their instantaneous disqualification.

143

and 12 are pooled in one sample and tested with respect to method of analysis, data, and sample period.

This examination is important for several reasons. Results that cannot be duplicated over diverse sample periods are likely to be the artifacts of that particular period. In contrast, findings that persist through time can lead to the development of more descriptive models. Finally, results that change over time can be indicative of changes in the return-generating mechanism (Amihud and Mendelson, 1987).

## 11.1 METHOD OF ANALYSIS

We use the categorical data analysis method (CDAM) to determine whether the method of analysis, observation frequency, and sample period can be used to predict and explain the results of a study. CDAM is a specialized, multivariate analysis technique for the evaluation of response and explanatory variables using weighted least-squares (WLS) procedures. This approach is useful in the examination of dichotomous (i.e., studies in early or late sample periods) and nonordered, polytomous (i.e., differences in method of analysis and data type) studies.

According to Feinberg (1978), CDAM is a multivariate method of analysis that was developed around the turn of the century. The technique uses a multidimensional contingency table to cross-classify data into categories. Each category count represents the frequency of a unique combination of categorical variables in the sample. The population variable-level combination probability is estimated using iterative WLS and the observed frequency.

Iterative WLS improves WLS estimates by first estimating the weights, fitting the regression function, and calculating the residuals. Next, the residuals from the first estimation are used to reestimate the weights and to refit the regression. The iterative process continues until no significant changes occur in the weights of the least squares.

The explanatory variables used in the analysis are assumed to represent true categorical variables and are not a blend or combination of the explanatory variables. Each of the variables we pick for the analysis is an independent categorical variable. In addition, explanatory variables are assumed to be fixed and to play a defining role, and can be either continuous or discrete.

The CADM method of analysis also assumes that explanatory variables are mutually independent—the knowledge of one of the independent categorical variable does not ensure correct prediction of another explanatory variable. In CDAM, it is further assumed that the table frequencies follow a product multinomial distribution. The product multinomial distribution requires that each observation in the sample be classified based on its unique combination of explanatory variables.

CDAM and analysis of variance (ANOVA) are similar methods of analysis in one respect: both estimate the interaction between variables. Yet, there is a difference. ANOVA models estimate the effects of independent variables on the dependent variable and partition the overall variability of the model, whereas CDAM estimates the structural relation between the variables by estimating the parameters and testing hypotheses about linear combinations of these parameters.

The null hypothesis is formulated so as to test the fit of the model. The test statistics calculated are generalized Wald (1943) statistics that approximate an asymptotic $\chi^2$ distribution.

The multidimensional contingency table displays cross-classified counts based on each of several sets of categories and facilitates CDAM. The table rows represent samples determined by unique combinations of independent variables, while the table columns are determined by the dependent variable's response. The count in the $(i,j)^{\text{th}}$ cell is the quantity of individuals in the $i$th population that have the $j$th response. The sample proportion, $p_{ij} = n_{ij}/n_j$, estimates the probability of the $j$th response $(\pi_{ij})$. The proportion vector $\mathbf{p}$ is converted into a function vector

$$\mathbf{F} = \mathbf{F}(\mathbf{p}).$$

If the true probabilities for the entire table are represented by the vector $\pi$, the functions of the probabilities $\mathbf{F}(\pi)$ follow the linear model:

$$\mathbf{E_A}(\mathbf{F}) = \mathbf{F}(\pi) = \mathbf{X}\beta,$$

where $\mathbf{E_A}$ indicates the asymptotic expectation, $\mathbf{X}$ is the fixed constant design matrix, and $\beta$ is the parameter vector to be estimated.

WLS is used to estimate the structural relation between the variables. The weights are determined from the inverse covariance matrix of the $\mathbf{F(p)}$ functions of $\mathbf{F}$ and b (where b is the estimate of $\beta$) and the weighted residual sum of squares is minimized. If $\mathbf{S}$ is defined as the estimated covariance matrix of $\mathbf{F}$, the fit of the model is determined using the test statistic:

$$\mathbf{F'S^{-1}F} - \mathbf{b'(X'S^{-1}X)}b,$$

which is asymptotically distributed $\chi^2$. The goodness of fit of the model is tested with the null hypothesis

$$\mathbf{H_0}\text{: } \mathbf{C}\beta = \mathbf{0},$$

where $\mathbf{C}$ is a matrix of arbitrary constants, against the alternate hypothesis

$$\mathbf{H_A}\text{: } \mathbf{C}\beta \neq \mathbf{0}.$$

The test statistic for the null

$$\mathbf{B'C'[C(X'S^{-1}X)^{-1}C']^{-1}Cb}$$

follows an asymptotically $\chi^2$ distribution if $\mathbf{H_0}$ is true.

**Table 11.1**

**The CDAM Classification Framework**

| Method of analysis | Data type | Sample period |
|---|---|---|
| Abnormal returns[a] | Daily | Pre-1976 |
| | | Post-1976 |
| | Other[b] | Pre-1976 |
| | | Post-1976 |
| Other[c] | Daily | Pre-1976 |
| | | Post-1976 |
| | Other | Pre-1976 |
| | | Post-1976 |
| Abnormal returns | Daily | Pre-1976 |
| | | Post-1976 |
| | Other | Pre-1976 |
| | | Post-1976 |
| Other | Daily | Pre-1976 |
| | | Post-1976 |
| | Other | Pre-1976 |
| | | Post-1976 |

[a]Abnormal returns methods of analysis include event study and abnormal returns. A listing of method of analysis classifications is found in the Appendix.
[b]Other data include weekly, monthly, quarterly, semiannual, and annual observations.
[c]Other methods of analysis include regression analyses and other methods (see Appendix).

Although the maximum likelihood estimation method of CDAM has a smaller variance, WLS regression CDAM is less complex and the difference in variance is not significant (Grizzle *et al.*, 1969). The implementation of CDAM is facilitated by the assignment of the sample's observations into classes based on some explanatory variable characteristic. The table developed from this classification process provides a concise summary of the data. The technique then uses a series of dummy variables representing the explanatory variable classes and tests the model using WLS estimation techniques.

## 11.2 DATA

Data are the set of empirical studies performed to support or reject the theoretical models discussed in the preceding chapters. Table 11.1 displays the framework used in the assignment of the individual studies to CDAM populations.

A population profile succinctly summarizes the assignment of individual empirical studies to groups based on explanatory variable combinations. The sample size of each population is the frequency that each combination of categorical variables appears in the overall sample.[2] Table 11.2 is the list of these studies by theoretical categories.

The three attributes of each study are the variables of the tests. These variables, in order, are as follows.

1. Method of analysis used, classified either as methods analyzing changes in price or average return (event study or price change methods of analyses), or as using regression analyses (least-square analysis, logit analysis, etc.) or other methods.[3]
2. Data type, classified as either daily data or less frequent data (weekly, monthly, etc.).
3. Sample period, where, based on the midpoint of the sample period, the study is classified as either pre-1976 or post-1976.[4]

## 11.3 RESULTS

The CDAM hypothesis tested is that any of the three explanatory variables (individually or in combination with others) is significant in its ability to predict the outcome of the study as it either supports or fails to support the hypothesis tested. CADM tests are presented in Table 11.3. Table 11.3A is for all studies, and Table 11.3B is for studies dealing with the information content of dividends only.

As shown in Table 11.3, the WLS estimates of method of analysis, data type, and sample period coefficients do not differ significantly from zero and therefore do not influence the outcome of the analyses. The estimates of each explanatory variable are extremely small, and the reported $p$ values range from 0.152 to 0.976.

The intercept term representing the mean of the dependent variable is highly significant, with a $p$ value of $<0.001$. These conclusions hold for both the total population and the information content population. The intercept term is highly significant in both the overall analysis and the information content of dividend hypothesis analysis. Because the term represents all variables not

*Text continued on p. 152*

---

[2]In the interest of economy, the classification into CDAM populations and the relative frequencies are not presented here, but are available upon request from the authors.

[3]See Appendix A for the assignment of methods of analysis to classes.

[4]The choice of 1976 as the dividing point is based on the publication of Jensen and Meckling's (1976) agency theory, which gave rise to intense examination of the costs of asymmetric information. In addition, this choice divides the studies in our sample into two approximately equal groups. We wish to emphasize, however, that our results are quite robust to the selection of the time period. Classifying the sample period using several other criteria did not alter results presented in this paper.

Table 11.2

**Empirical Studies of Corporate Dividend Policy**

| Author(s) | Period | Data | Method of analysis[a] |
|---|---|---|---|
| Empirical studies of the Miller and Modiglini (1961) dividend irrelevance proposition | | | |
| Dhrymes and Kurz (1967) | 1951–1960 | Annual | XSRA, OLS, 2SLS, 3SLS |
| Brigham and Gordon (1968) | 1958–1962 | Annual | MRA |
| Higgins (1972) | 1961–1965 | Annual | XSRA |
| Fama (1974) | 1946–1968 | Annual | TSRA, OLS, 2SLS |
| McDonald et al. (1975) | 1962–1968 | Annual | XSRA, OLS, 2SLS |
| Bar-Yosef and Kolodny (1976) | 1963–1971 | Annual | XSRA |
| McCabe (1979) | 1966–1973 | Annual | XSRA, OLS, 2SLS |
| Anderson (1983) | 1963–1977 | Quarterly | TSRA |
| Peterson and Benesh (1983) | 1975–1979 | Annual | XSRA, 2SLS, 3SLS, SUR |
| Smirlock and Marshall (1983) | 1958–1977 | Annual | GC |
| Jensen et al. (1992) | 1982, 1987 | Annual | XSRA, 3SLS |
| Frankfurter and Gong (1993) | 1979–1990 | Quarterly | TSRA, XSRA, VAR |
| Empirical studies pricing the tax on dividends by adding a variable to the capital asset pricing model | | | |
| Black and Scholes (1974) | 1936–1966 | Monthly | MRA |
| Litzenberger and Ramaswamy (1979) | 1936–1977 | Monthly | MRA |
| Rosenberg and Marathe (1979) | 1931–1966 | Monthly | MRA, 2SLS |
| Litzenberger and Ramaswamy (1980) | 1936–1977 | Monthly | XSRA |
| Gordon and Bradford (1980) | 1926–1978 | Monthly | MRA |
| Green (1980) | 1962–1977 | Daily | XSRA, TSRA |
| Blume (1980) | 1936–1976 | Quarterly | XSRA |
| Morgan (1982) | 1931–1977 | Monthly | MRA, OLS, BJM |
| Litzenberger and Ramaswamy (1982) | 1936–1980 | Monthly | XSRA |
| Miller and Scholes (1982) | 1940–1978 | Monthly | XSRA |
| Hess (1982) | 1962–1979 | Daily | MRA |
| Hess (1983) | 1951–1980 | Monthly | MRA |
| Auerbach (1983) | 1963–1977 | Daily | MRA |
| Elton et al. (1983) | 1936–1976 | Annual | MRA |
| Ang and Peterson (1985) | 1973–1983 | Annual | XSRA |
| Christie (1990) | 1946–1985 | Monthly | MRA |
| Naranjo et al. (1998) | 1963–1994 | Monthly | MRA |
| Empirical studies of changes in price during the period surrounding ex-dividend days | | | |
| Elton and Gruber (1970) | 1966–1967 | Daily | EG |
| Long (1978) | 1956–1976 | Daily | $P_A/P_B$ |
| Finnerty (1981) | 1978 | Daily | EG |
| Kalay (1982) | 1966–1967 | Daily | MEG |
| Eades et al. (1984) | 1962–1980 | Daily | MEG |
| Lakonishok and Vermaelen (1986) | 1970–1981 | Daily | ES |
| Kaplanis (1986) | 1979–1984 | Daily | OP |

**Table 11.2** (*continued*)

| Author(s) | Period | Data | Method of analysis[a] |
|---|---|---|---|
| Poterba (1986) | 1965–1984 | Daily | $P_A/P_B$ |
| Bailey (1988) | 1976–1983 | Daily | $C_A/C_B$ |
| Karpoff and Walkling (1988) | 1964–1985 | Daily | XSRA, OLS |
| Bajaj and Vijh (1990) | 1962–1987 | Daily | ES |
| Karpoff and Walkling (1990) | 1973–1985 | Daily | ES |
| Skinner and Gilster (1990) | 1980–1985 | Daily | EG |
| Sterk and Vandenberg (1990) | 1984–1986 | Daily | $P_A/P_B$ |
| Venkatesh (1991) | 1988 | Intraday | MEG |
| Stickel (1991) | 1972–1980 | Daily | ES |
| Dubofsky (1992) | 1962–1987 | Daily | MEG |

Empirical studies of changes in the tax liability of dividends

| | | | |
|---|---|---|---|
| Feldstein (1970) | 1953–1964 | Quarterly | XSRA, OLS, GLS, IV, ALS |
| Khoury and Smith (1970) | 1962–1973 | Annual | TSRA |
| Morgan (1980) | 1968–1977 | Monthly | MRA, OLS, GLS |
| Lakonishok and Vermaelen (1983) | 1971–1972 | Daily | MEG |
| Amoako-Adu (1983) | 1968–1978 | Monthly | ES |
| Booth and Johnston (1984) | 1970–1980 | Daily | EG |
| Poterba and Summers (1984) | 1955–1981 | Daily | XSRA, GLS |
| Barclay (1987) | 1900–1910 | Daily | EG |
| Crockett and Friend (1988) | 1940–1985 | Annual | TSRA, OLS |
| Grammatikos (1989) | 1975–1985 | Daily | MEG, ES |
| Robin (1991) | 1984–1988 | Daily | ES |
| Michaely (1991) | 1986–1989 | Daily | MEG |
| Ang et al. (1991) | 1969–1982 | Annual | Means |
| Givoly et al. (1992) | 1983–1987 | Annual | XSRA |
| Hearth and Rimbey (1992) | 1984–1988 | Daily | EG, NP |
| Wu and Hsu (1992) | 1984–1990 | Daily | ES |
| McKenzie and Thompson (1995) | 1985–1986 | Daily | ES |
| Bond et al. (1996) | 1970–1990 | Annual | OLS |
| Kalay and Michaely (2000) | 1936–1977 | Multiple | OLS, GLS, MLE |

Early empirical studies of the information content of dividends hypothesis

| | | | |
|---|---|---|---|
| Fama et al. (1969) | 1927–1959 | Monthly | ES, TSRA |
| Pettit (1972) | 1964–1969 | Daily | ES, XSRA |
| Watts (1973) | 1946–1965 | Monthly | XSRA, OLS |
| Ezell (1974) | 1966–1970 | Annual | MRA |
| Ang (1975) | 1966–1971 | Quarterly | CSA |
| Griffen (1976) | 1968–1973 | Monthly | XSRA, ES |
| Laub (1976) | 1946–1965 | Annual | MRA |
| Petitt (1976) | 1946–1965 | Monthly | MRA |
| Charest (1978) | 1962–1969 | Daily | ES |
| Gonedes (1978) | 1946–1972 | Annual | XSRA |

(*continued*)

**Table 11.2** (*continued*)

| Author(s) | Period | Data | Method of analysis[a] |
|---|---|---|---|
| Empirical studies supporting the information content of dividend hypothesis | | | |
| Aharony and Swary (1980) | 1963–1976 | Daily | ES |
| Kalay (1980) | 1956–1975 | Annual | DCA |
| Kwan (1981) | 1973–1977 | Quarterly | ES |
| Woolridge (1982) | 1970–1977 | Daily | ES |
| Eades (1982) | 1960–1979 | Monthly | MRA, ES |
| Woolridge (1983) | 1971–1977 | Daily | ES, NP |
| Asquith and Mullins (1983) | 1964–1980 | Daily | ES |
| Brickley (1983) | 1969–1979 | Daily | ES |
| Divecha and Morse (1983) | 1977–1979 | Daily | ES |
| Penman (1983) | 1968–1973 | Annual | TSRA, Means |
| Kane *et al.* (1984) | 1979–1981 | Daily | ES, MRA |
| Handjinicolaou and Kalay (1984) | 1975–1976 | Daily | ES |
| Benesh *et al.* (1984) | 1971–1978 | Daily | ES |
| Dielman and Oppenheimer (1984) | 1969–1977 | Daily | RCRA |
| Kalay and Lowenstein (1985) | 1962–1980 | Daily | ES |
| Eades *et al.* (1985) | 1962–1980 | Daily | ES |
| Asquith and Mullins (1986) | 1964–1980 | Daily | ES |
| Kalay and Lowenstein (1986) | 1979–1981 | Daily | ES |
| Richardson *et al.* (1986) | 1969–1982 | Daily | XSRA |
| Ofer and Siegel (1987) | 1976–1984 | Daily | MRA, IV |
| Healy and Palepu (1988) | 1954–1982 | Quarterly | XSRA |
| Eddy and Seifert (1988) | 1983–1985 | Daily | ES |
| Fehrs *et al.* (1988) | 1980–1984 | Daily | ES |
| Damodaran (1989) | 1981–1985 | Daily | EPS/DPS, NP |
| Venkatesh (1989) | 1972–1983 | Daily | NP |
| Manakyan and Carroll (1990) | 1979–1983 | Quarterly | NP, GC |
| Easton (1991) | 1978–1980 | Semiannual | MRA |
| Wansley *et al.* (1991) | 1973–1986 | Daily | ES, XSRA |
| Ghosh and Woolridge (1991) | 1962–1984 | Daily | ES |
| Shrader and Milkman (1991) | 1987–1988 | Daily | ES |
| DeAngelo *et al.* (1992) | 1980–1985 | Annual | LOGIT, NP |
| Eddy and Seifert (1992) | 1983–1985 | Daily | ES |
| Kao *et al.* (1992) | 1965–1990 | Quarterly | TOBIT |
| Kim and Viswanath (1992) | 1971–1980 | Daily | ES |
| Schatzberg and Datta (1992) | 1963–1988 | Daily | ES, NP |
| Wong and Swindle (1992) | 1970–1986 | Daily | NP |
| Gu and Clayton (1993) | 1982–1986 | Quarterly | ANOVA RBD |
| Denis *et al.* (1994) | 1962–1988 | Daily | ES |
| Bajaj and Vijh (1995) | 1962–1987 | Daily | ES |
| Bernheim and Wantz (1995) | 1962–1988 | Daily | OLS |
| Michaely *et al.* (1995) | 1964–1988 | Daily | ES |
| Akhigbe and Madura (1996) | 1972–1990 | Daily | ES |

**Table 11.2** (*continued*)

| Author(s) | Period | Data | Method of analysis[a] |
|---|---|---|---|
| Firth (1996) | 1980–1991 | Daily | ES |
| Amihud and Murgia (1997) | 1988–1992 | Daily | ES |
| Desai and Jain (1997) | 1976–1991 | Monthly | Bootstrap |
| Brook *et al.* (1998) | N/A | Annual | AR |
| Dyl and Weigand (1998) | 1972–1993 | Daily | ES, OLS |
| Howe and Shen (1998) | 1968–1992 | Daily | ES |
| Lipson *et al.* (1998) | 1980–1986 | Daily | ES |
| DeAngelo *et al.* (2000) | 1962–1995 | Daily | ES |
| Garrett and Priestley (2000) | 1977–1997 | Annual | ECM |
| Guay and Harford (2000) | 1981–1993 | Quarterly | MRA |
| Kosedag and Michalyluk (2000) | 1980–1996 | Daily | ES |
| Pan (2001) | 1971–1993 | Annual | CCA |

Empirical studies not supportive of the information content of
dividend hypothesis and signaling models

| | | | |
|---|---|---|---|
| Riding (1984) | 1974–1979 | Monthly | RRA, ES |
| Born *et al.* (1988) | 1962–1985 | Daily | ES, MRA |
| McCann and Webb (1992) | 1975–1987 | Daily | ES, MRA |
| Frankfurter and Gong (1992) | 1986–1990 | Daily | ES |
| DeAngelo *et al.* (1996) | 1980–1987 | Annual | AR |
| Benartzi *et al.* (1997) | 1979–1991 | Annual | OLS |
| DeAngelo *et al.* (2000) | 1962–1995 | Daily | ES |
| Jagannathan *et al.* (2000) | 1985–1996 | Annual | NP, Means |

Empirical studies of agency cost theory

| | | | |
|---|---|---|---|
| Rozeff (1982) | 1974–1980 | Annual | MRA |
| Dyl and Hoffmeister (1986) | 1979 | Weekly | MRA |
| Crutchley and Hansen (1989) | 1981–1985 | Annual | MRA |
| DeAngelo and DeAngelo (1990) | 1980–1985 | Annual | LOGIT |
| Collins *et al.* (1992) | 1989–1990 | Annual | MRA, OLS |
| Dempsey and Laber (1992) | 1981–1987 | Annual | MRA |
| Sun (1992) | 1979–1983 | Annual | MRA |
| Lippert *et al.* (2000) | 1992 | Annual | OLS |

Empirical studies of signaling versus free cash flow hypotheses

| | | | |
|---|---|---|---|
| Lang and Litzenberger (1989) | 1979–1984 | Intraday | AARA |
| Barber and Castanias (1992) | 1977–1989 | Annual | LOGIT, NP |
| Denis *et al.* (1992) | 1962–1987 | Daily | XSRA |
| Lee and Roberts-Glandoff (1992) | 1975–1987 | Daily | ES |
| Maquiera and Megginson (1992) | 1980–1990 | Daily | ES, MRA, NP |
| Moh'd *et al.* (1995) | 1972–1989 | Annual | XSRA |

[a]See Appendix for abbreviations.

**Table 11.3**

**CDAM Analyses—WLS Models: Empirical Studies of Corporate Dividend Policy[a]**

| Variable | Estimate | Standard error | $\chi^2$ | Probability ($p$ value) |
|---|---|---|---|---|
| A: All studies | | | | |
| Intercept | 0.2094 | 0.0321 | 41.54[b] | 0.001 |
| Method of Analysis | 0.0116 | 0.0417 | 0.07[b] | 0.777 |
| Data Type | −0.0019 | 0.0416 | 0.00[b] | 0.976 |
| Sample Period | 0.0448 | 0.0332 | 1.85[b] | 0.152 |
| B: Information content hypothesis | | | | |
| Intercept | 0.2469 | 0.0472 | 26.92[c] | 0.001 |
| Method of Analysis | −0.0029 | 0.0521 | 0.00[c] | 0.957 |
| Data Type | −0.0431 | 0.0576 | 0.55[c] | 0.459 |
| Sample Period | 0.0249 | 0.0499 | 0.23[c] | 0.619 |

[a]Empirical studies evaluated are listed in Table 11.2.
[b]$N = 150$.
[c]$N = 85$.

included, factors absent from the model can cause the diverse results of the empirical tests. In addition, a finer qualitative classification might find some, or all, of the explanatory variables significant. Such significance might have cancelled out in the model tested thus far.

As stated earlier, a rationale used commonly to explain different results from empirical analyses is to attribute the inconsistencies to differences in method of analysis, data type, or sample period. Additional CDAM is performed using finer divisions of the explanatory variables. The "method of analysis" variable is divided into four groups: abnormal returns, price change, regression, and other methods of analysis. The variable representing data type is divided into studies using annual, quarterly, monthly, and daily data samples. The results of these refined tests are shown in Tables 11.4A–Table 11.4C, respectively.

As can be gleaned from Table 11.4, finer categorizations do not alter the results of the previous findings: none of the independent variables show any significant explanatory power. Consequently, in contrast to commonly held beliefs, the choice of method of analysis, data type, and sample period does not significantly affect the results of a study.

Although the outcomes of the experiments presented here are quite robust, a caveat is in order. It should be recognized that the length of the sample period and/or the total number of observations used in the analysis might be significant. Studies using data drawn from a narrower time horizon can reflect anomalies that disappear over longer sample periods. This may be something that is not in the best interest of advancing scientific knowledge. Model specification, variable definition, and proxy choice can also affect findings.

**Table 11.4**

**Analysis of Weighted Least-Squares Estimates Obtained from Categorical Variable Analysis of Empirical Analyses of Corporate Dividend Policy**[a]

| Variable | Estimate | Standard error | $\chi$[b] | Probability ($p$ value) |
|---|---|---|---|---|
| Explanatory variable | | | | |
| A: Method of analysis | | | | |
| Intercept | 0.2045 | 0.0357 | 29.99 | 0.0001 |
| Price Change | −0.0641 | 0.0521 | 1.45 | 0.2241 |
| Regression Analysis | 0.0968 | 0.0817 | 1.44 | 0.2368 |
| Other | 0.0531 | 0.0514 | 1.01 | 0.3061 |
| B: Data type | | | | |
| Intercept | 0.2158 | 0.0391 | 29.82 | 0.0001 |
| Quarterly | 0.0563 | 0.0672 | 0.69 | 0.4001 |
| Monthly | −0.0284 | 0.0510 | 0.33 | 0.5712 |
| Daily | 0.0441 | 0.0761 | 0.32 | 0.5548 |
| C: Study midpoint | | | | |
| Intercept | 0.2167 | 0.0360 | 41.32 | 0.0001 |
| Late[c] | 0.0438 | 0.0320 | 1.68 | 0.1923 |

[a]Empirical studies evaluated are listed in Table 11.2.
[b]$N = 150$.
[c]Late studies are those with sample period midpoints of 1976 or later.

# 11.4 CONCLUSIONS

Following Black (1976), Feldstein and Green (1983) remarked that "the nearly universal policy of paying substantial dividends is the primary puzzle in the economics of corporate finance." A number of conflicting theoretical models, all lacking strong empirical support, define current attempts by research in finance to explain the dividend phenomenon. Nor can corporate dividend policy be ascribed to existing regulatory constraints. The incomplete nature of current theories and the sensitivity of data to changes in specifications preclude any dogmatism (Brealy and Myers, 1991).

It is known that dividend policy is "sticky"—managers decrease dividends only when absolutely necessary—in the event of poor earnings with reserves insufficient to fund the dividend (Myers, 1984; DeAngelo et al., 1992). Furthermore, individual market imperfections do little to explain the underlying reasons for dividend payments (Black, 1976). The systematic time series behavior of corporate dividend policy implies that firm-specific, theoretical explanations of dividend policy—signaling and agency theories—cannot explain the practice (Marsh and Merton, 1987).

The majority of empirical works support the hypothesis that the returns on dividend-paying stocks are increased to offset the tax liability of dividend payment. The absence of a pronounced difference in the portfolios of high-tax-bracket and low-tax-bracket individuals casts doubts, however, as to the significance of taxes in the determination of corporate dividend policy.

The majority of shareholders must pay taxes on dividend income. In a commentary appearing in the *Wall Street Journal*, Jeremy Siegel (2002) blames the Enron fiasco on the double taxation of dividends. He also insinuates that dividends are the best signal of the financial health of the firm (p. A20). To convince the reader, Siegel contends that in the past (i.e., the 19th century), investors relied on the amount of dividends paid, without SEC and FASB, in judging the financial health of the firm. It is sincerely hoped that the reader of this book will see how false this claim is.

Dividends can relay information, but the use of dividends for this purpose fails to explain why firms pay dividends. The impact of signaling on the investor's preference for dividends is even less certain because of the ambiguity associated with signals. Further, if dividends are changed only to signal firm-specific information, aggregate dividend changes should be small and random rather than have a systematic time series pattern and a demonstrated positive trend (Marsh and Merton, 1987; Fama and French, 2001).

No single economic rationale can explain the dividend phenomenon. The preference of shareholders for dividends (Crockett and Friend, 1988) can instead be partially explained by a combination of factors: risk-averse shareholders who have invested in capital-constrained firms, the costs associated with systematic liquidation of holdings, agency costs, and information transmission. The incompleteness of the theoretical models is largely due to a misconception of the nature of dividend payments. The continuance of dividends is based in the main on long-standing corporate traditions (Brealy and Myers, 1991).

The corporate tradition of paying dividends is the sum total of more than 300 years of *evolution* of the practice of dividend payments. Despite individual differences in policy, consistent, identifiable patterns of dividend payment recur through corporations. Managers are reluctant to reduce dividend payments, even in periods of financial distress. Moreover, dividends are increased only if a corporation's management is confident that the higher levels can be maintained. Executives believe that shareholders expect significant dividends to be paid, and shareholders believe that they deserve these dividends.

Finally, shareholders prefer dividend payments, despite the tax liability (see, e.g., DRIPs). Myers (1990) surmised that dividend payments are in reality an unwritten contract between shareholders and corporate management, and, therefore, are "sticky."

Current models of corporate dividend policy by and large ignore behavioral and socioeconomic influences on managerial and shareholder activities. Unless these influences are incorporated into future models, dividend preference is difficult to explain, other than as an irrational desire by investors for dividends (Shiller, 1984).

The exclusion of these motivations from financial models severely limits their application to corporate activities and policy determination. Dividend policy is influenced by the same fads and fashions that affect stock prices because the managers who determine dividend policy are motivated by behavioral and socioeconomic influences (Shiller, 1990). As Shiller (1986) argues, a model incorporating a combination of modern financial theories and behavioral and psychological influences might best explain corporate dividend policy. Until such models are developed, we are confident to argue that tests of dividend policy theories will remain both inconclusive and inconsistent. The study discussed in this chapter gives a solid basis for such confidence.

# REFERENCES

Aharony, Joseph, and Itzhak Swary. 1980. "Quarterly dividend and earnings announcements and stockholders' returns: An empirical analysis." *The Journal of Finance* 35:1–12.

Akhigbe, Aigbe, and Jeff Madura. 1996. "Dividend policy and corporate performance." *Journal of Business Finance and Accounting* 23:1267–1287.

Amihud, Yakov, and Haim Mendelson. 1987. "Trading mechanisms and stock returns: an empirical investigation." *The Journal of Finance* 42:533–555.

Amihud, Yakov, and Maurizio Murgia. 1997. "Dividends, taxes, and signaling: evidence from Germany." *The Journal of Finance* 52:397–408.

Amoako-Adu, Ben. 1983. "The Canadian tax reform and its effect on stock prices: a note." *The Journal of Finance* 38:1669–1675.

Anderson, G. J. 1983. "The internal financing decisions of the industrial and commercial sector: a reappraisal of the Lintner model of dividend disbursements." *Economica* 50:235–248.

Ang, James S. 1975. "Dividend policy: informational content or partial adjustment." *The Review of Economics and Statistics* 57:65–70.

Ang, James S., David W. Blackwell, and William L. Megginson. 1991. "The effect of taxes on the relative valuation of dividends and capital gains: evidence from dual-class british investment trusts." *The Journal of Finance* 46:383–399.

Ang, James S., and David R. Peterson. 1985. "Return, risk, and yield: evidence from ex ante data." *The Journal of Finance* 40:537–548.

Asquith, Paul, and David W. Mullins, Jr. 1983. "The impact of initiating dividend payments on shareholders' wealth." *The Journal of Business* 56:77–96.

Asquith, Paul, and David W. Mullins, Jr. 1986. "Signalling with dividends, stock repurchases, and equity issues." *Financial Management* 15(Autumn):27–44.

Auerbach, Alan J. 1983. "Stockholder tax rates and firm attributes." *Journal of Public Economics* 21:107–127.

Bailey, Warren. 1988. "Canada's dual class shares: further evidence on the market value of cash dividends." *The Journal of Finance* 43:1143–1160.

Bajaj, Mukesh, and Anand M. Vijh. 1990. "Dividend clienteles and the information content of dividend changes." *Journal of Financial Economics* 26:193–219.

Bajaj, Mukesh, and Anand M. Vijh. 1995. "Trading behavior and the unbiasedness of the market reaction to dividend announcements." *The Journal of Finance* 50:255–279.

Baker, H. Kent, and Gail E. Farrelly. 1988. "Dividend achievers: a behavioral perspective." *Akron Business and Economic Review* 19:79–92.

Barber, Brad M., and Richard C. Castanias. 1992. "Why do firms initiate dividends?" Unpublished working paper.

Barclay, Michael J. 1987. "Dividends, taxes, and common stock prices." *Journal of Financial Economics* 19:31–44.

Bar-Yosef, Sasson, and Richard Kolodny. 1976. "Dividend policy and capital market theory." *The Review of Economics and Statistics* 58:181–190.

Benartzi, Shlomo, Michaely, Roni and Richard Thaler. 1997. "Do changes in dividends signal the future or the past?" *The Journal of Finance* 52:1007–1034.

Benesh, Gary A., Arthur J. Keown, and John M. Pinkerton. 1984. "An examination of market reaction to substantial shifts in dividend policy." *The Journal of Financial Research* 7:131–142.

Bernheim, B. Douglas, and Adam Wantz. 1995. "A tax-based test of the dividend signaling hypothesis." *The American Economic Review* 85:532–551.

Black, Fisher. 1976. "The dividend puzzle." *The Journal of Portfolio Management* 2:5–8.

Black, Fisher, and Myron Scholes. 1974. "The effects of dividend yield and dividend policy on common stock prices and returns." *Journal of Financial Economics* 1:1–22.

Blume, Marshall E. 1980. "Stock returns and dividend yields: some more evidence." *The Review of Economics and Statistics* 62:567–577.

Bond, Stephen R., Lucy Chennells, and Michael P. Devereus. 1996. "Taxes and company dividends: a microeconometric investigation exploiting cross-section variation in taxes." *The Economic Journal* 106:320–333.

Booth, L. D., and Johnston, D. J. 1984. "The ex-dividend day behavior of Canadian stock prices: tax changes and clientele effects." *The Journal of Finance* 39:457–476.

Born, Jeffery A., James T. Moser, and Dennis T. Officer. 1988. "Changes in dividend policy and subsequent earnings." *The Journal of Portfolio Management* 14:56–62.

Brealey, Richard, and Stewart Myers. 1991. *Principles of Corporate Finance.* 4th ed. New York: McGraw-Hill Book Company.

Brickley, James A. 1983. "Shareholder wealth, information signaling and the specially designated dividend." *Journal of Financial Economics* 12:187–209.

Brigham, Eugene F., and Myron J. Gordon. 1968. "Leverage, dividend policy, and the cost of capital." *The Journal of Finance* 23:85–103.

Brook, Yaron, William T. Charlton, Jr., and Robert J. Hendershott. 1998. "Do firms use dividends to signal large future cash flow increases?" *Financial Management* 27(3):46–57.

Charest, Guy. 1978. "Dividend information, stock returns, and market efficiency—II." *Journal of Financial Economics* 6:297–330.

Christie, William G. 1990. "Dividend yield and expected returns." *Journal of Financial Economics* 28:95–125.

Collins, M. Cary, Atul K. Saxena, and James T. Wansley. 1992. "Delegated monitoring and dividend policy: a comparison of regulated and unregulated firms." Unpublished working paper.

Crockett, Jean, and Irwin Friend. 1988. "Dividend policy in perspective: can theory explain behavior?" *The Review of Economics and Statistics* 70:603–613.

Crutchley, Claire E., and Robert S. Hansen. 1989. "A test of the agency theory of managerial ownership, corporate leverage, and corporate dividends." *Financial Management* 18:36–46.

Damodaran, Aswath. 1989. "The weekend effect in information releases: a study of earnings and dividend announcements." *Review of Financial Studies* 2:607–623.

DeAngelo, Harry, and Linda DeAngelo. 1990. "Dividend policy and financial distress: an empirical investigation of troubled NYSE firms." *The Journal of Finance* 55:1415–1431.

DeAngelo, Harry, Linda DeAngelo, and Douglas J. Skinner. 1992. "Dividends and losses." *The Journal of Finance* 57:1837–1863.

DeAngelo, Harry, Linda DeAngelo, and Douglas J. Skinner. 1996. "Reversal of fortune: dividend signaling and the disappearance of sustained earnings growth." *Journal of Financial Economics* 40:341–371.

DeAngelo, Harry, Linda DeAngelo, and Douglas J. Skinner. 2000. "Special dividends and the evolution of dividend signaling." *Journal of Financial Economics* 57:309–354.

Dempsey, Stephen J., and Gene Laber. 1992. "Effects of agency and transaction costs on dividend payout ratios: further evidence of the agency-transaction cost hypothesis." *The Journal of Financial Research* 15:317–321.

Denis, David J., Diane K. Denis, and Atulya Sarin. 1994. "The information content of dividend changes: cash flow signaling, overinvestment, and dividend clienteles." *Journal of Financial and Quantitative Analysis* 29:567–587.

Desai, Hemang, and Prem C. Jain. 1997. "Long-run common stock returns following stock splits and reverse splits." *Journal of Business* 70:409–433.

Dhrymes, Phoebus J., and Mordecai Kurz. 1967. "Investment, dividend, and external finance behavior of firms." in *Determinants of Investment Behavior: A Conference of the Universities-National Bureau Committee for Economic Research*. Robert Ferber. ed. New York: National Bureau of Economic Research.

Dielman, Terry E., and Henry R. Oppenheimer. 1984. "An examination of investor behavior during periods of large dividend changes." *Journal of Financial and Quantitative Analysis* 19:197–216.

Divecha, Arjun, and Dale Morse. 1983. "Market responses to dividend increases and changes in payout ratios." *Journal of Financial and Quantitative Analysis* 18:163–173.

Dubofsky, David A. 1992. "A market microstructure explanation of ex-day abnormal returns." *Financial Management* 21:32–43.

Dyl, Edward A., and Ronald Hoffmeister. 1986. "A note on dividend policy and beta." *Journal of Business Finance and Accounting*, 13:107–115.

Dyl, Edward A., and Robert A. Weigand. 1998. "The informational content of dividend initiations: additional evidence." *Financial Management* 27(2):27–35.

Eades, Kenneth M. 1982. "Empirical evidence on dividends as a signal of firm value." *Journal of Financial and Quantitative Analysis* 17:471–500.

Eades, Kenneth M., Patrick J. Hess, and E. Han Kim. 1984. "On interpreting security returns during the ex-dividend period." *Journal of Financial Economics* 13:3–34.

Eades, Kenneth M., Patrick J. Hess, and E. Han Kim. 1985. "Market rationality and dividend announcements." *Journal of Financial Economics* 14:581–604.

Easton, Stephen, 1991. "Earnings and dividends: is there an interaction effect." *Journal of Business Finance and Accounting* 18:255–266.

Eddy, Albert, and Bruce Seifert. 1988. "Firm size and dividend announcements." *The Journal of Financial Research* 11:295–302.

Eddy, Albert, and Bruce Seifert. 1992. "Stock price reactions to dividends and earnings announcements: contemporaneous versus non-contemporaneous announcements." *The Journal of Financial Research* 15:207–217.

Elton, Edward J., and Martin J. Gruber. 1970. "Marginal stockholder tax rates and the clientele effect." *The Review of Economics and Statistics* 52:68–74.

Elton, Edward J., Martin J. Gruber, and Joel Rentzler. 1983. "A simple examination of the empirical relationship between dividend yields and deviations from the CAPM." *Journal of Banking and Finance* 7:135–146.

Ezell, John R. 1974. "The informational content of dividends hypothesis: some empirical evidence." *The Journal of Business Research* 2:99–103.

Fama, Eugene F. 1974. "The empirical relationships between the dividend and investment decisions of firms." *The American Economic Review* 64:304–318.

Fama, Eugene F., Lawrence Fisher, Michael C. Jensen, and Richard Roll. 1969. "The adjustment of stock prices to new information." *International Economic Review* 10:1–21.

Fama, Eugene F., and Kenneth R. French. 2001. "Disappearing dividends: changing firm characteristics or lower propensity to pay." *Journal of Financial Economics* 60:3–43.

Fehrs, Donald H., Gary A. Benesh, and David R. Peterson. 1988. "Evidence of a relation between stock price reactions around cash dividend changes and yields." *The Journal of Financial Research* 11:111–123.

Feldstein, Martin S. 1970. "Corporate taxation and dividend behavior." *Review of Economic Studies* 37:57–72.

Feldstein, Martin S., and Jerry Green. 1983. "Why do companies pay dividends?" *The American Economic Review* 73:17–30.

Fienberg, Stephen E. 1980. *The Analysis of Cross-Classified Categorical Data.* 2nd Ed. Cambridge, MA: The MIT Press.

Finnerty, John D. 1981. "The behavior of electric utility common stock prices near the ex-dividend date." *Financial Management* 10:59–69.

Firth, Michael. 1996. "Dividend changes, abnormal returns, and intra-industry firm valuations." *Journal of Financial and Quantitative Analysis* 31:189–211.

Frankfurter, George M., and Jaisik Gong. 1992. "Empirical tests of a dividend signaling equilibrium model." Unpublished working paper.

Frankfurter, George M., and Jaisik Gong. 1993. "Time-series cross-sectional tests of dividend policy determinants." Unpublished working paper.

Garrett, Ian, and Richard Priestley. 2000. "Dividend behavior and dividend signaling." *Journal of Financial and Quantitative Analysis* 35:173–189.

Ghosh, Chinmoy, and J. Randall Woolridge. 1991. "Dividend omissions and stock market rationality." *Journal of Business Finance and Accounting,* 18:315–330.

Givoly, Dan, Carla Hayn, Aharon R. Ofer, and Oded Sarig. 1992. "Taxes and capital structure: evidence from firms' response to the Tax Reform Act of 1986." *The Review of Financial Studies* 5:331–355.

Gonedes, Nicholas J. 1978. "Corporate signaling, external accounting, and capital market equilibrium: evidence on dividends, income, and extraordinary items." *Journal of Accounting Research* 16:26–79.

Gordon, Roger H., and David F. Bradford. 1980. "Taxation and the stock market valuation of capital gains and dividends." *Journal of Public Economics* 14:109–136.

Grammatikos, Theoharry. 1989. "Dividend stripping, risk exposure, and the effect of the 1984 tra on the ex-dividend day behavior." *The Journal of Business* 62:157–173.

Green, Jerry. 1980. "Taxation and the Ex-dividend day behavior of common stock prices." NBER working paper.

Griffen, Paul A. 1976. "Competitive information in the stock market: an empirical study of earnings, dividends, and analysts' forecasts." *The Journal of Finance* 31:631–650.

Gu, Zheng, and Ronnie Clayton. 1993. "Dividend signaling and cash flow: an empirical examination." Unpublished working paper.

Guay, Wayne, and Jarrad Harford. 2000. "The cash-flow permanence and information content of dividend increases versus repurchases." *Journal of Financial Economics* 57:385–415.

Handjinicolaou, George, and Avner Kalay. 1984. "Wealth redistributions or changes in firm value: an analysis of returns to bondholders and stockholders around dividend announcements." *Journal of Financial Economics* 13:35–63.

Healy, Paul M., and Krishna G. Palepu. 1988. "Earnings information conveyed by dividend initiations and omissions." *Journal of Financial Economics* 21:149–175.

Hearth, Douglas, and James H. Rimbey. 1992. "The dividend-clientele controversy and the Tax Reform Act of 1986." Unpublished working paper.

Hess, Patrick. 1982. "The Ex-dividend day behavior of stock returns: further evidence on tax effects." *The Journal of Finance* 37:445–456.

Hess, Patrick. 1983. "Test for tax effects in the pricing of financial assets." *Journal of Business* 56:537–554.

Higgins, Robert C. 1972. "The corporate dividend-saving decision." *Journal of Financial and Quantitative Analysis* 7:1527–1541.

Howe, John S., and Yang-pin Shen. 1998. "Information associated with dividend initiations: firm-specific or industry-wide?" *Financial Management* 27(3):17–26.

Jagannarthan, Murali, Clifford P. Stephens, and Michael S. Weisbach. 2000. "Financial flexibility and the choice between dividends and stock repurchases." *Journal of Financial Economics* 57: 355–384.

Jensen, Gerald R., Donald P. Solberg, and Thomas S. Zorn. 1992. "Simultaneous determination of insider ownership, debt, and dividend policies." *Journal of Financial and Quantitative Analysis* 27:247–263.

Jensen, Michael C., and William H. Meckling. 1976. "Theory of the firm: managerial behavior, agency costs and ownership structure." *Journal of Financial Economics* 3:305–360.

Kalay, Avner. 1980. "Signaling, information content, and the reluctance to cut dividends." *Journal of Financial and Quantitative Analysis* 15:855–869.

Kalay, Avner. 1982. "Stockholder-bondholder conflict and dividend constraints." *Journal of Financial Economics* 10:211–233.

Kalay, Avner. 1984. "The ex-dividend day behavior of stock prices; a re-examination of the clientele effect: a reply." *The Journal of Finance* 37:557–561.

Kalay, Avner, and Uri Loewenstein. 1985. "Predictable events and excess returns: the case of dividend announcements." *Journal of Financial Economics* 14:423–449.

Kalay, Avner, and Uri Loewenstein. 1986. "The informational content of the timing of dividend announcements." *Journal of Financial Economics* 16:373–388.

Kalay, Avner, and Roni Michaely. 2000. "Dividends and taxes: a re-examination." *Financial Management* 29(2):55–75.

Kane, Alex, Young Ki Lee, and Alan Marcus. 1984. "Earnings and dividend announcements: is there a corroboration effect?" *The Journal of Finance* 39:1091–1099.

Kao, Chinwa, Chunchi Wu, and Yuah-Chiao Lin. 1992. "Corporate dividend dynamics and information signaling." Unpublished working paper.

Kaplanis, Costas P. 1986. "Options, taxes, and ex-dividend day behavior." *The Journal of Finance* 41:411–424.

Karpoff, Jonathan M., and Ralph A. Walkling. 1988. "Short-term trading around ex-dividend days." *Journal of Financial Economics* 21:291–298.

Karpoff, Jonathan M., and Ralph A. Walkling. 1990. "Dividend capture in NASDAQ stocks." *Journal of Financial Economics* 28:39–65.

Khoury, N. T., and Smith, K. V. 1977. "Dividend policy and the capital gains tax in Canada." *Journal of Business Administration* 8:19–37.

Kim, Yu Kyung, and P. V. Viswanath. 1992. "Financing slack, investment opportunities and market reaction to dividend changes." Unpublished working paper.

Kosedag, Arman, and David Michayluk. 2000. "Dividend initiations in reverse-LBO firms." *Review of Financial Economics* 9:55–63.

Kwan, Clarence C. Y. 1981. "Efficient market tests of the informational content of dividend announcements: critique and extension." *Journal of Financial and Quantitative Analysis* 16:193–206.

Lakonishok, Josef, and Theo Vermaelen. 1983. "Tax reform and ex-dividend day behavior." *The Journal of Finance* 38:1157–1179.

Lakonishok, Josef, and Theo Vermaelen. 1986. "Tax-induced trading around ex-dividend days." *Journal of Financial Economics* 16:287–319.

Lang, Larry H. P., and Robert H. Litzenberger. 1989. "Dividend announcements: cash flow signalling vs. free cash flow hypothesis?" *Journal of Financial Economics* 24:181–191.

Laub, P. Michael. 1976. "On the informational content of dividends." *The Journal of Business* 49: 73–80.

Lee, Hei-Wei, and Patricia A. Robert-Grandoff. 1992. "The role of growth opportunities in dividend initiations and omissions: dividend signaling hypothesis or free cash flow hypothesis." Unpublished working paper.

Lippert, Robert L., Terry D. Nixon, and Eugene A. Pilotte. 2000. "Incentive compensation and the stock price response to dividend increase announcements." *The Financial Review* 35:69–94.

Lipson, Marc L., Carlos P. Maquieira, and William Megginson. 1998. "Dividend initiations and earnings surprises." *Financial Management* 27(3):36–45.

Litzenberger, Robert H., and Krishna Ramaswamy. 1979. "The effect of personal taxes and dividends on capital asset prices: theory and empirical evidence." *Journal of Financial Economics* 7:163–195.

Litzenberger, Robert H., and Krishna Ramaswamy. 1980. "Dividends, short selling restrictions, tax-induced investor clienteles and market equilibrium." *The Journal of Finance* 35:469–485.

Litzenberger, Robert H., and Krishna Ramaswamy. 1982. "The effects of dividends on common stock prices tax effects or information effects." *The Journal of Finance* 37:429–443.

Long, John B., Jr. 1978. "The market valuation of cash dividends: a case to consider." *Journal of Financial Economics* 6:235–264.

Manakyan, Herman, and Carolyn Carroll. 1990. "An empirical examination of the existence of a signaling value function for dividends." *The Journal of Financial Research* 13:201–209.

Maquieira, Carlos P., and William L. Megginson. 1992. "Why do public companies begin paying dividends?" Unpublished working paper.

Marsh, Terry A., and Robert C. Merton. 1987. "Dividend behavior for the aggregate stock market." *The Journal of Business* 60:1–40.

McCabe, George M. 1979. "The empirical relationship between investment and financing: a new look." *Journal of Financial and Quantitative Analysis* 14:119–135.

McCann, P. Douglas, and Gwendolyn P. Webb. 1992. "The information content of the initial dividend." Unpublished working paper.

McDonald, John G., Bertrand Jacquillat, and Maurice Nussenbaum. 1975. "Dividend, investment and financing decisions: empirical evidence on French firms." *Journal of Financial and Quantitative Analysis* 10:741–755.

McKenzie, Kenneth J., and Aileen J. Thompson. 1995. "Dividend taxation and equity value: the Canadian tax changes of 1986." *Canadian Journal of Economics* 28:463–472.

Michaely, Roni. 1991. "Ex-dividend day stock price behavior: the case of the 1986 Tax Reform Act." *The Journal of Finance* 46:845–859.

Michaely, Roni, Richard Thaler, and K. Womack. 1995. "Price reactions to dividend initiations and omissions: overreaction or drift?" *The Journal of Finance* 50:573–608.

Miller, Merton H., and Myron S. Scholes. 1982. "Dividends and taxes: some empirical evidence." *Journal of Political Economy* 90:1118–1141.

Moh'd Mahmoud A., Larry G. Perry, and James N. Rimbey. 1995. "An investigation of the dynamic relationship between agency theory and dividend policy." *The Financial Review* 30:367–385.

Morgan, I. G. 1980. "Dividend and stock price behavior in Canada." *Journal of Business Administration*, 12:91–107.

Morgan, I. G. 1982. "Dividends and capital asset prices." *The Journal of Finance* 37:1071–1086.

Myers, Stewart C. 1984. "The capital structure puzzle." *The Journal of Finance* 39:575–592.

Myers, Stewart C. 1990. "Still searching for capital structure." Keynote address delivered at HEC International Conference.

Naranjo, Andy, M. Nimalendran, and Mike Ryngaert. 1998. "Stock returns, dividend yields, and taxes." *The Journal of Finance* 53:2029–2057.

Ofer, Aharon R., and Daniel R. Siegel. 1987. "Corporate financial policy, information, and market expectations: an empirical investigation of dividends." *The Journal of Finance* 42:889–911.

Pan, Ming-Shiun. 2001. "Aggregate dividend behavior and permanent earnings hypothesis." *The Financial Review* 36:23–38.

Penman, Stephen H. 1983. "The predictive content of earnings forecasts and dividends." *The Journal of Finance* 38:1181–1199.

Peterson, Pamela P., and Gary A. Benesh. 1983. "A re-examination of the empirical relationship between investment and financing decisions." *Journal of Financial and Quantitative Analysis* 18:439–453.

Pettit, R. Richardson. 1972. "Dividend announcements, security performance, and capital market efficiency." *The Journal of Finance* 27:993–1007.

Pettit, R. Richardson. 1976. "The impact of dividend and earnings announcements: a reconciliation." *The Journal of Business* 49:86–96.

Poterba, James M. 1986. "The market valuation of cash dividends." *Journal of Financial Economics* 15:395–405.

Poterba, James M., and Lawrence H. Summers. 1984. "New evidence that taxes affect the valuation of dividends." *The Journal of Finance* 39:1397–1415.

Richardson, Gordon, Stephan E. Sefcik, and Rex Thompson. 1986. "Test of dividend irrelevance using volume reactions to a change in dividend policy." *Journal of Financial Economics* 17:313–333.

Riding, Allan L. 1984. "The information content of dividends: an other test." *Journal of Business Finance & Accounting*, 11:163–176.

Robin, Ashok J. 1991. "The impact of the 1986 Tax Reform Act on ex-dividend day returns." *Financial Management* 20:60–70.

Roll, Richard. 1977. "A critique of the asset price theory's test; part I: on past and potential testability of theory." *Journal of Financial Economics* 4:129–176.

Rosenberg, Barr, and V. Marathe. 1979. "Tests of capital asset pricing hypothesis." *Research in Finance* 1:115–223.

Rozeff, Michael S. 1982. "Growth, beta and agency costs as determinants of dividend payout ratios." *The Journal of Financial Research* 5:249–259.

Schatzberg, John D., and Prabir Datta. 1992. "The weekend effect and corporate dividend announcements." *The Journal of Financial Research* 15:69–76.

Shiller, Robert J. 1984. "Stock prices and social dynamics." *Brookings Papers on Economic Activity*, 457–510.

Shiller, Robert J. 1986. "The marsh-merton model of managers' smoothing of dividends." *The American Economic Review* 76:499–503.

Shiller, Robert J. 1990. "Market volatility and investor behavior." *The American Economic Review* 80(2):58–62.

Siegel, Jeremy. 2002. "The dividend deficit." *The Wall Street Journal* 239:A20.

Shrader, Mark J., and Martin Milkman. 1991. "The effects of growth opportunities on dividend signaling." Unpublished working paper.

Skinner, David L., and John E. Gilster, Jr. 1990. "Dividend clienteles, the tax-clientele hypothesis, and utilities." *The Financial Review* 25:287–296.

Smirlock, Michael, and William Marshall. 1983. "An examination of the empirical relationship between the dividend and investment decisions: a note." *The Journal of Finance* 38:1659–1667.

Sterk, William E., and Pieter A. Vanderberg. 1990. "The market valuation of cash dividends and the tax differential theory of dividend policy: a case revisited." *The Financial Review* 25:441–455.

Stickel, Scott E. 1991. "The ex-dividend behavior on nonconvertible preferred stock returns and trading volume." *Journal of Financial and Quantitative Analysis* 26:45–61.

Sun, Y. Elizabeth. 1992. "Corporate dividend policy in an agency costs framework." Unpublished working paper.

Venkatesh, P. C. 1989. "The impact of dividend initiation on the information content of earnings announcements and returns volatility." *The Journal of Business* 62:175–198.

Venkatesh, P. C. 1991. "Trading costs and ex-day behavior: an examination of primes and stocks." *Financial Management* 20:84–95.

Wald, A. 1943. "Tests of statistical hypotheses concerning general parameters when the number of observations is large." *Transactions of the American Mathematical Society* 54:426–482.

Wansley, James W., Sirmans, C. F., James D. Shilling, and Young-jin Lee. 1991. "Dividend change announcement effects and earnings volatility and timing." *The Journal of Financial Research* 14:37–49.

Watts, Ross. 1973. "The information content of dividends." *The Journal of Business.*" 46:191–211.

Watts, Ross. 1976a. "Comments on 'The Informational Content of Dividends.'" *The Journal of Business* 49:81–85.

Watts, Ross. 1976b. "Comments on 'The impact of dividend and earnings announcements: a reconciliation.'" *The Journal of Business* 49:97–106.

Woolridge, J. Randall. 1982. "The information content of dividend changes." *The Journal of Financial Research* 5:237–247.

Woolridge, J. Randall. 1983. "Dividend changes and security prices." *The Journal of Finance* 38:1607–1615.

Wong, Thian S., and C. Sloan Swindle. 1992. "Dividends as an information transmission mechanism." Unpublished working paper.

Wu, Chunchi, and Junming Hsu. 1992. "The impact of the 1986 tax reform on ex-dividend day volume and price behavior." Unpublished working paper.

# APPENDIX A

# Method of Analysis Abbreviations

## A. Abnormal Return Methods of Analysis

| | |
|---|---|
| ARA | Abnormal returns analysis |
| ES | Event study method of analysis |

## B. Price Change Methods of Analysis

| | |
|---|---|
| $C_A/C_B$ | Price ratio between two classes of common stock |
| DCA | Dividend change analysis |
| EG | Elton and Gruber |
| EPS/DPS | Earnings per share/dividends per share |
| MEG | Modified Elton and Gruber |
| OP | Changes in option prices |
| $P_A/P_B$ | Price ratio between two issues |

## C. Regression Analysis Methods of Analysis

| | |
|---|---|
| ALS | Augmented least-squares regression |
| Bootstrap | Bootstrap |
| IV | Instrumental variables |
| LOGIT | Logit |
| MRA | Multiple regression |
| OLS | Ordinary least-squares regression |
| RCRA | Random coefficient regression |
| RRA | Recursive regression |
| SUR | Seemingly unrelated regressions |
| TSRA | Time series regression |
| 2SLS | Two-stage least squares |
| 3SLS | Three-stage least squares |
| TOBIT | Tobit |
| XSRA | Cross-sectional regression |

## D. Other Methods of Analysis

| | |
|---|---|
| ANOVA RBD | Analysis of variance randomized block design |
| BJM | Box Jenkins method |
| CCA | Canonical correlation analysis |
| CSA | Cross-spectral analysis |
| DA | Aggregate data analysis |
| ECM | Error correction model |
| GC | Granger causality test |
| Means | Means test |
| NP | Nonparametric tests |
| VAR | Vector autoregression |

# PART IV

## New Ways of Thinking about Dividends and Dividend Policy

# CHAPTER 12

# Unconventional Explanations

No theory based on the economic paradigm developed thus far completely explains the persistence of corporate dividend policy. Empirical attempts to validate these theories are inconclusive or contradictory (Baker and Farrelly, 1988). Shiller (1984) argued that investor behavior is influenced substantially by societal norms and attitudes, unfortunately, this motivation has been ignored by financial theorists for the most part because of the difficulty of introducing investor behavior into traditional financial pricing models (Arbel *et al.*, 1988). The inclusion of these factors and effects into theoretical models is not an easy task. Nevertheless, the effect can enrich the development of a theory to explain corporate dividend policy as an enduring tradition (Shiller, 1989).

It has been well articulated by Knight (1964) that ordinary investors are not actually faced with risk but rather with uncertainty—a lack of concise judgment and sense of objective evidence. Shiller (1984) added that social pressures can lead to errors in judgment and trading activities by shareholders that defy logical explanation. These errors in judgment may just be mistakes rather than lapses of rational investment activity. Mass investor psychology profoundly influences aggregate market activity.

Dividend policy is inconsistent with wealth maximization of the shareholder and is better explained by the addition of sociopsychological elements of behavior explicitly included in a paradigm that is set out to explain this phenomenon. Dividend payouts can be viewed as the socioeconomic repercussion of corporate evolution—the ever-increasing separation between managers and shareholders—that causes dividends to be paid to increase the attractiveness of equity issues (Frankfurter and Lane, 1992). Frankfurter and Lane (1992) also argued that managers discern shareholders' desire for dividends and pay or increase dividends as a method of mollifying investors. The systematic relation between industry type and dividend policy reported by Michel (1979) implies that managers are influenced by the actions of competitive firm executives when determining dividend payout levels. Dividend payments to shareholders should help increase the corporation's stability by serving as a ritualistic reminder of the managerial and owner relationship (Ho and Robinson, 1992). Dividends are partially a tradition and partially a method to allay investor anxiety (Frankfurter and Lane, 1992).

## 12.1  MANAGERIAL SURVEYS

Lintner (1956) surveyed corporate chief executive officers (CEOs) and chief financial officers (CFOs) and found that dividend policy is an active decision variable because managers believe that stable dividends lessen negative investor reactions. The active determination of dividend policy implies that the levels of retained earnings and savings are dividend decision by-products. Corporate management believes that shareholders should receive an equitable portion of earnings.

Lintner also reported that the majority of managers develop long-term payout ratio targets and use periodic partial adjustments to reach target levels. The *magnitude* of the percentage change in payout levels is more important than the absolute dollar amount. Unexpected changes in earnings are one of the most important dividend determinants. Managers are reluctant to renege on changes— dividend decreases are met with considerable managerial resistance and dividend increases occur *only* if managers are convinced that future cash flows will cover the higher levels of payout. Dividends are smoothed in the short run to conceal the variability of earnings. According to many (present company included), this empirical work is still the best of all empirical works done in the subject. Nevertheless, Lintner's (1956) results failed to explain why companies pay dividends.

A change in dividend policy implies a change in managerial expectations of future cash flows and depends substantially on current and past earnings. Darling (1957), Turnovsky (1967), and Fama and Babiak (1968) found empirical support for Lintner's findings. Dividends are a function of current and past profit levels, expected future earnings, and are negatively correlated with changes in the level of sales. Current income remains the critical determinant of corporate dividend policy 30 years after Lintner's original survey (DeAngelo *et al.*, 1992).

Other factors not considered by Lintner (regulatory constraints, investment magnitude, debt, and firm size) also affect dividend policy. Variations in dividend policy are primarily because of a combination of endogenous and exogenous elements (Dhrymes and Kurz, 1964).

Harkins and Walsh (1971) found that shareholder dividend desires and management need of retained earnings for investment opportunities conflict. A compromise policy partially satisfying both parties is chosen. Managers consider current and expected earnings, dividend payment history, dividend level stability, cash flows and investment opportunities, and shareholder desires in their determination of the payout level. One-half of the firms surveyed have target dividend payout levels. Dividends are adjusted gradually over some period to reach this target level. Although costly, dividend payments are important.

A survey of 318 New York Stock Exchange firm CFOs by Baker *et al.* (1985) found attitudes similar to those found by Lintner (1956). The CFOs cited the importance of dividend continuity, the belief that share prices are affected by dividend policy, and the difference in classification of regular and unusual cash flows as important determinants of dividend policy. Dividends are changed only if managers are sure of the changed cash flows' permanence. Financial managers view the efforts on share price from dividend payment and earnings retention differently. Regulated firm CFOs have different attitudes toward dividend policy.

In a survey of corporate managers of dividend achievers (defined as firms with 10 consecutive years of dividend increases) Baker and Farrelly (1988) found that the amount of dividend payment is less important than the consistency of payment. Managerial views of dividend policy are essentially unchanged 30 years after Lintner's study. Dividends are paid because shareholders expect continued dividend growth and because managers believe investors want to receive dividends. Managers believe that dividend payments are necessary to maintain or increase share price and to attract new investors. Dividend payout policy is determined using criteria including sustainability, current firm profitability, future cash flow expectations, and industry norms.

The majority of firms develops target payout ratios and use dividends as an active decision variable. Although financial managers view changes in dividend policy as the release of information, the message is often ambiguous and can actually misinform investors. Baker and Farrelly (1988) found that less than one-half of the CFOs questioned in their study attempted to signal through dividend policy.

## 12.2 THEORETICAL BEHAVIORAL MODELS

Feldstein and Green (1983) modeled the corporate dividend decision as the last step in a process that evaluates inputs from five sources. First, dividend policy is a consequence of investor consumption needs. (The tax liabilities from dividend payment are less than the transaction costs of selling shares to provide income if earnings are retained.) Second, the market value of retained earnings is less than the market value of dividends. Third, dividend payment is consistent with steady-state growth and an optimal debt/equity ratio. Fourth, dividend payments are a by-product of the separation of corporation owners and managers; dividend payments help diminish the agency costs arising from separation of these parties and are used for signaling activities. Finally, the model is independent of market imperfections such as asymmetric information and agency costs.[1] Shareholders with diverse tax liabilities and diversification goals in an equilibrium with uncertainty result in dividend payments.

Shefrin and Statman (1984) explained dividend preference by applying the theory of self-control (Thaler and Shefrin, 1981) and the descriptive theory of choice under uncertainty (Kahneman and Tversky, 1979). Information models are used to justify the presence of corporate dividends, whereas the tax liability of dividends is used as a counterargument. This model is also consistent with dividend clienteles. Dividends and capital gains are not always perfect substitutes (even in a world without taxes and transaction costs) because of a lack of self-control to delay gratification (Thaler and Shefrin, 1981). In financial theory, dividends and capital gains have the same value. This is not the case in a world described by the theory of self-control.

Dividend checks are appreciated more than capital gains and provide an automatic control device on spending levels (Thaler, 1980). Risky alternatives, costs, and payoffs are evaluated separately. The greater effects shown following dividend decreases also support this theory; losses are more meaningful than gains. Kahneman and Tversky (1982) posited that the sale of shares of stock causes more investor regret and anxiety than spending the cash received from dividend payments. A subsequent price rise of shares sold for income needs increases the shareholders' contrition. Clearly, in this model, capital gains and dividends are not perfect substitutes. Regret aversion can induce a preference for dividends through a consumption rule based on the use of dividends, not invested capital. Dividend yields are positively correlated with the planned dissaving rate. If dissaving is positively related to age and negatively to income, portfolio dividend yields will be positively correlated with age and negatively with income.

Marsh and Merton (1986) developed a rational expectations model of dividend policy as management's response to permanent earnings. In equilibrium, dividend levels are determined using future earnings expectations. Using dividends as signals is incompatible with this model.

Marsh and Merton (1987) studied an aggregate stock market dividend process using 55 years of aggregate data and economic earnings. They found that market prices adequately reflect permanent earnings. Managers systematically

---

[1]In fact, Feldstein and Green (1983) severely criticized all then known and existing dividend models, including the early attempts of Bhattacharya (1979, 1980) at dissipative signaling.

change the dividend payout following unexpected changes in permanent earnings by partially adjusting dividend levels. This partial adjustment causes dividends to be less volatile than share prices. The change in dividends is unrelated to later changes in share price. Lagged dividends explain little aggregate dividend variance when previous period stock price changes are included in the model. Dividends exhibit a systematic time series behavior—the aggregate dividend change is driven by the one period lagged stock price change.

Managerial and shareholder behavioral and socioeconomic influences affect corporate dividend policy profoundly. In surveys of corporate managers, Marsh and Merton (1987) found that the attitudes toward dividend payments have remained largely unchanged over the past 40 years. Managers believe that shareholders expect and are entitled to significant and regular dividend payments. The managers also believe that share price is affected substantially by dividend policy and that shareholders use dividend payments as a major input in firm valuation. However, these surveys are incapable of explaining why corporations began to pay and continue to pay dividends and why instead they did not try to modify behavior by "educating" shareholders.

Behavioral influences affect shareholder attitudes toward dividend payments. Dividends and capital gains are not perfect substitutes in the eyes of shareholders because of psychological and behavioral influences affecting the evaluation of the two alternatives. Incorporating investor behavioral and psychological influences into theoretical models could greatly enrich the development of a theory to explain corporate dividend policy persistence.

# REFERENCES

Arbel, Avner, Steven Carvell, and Erik Postnieks. 1988. "The smart crash of October 19th." *Harvard Business Review* 66:124–136.

Baker, H. Kent, and Gail E. Farrelly. 1988. "Dividend achievers: a behavioral perspective." *Akron Business and Economic Review* 19:79–92.

Baker, H. Kent, Gail E. Farrelly, and Richard B. Edelman. 1985. "A survey of management views on dividend policy." *Financial Management* 14:78–84.

Bhattacharya, Sudipto. 1979. "Imperfect information, dividend policy, and 'the bird in the hand' fallacy." *Bell Journal of Economics* 10:259–270.

Bhattacharya, Sudipto. 1980. "Nondissipative signaling structures and dividend policy." *The Quarterly Journal of Economics* 95:1–24.

Darling, Paul G. 1957. "The influence of expectations and liquidity on dividend policy." *Journal of Political Economy* 65:209–224.

DeAngelo, Harry, Linda DeAngelo, and Douglas J. Skinner. 1992. "Dividends and losses." *The Journal of Finance* 57:1837–1863.

Dhrymes, Phoebus J., and Mordecai Kurz. 1964. "On the dividend policy of electric utilities." *The Review of Economics and Statistics* 46:76–81.

Fama, Eugene F., and Harvey Babiak. 1968. "Dividend policy: an empirical analysis." *Journal of American Statistical Association* 63:1132–1161.

Feldstein, Martin S., and Jerry Green. 1983. "Why do companies pay dividends?" *The American Economic Review* 73:17–30.

Frankfurter, George M., and William R. Lane. 1992. "The rationality of dividends." *International Review of Financial Analysis* 1:115–129.

Harkins, Edwin P., and Francis J. Walsh, Jr. 1971. *Dividend Policies and Practices*. New York: The Conference Board, Inc.

Ho, Kwok, and Chris Robinson. 1992. "Dividend policy is relevant in perfect markets." York University. Unpublished working paper.

Kahneman, Daniel, and Amos Tversky. 1979. "Prospect theory: an analysis of decision under risk." *Econometrica* 47:263–291.

Kahneman, Daniel, and Amos Tversky. 1982. "The psychology of preferences." *Scientific American* 246:167–173.

Knight, Frank H. 1964. *Uncertainty and Profit*. London: Augustus M. Kelley, bookseller.

Lintner, John. 1956. "Optimal dividends and corporate growth under uncertainty." *The Quarterly Journal of Economics* 78:49–95.

Marsh, Terry A., and Robert C. Merton. 1986. "Dividend variability and variance bounds tests for the rationality of stock market prices." *The American Economic Review* 76:483–498.

Marsh, Terry A., and Robert C. Merton. 1987. "Dividend behavior for the aggregate stock market." *The Journal of Business* 60:1–40.

Michel, Allen J. 1979. "Industry influence on dividend policy." *Financial Management* 8:22–26.

Shefrin, Hersh M., and Meir Statman. 1984. "Explaining investor preference for cash dividends." *Journal of Financial Economics* 13:253–282.

Shiller, Robert J. 1984. "Stock prices and social dynamics." *Brookings Papers on Economic Activity* 457–510.

Shiller, Robert J. 1989. "Fashions, fads, and bubbles in financial markets." In *Market volatility*, Cambridge, MA: MIT Press.

Thaler, Richard H., 1980. "Toward a positive theory of consumer choice." *Journal of Economic Behavior and Organization* 1:39–60.

Thaler, Richard H., and Hersh M. Shefrin. 1981. "An economic theory of self control." *Journal of Political Economy* 89:392–410.

Turnovsky, Stephen J. 1967. "The allocation of corporate profits between dividends and retained earnings." *The Review of Economics and Statistics* 49:583–589.

# CHAPTER 13

# Dividend Policy of Regulated Industries

Modern financial theory/financial economics suggests that a firm's dividend policy[1] is dictated by its investment and financing choices. That is, a firm accepts all favorable investment opportunities and finances those investments based on its optimal mix of debt and equity. This, in turn, indicates how the firm should dispose of its earnings available after taxes.[2]

For firms in regulated industries, however, additional constraints on the payment of dividends are frequently imposed. These constraints are based on either legislation, as in the case of Real Estate Investment Trusts (REITs), or concern by the appropriate regulatory body for interest groups other than stockholders. For example, bank regulators focus primarily on the interests of depositors, and historically, utility regulators have been primarily concerned about the ratepayer.

As stressed so far in this book, several notable authors (e.g., Miller, 1986; Black, 1976) have struggled to provide a rational explanation for the payment of dividends. Black (1976) called these payments a "puzzle," and Miller (1986) suggested that one of the primary tasks of corporate finance theory is to provide a rational explanation for this pervasive practice.[3]

[1]Throughout this chapter we discuss and measure dividend policy based on dividend payout ratio and yield. The payout ratio is defined as the ratio of dividends paid per share to earnings per share. Dividend yield is defined as dividends paid per share divided by the firm's share price.

[2]In practice, firms rarely follow this "residual" dividend policy because of the large fluctuations it causes in payout and the uncertainty for investors regarding the continuity and level of dividends.

[3]Miller himself in a period of a quarter of a century suggested six different "rational" explanations for the persistence of dividend as a practice. The most convincing one of these is the indifference proposition (Miller and Modigliani, 1961), according to which in a world of no corporate or personal income tax, the investor should be indifferent between dividends and retained earnings.

Explanations for dividend payments typically involve an informational component. In the Miller and Rock (1985) model, dividends form the missing component of the sources and uses of funds constraint and help investors form expectations about future earnings. Thus, dividend payments have an informational aspect, and this information relates to future earnings.

Miller and Modigliani (1961) showed that a firm's value was invariant with respect to its dividend policy, under certain limiting assumption. These assumptions included perfect markets, rational investor behavior, and perfect certainty. The assumption of perfect certainty eliminated uncertainty with respect to future investments and future profits. Miller and Modigliani (1961) also asserted that dividend policy is irrelevant under uncertainty, although they recognize that changes in dividend payout are frequently associated with changes in market price. Modigliani and Miller reconciled these two seemingly conflicting viewpoints with what they refer to as the "informational content" of dividends. They define the "informational content" of dividends in the following way:

> That is, where a firm has adopted a policy of dividend stabilization with a long-established and generally appreciated "target payout ratio," investors are likely to (and have good reason to) interpret a change in the dividend rate as a change in management's view of future prospects for the firm. The dividend change, in other words, provides the occasion for the price change though not its cause, the price still being solely a reflection of future earnings and growth opportunities (p. 430).

Asquith and Mullins (1986) supported the view that dividends are informative signals, although they are dissipative. They are valuable, in the view of Asquith and Mullins (1986), because they are backed by ". . . cold, hard, cash."

Regardless of the rationale for dividend payment, it is generally recognized that fundamental differences exist in the dividend policies of unregulated and regulated firms.[4] A reason for this difference in dividend policy is that historically the investment opportunity set available to regulated firms has been restricted, and these restrictions have limited the capital gains potential from equity investments in regulated firms.

In order for these firms to compete for capital in the capital markets, the total return, adjusted for risk, for regulated firms must be comparable with unregulated firms. Thus, if the capital gains component of return is limited, then these firms must make up any shortfall in the dividend yield component of the return. Differences in dividend policy between unregulated and regulated

---

[4]Because of the recognition of fundamental differences in dividend policy between regulated and unregulated firms, most academic research studying dividend policy explicitly excludes regulated firms from their sample.

firms can be seen most clearly through their dividend payout ratios or dividend yields.

Table 13.1 reports the average annual dividend payout ratio for many publicly traded companies for the 21-year period from 1980 through 2000.[5] Differences in dividend payout ratios between unregulated firms and firms in a number of regulated industries, most noticeably utilities and REITs, are immediately apparent. The average dividend payout ratio for unregulated firms over this 21-year period has ranged from a low of 15.9% in 1994 to a high of 31.5% in 1982. During the very same period, dividend payout ratios for utilities and REITS ranged from 62.0 to 175.5%.[6] Differences in payout between unregulated firms and several of the other industries, such as transportation and insurance, are less apparent.

Table 13.2 shows the dividend yield for the same firms included in Table 13.1. Using this alternative measure of dividend policy, differences between regulated and unregulated firms are more evident. The average dividend yield for unregulated firms over the 1980–2000 period is 1.6% compared with 6.6% for utilities and 9.8% for REITs.

Tables 13.3 and 13.4 report the average dividend payout ratio and dividend yield only for those firms that paid dividends. These results are much consistent with what is shown in Tables 13.1 and 13.2. Unregulated firms pay out a substantially smaller portion of their earnings than do most regulated industries, especially utilities and REITs, and the dividend yield of unregulated firms is significantly smaller than the corresponding yield of most regulated firms, with insurance companies being an exception.

## 13.1 DIVIDEND POLICY AND CORPORATE MONITORING

Several authors have focused on the role that dividends play in mitigating or supplementing capital market monitoring,[7] which reduces the firm's agency

*Text continued on p. 180.*

[5]Data in Tables 13.1–13.4 were taken from the annual Standard and Poor's Compustat data tapes. In order to screen out outliers, firms whose dividend payout ratios exceeded 10.0 were deleted. While the number of firms varies from year to year, data in these tables represent a broad cross section of publicly traded firms. In 1999, for example, there were 1305 unregulated firms, 40 firms in the petroleum and natural gas industries, 57 transportation firms, 46 telecommunication firms, 101 utilities, 341 banking and financial services firms, 105 insurance companies, and 116 REITs represented in Table 13.1.

[6]Note that REITs can pay dividends from cash flows, which typically exceed accounting earnings. Thus, it is possible, and even common, for REITS to have a dividend payout ratio, as commonly formulated, that exceeds 100%.

[7]The discussion of corporate monitoring draws heavily on Hansen *et al.* (1994).

## Table 13.1
### Dividend Payout Ratios for Unregulated and Regulated Firms: All Firms[a]

| Year | Unregulated | Petroleum | Transportation | Tele-com | Utilities | Banking and financial services | Insurance | REITs |
|---|---|---|---|---|---|---|---|---|
| 1980 | 25.9% | 15.3% | 29.0% | 33.9% | 68.3% | 38.0% | 30.1% | 82.5% |
| 1981 | 26.6% | 15.8% | 30.6% | 44.4% | 66.3% | 41.0% | 43.4% | 84.1% |
| 1982 | 31.5% | 58.0% | 39.2% | 32.6% | 67.7% | 39.7% | 35.4% | 78.8% |
| 1983 | 23.8% | 33.7% | 19.7% | 34.1% | 65.3% | 32.1% | 31.7% | 85.1% |
| 1984 | 25.7% | 42.4% | 23.5% | 36.5% | 62.0% | 41.3% | 48.2% | 96.3% |
| 1985 | 26.2% | 94.5% | 27.0% | 31.1% | 67.8% | 32.0% | 26.0% | 140.6% |
| 1986 | 26.3% | 1.1% | 20.4% | 55.9% | 74.0% | 25.6% | 23.6% | 112.7% |
| 1987 | 23.2% | 1.2% | 20.1% | 42.4% | 78.5% | 41.2% | 22.3% | 153.0% |
| 1988 | 22.5% | 1.5% | 24.0% | 30.0% | 72.0% | 38.3% | 31.7% | 138.0% |
| 1989 | 29.0% | 64.2% | 31.5% | 34.3% | 70.2% | 45.3% | 25.6% | 167.1% |
| 1990 | 29.2% | 37.6% | 42.3% | 45.0% | 77.1% | 59.1% | 28.9% | 170.2% |
| 1991 | 29.8% | 63.1% | 19.4% | 48.3% | 83.5% | 65.2% | 27.3% | 175.5% |
| 1992 | 22.0% | 45.5% | 60.0% | 40.9% | 78.8% | 27.9% | 23.1% | 171.1% |
| 1993 | 21.8% | 64.6% | 40.4% | 32.7% | 81.1% | 22.0% | 18.1% | 135.4% |
| 1994 | 15.9% | 27.6% | 17.8% | 45.8% | 77.9% | 24.1% | 17.4% | 154.2% |
| 1995 | 17.1% | 30.0% | 22.2% | 40.6% | 86.9% | 29.7% | 23.4% | 143.3% |
| 1996 | 17.3% | 10.4% | 18.5% | 33.3% | 76.7% | 42.1% | 19.0% | 136.1% |
| 1997 | 16.3% | 20.6% | 19.1% | 26.4% | 80.1% | 33.2% | 22.8% | 122.0% |
| 1998 | 18.0% | 92.0% | 20.2% | 38.5% | 77.9% | 36.6% | 22.8% | 146.4% |
| 1999 | 20.7% | 26.8% | 38.0% | 30.1% | 85.6% | 40.0% | 25.3% | 153.3% |
| 2000 | 30.20% | 5.5% | 44.40% | 28.70% | 70.00% | 40.70% | 40.50% | 148.50% |
| Average | 23.7% | 35.8% | 28.9% | 37.4% | 74.6% | 37.9% | 27.9% | 133.1% |

[a]From Standard and Poor's COMPUSTAT data annual tapes from 1980 to 2000.

## Table 13.2

### Dividend Yields for Unregulated and Regulated Firms: All Firms[a]

| Year | Unregulated | Petroleum | Transportation | Tele-com | Utilities | Banking and financial services | Insurance | REITs |
|---|---|---|---|---|---|---|---|---|
| 1980 | 2.70% | 0.66% | 3.05% | 4.27% | 10.21% | 5.83% | 4.20% | 9.20% |
| 1981 | 2.71% | 1.24% | 3.21% | 4.36% | 10.42% | 5.64% | 4.21% | 8.41% |
| 1982 | 2.63% | 2.69% | 2.60% | 3.73% | 9.33% | 5.21% | 3.82% | 8.98% |
| 1983 | 1.51% | 1.76% | 1.72% | 3.80% | 9.40% | 3.80% | 2.93% | 6.99% |
| 1984 | 1.97% | 3.46% | 1.70% | 4.21% | 8.59% | 3.67% | 2.61% | 7.66% |
| 1985 | 1.52% | 3.04% | 1.54% | 3.45% | 7.20% | 2.83% | 1.60% | 21.73% |
| 1986 | 1.26% | 4.14% | 1.26% | 2.78% | 6.03% | 2.59% | 2.52% | 7.46% |
| 1987 | 1.67% | 5.11% | 1.78% | 3.04% | 7.02% | 3.56% | 2.21% | 11.07% |
| 1988 | 1.70% | 5.66% | 21.43% | 2.40% | 6.71% | 4.14% | 2.32% | 10.44% |
| 1989 | 2.10% | 2.23% | 6.98% | 1.92% | 5.99% | 3.61% | 1.98% | 12.30% |
| 1990 | 1.95% | 1.66% | 3.46% | 2.49% | 6.52% | 5.49% | 2.65% | 12.99% |
| 1991 | 1.59% | 2.73% | 1.88% | 1.95% | 5.66% | 3.11% | 1.79% | 10.18% |
| 1992 | 1.03% | 1.30% | 2.39% | 3.14% | 5.49% | 2.02% | 1.43% | 9.61% |
| 1993 | 0.96% | 1.42% | 1.64% | 1.23% | 5.12% | 1.64% | 1.24% | 5.68% |
| 1994 | 1.05% | 0.90% | 1.27% | 1.45% | 6.22% | 2.19% | 1.49% | 7.54% |
| 1995 | 0.97% | 1.00% | 1.67% | 1.34% | 5.56% | 1.90% | 1.25% | 8.01% |
| 1996 | 0.94% | 0.56% | 1.26% | 1.34% | 5.50% | 2.17% | 1.24% | 6.83% |
| 1997 | 0.80% | 0.86% | 0.86% | 1.25% | 4.44% | 1.45% | 1.12% | 5.92% |
| 1998 | 0.94% | 2.53% | 1.19% | 1.77% | 4.04% | 1.95% | 1.32% | 8.08% |
| 1999 | 1.15% | 1.30% | 1.22% | 1.09% | 4.94% | 2.77% | 2.07% | 14.63% |
| 2000 | 1.70% | 0.56% | 2.35% | 1.90% | 3.95% | 2.97% | 1.34% | 12.10% |
| Average | 1.6% | 2.1% | 3.1% | 2.5% | 6.6% | 3.3% | 2.2% | 9.8% |

[a]From Standard and Poor's COMPUSTAT data annual tapes from 1980 to 2000.

177

## Table 13.3

### Dividend Payout Ratios—Unregulated and Regulated Firms: Only Dividend-Paying Firms[a]

| Year | Unregulated | Petroleum | Transportation | Tele-com | Utilities | Banking and financial services | Insurance | REITs |
|---|---|---|---|---|---|---|---|---|
| 1980 | 35.5% | 32.5% | 41.5% | 39.9% | 71.3% | 40.0% | 32.3% | 93.6% |
| 1981 | 39.3% | 35.2% | 46.9% | 53.6% | 69.6% | 43.3% | 48.4% | 97.4% |
| 1982 | 48.2% | 73.9% | 58.8% | 40.7% | 70.6% | 43.4% | 40.1% | 90.7% |
| 1983 | 43.2% | 52.5% | 37.2% | 42.9% | 68.2% | 39.2% | 39.9% | 97.9% |
| 1984 | 44.1% | 63.6% | 44.1% | 49.1% | 66.1% | 39.3% | 62.5% | 108.4% |
| 1985 | 48.2% | 130.5% | 48.2% | 44.1% | 73.7% | 40.8% | 40.1% | 150.4% |
| 1986 | 52.0% | 156.0% | 39.9% | 83.9% | 80.5% | 32.6% | 34.8% | 123.3% |
| 1987 | 44.9% | 153.6% | 34.8% | 64.5% | 85.4% | 49.9% | 29.9% | 161.0% |
| 1988 | 43.4% | 178.5% | 38.5% | 44.4% | 75.5% | 42.8% | 43.7% | 143.1% |
| 1989 | 54.2% | 92.5% | 47.2% | 49.9% | 72.5% | 53.3% | 34.0% | 170.6% |
| 1990 | 51.9% | 61.0% | 65.6% | 65.2% | 81.0% | 66.9% | 40.6% | 170.2% |
| 1991 | 61.4% | 90.7% | 34.7% | 80.6% | 86.3% | 78.3% | 42.5% | 175.5% |
| 1992 | 51.4% | 100.7% | 103.6% | 56.7% | 82.7% | 38.2% | 33.6% | 171.2% |
| 1993 | 52.4% | 135.6% | 77.8% | 60.5% | 84.5% | 30.4% | 28.4% | 154.8% |
| 1994 | 37.7% | 67.4% | 37.0% | 93.3% | 82.2% | 31.4% | 26.1% | 159.0% |
| 1995 | 42.0% | 63.3% | 48.3% | 79.8% | 88.9% | 37.3% | 37.1% | 147.6% |
| 1996 | 43.7% | 32.1% | 39.0% | 67.8% | 80.3% | 52.1% | 28.3% | 140.1% |
| 1997 | 42.3% | 49.6% | 48.8% | 50.3% | 84.1% | 40.3% | 32.6% | 126.3% |
| 1998 | 44.2% | 117.2% | 47.6% | 60.3% | 81.4% | 43.6% | 32.3% | 150.2% |
| 1999 | 50.4% | 48.7% | 98.4% | 57.6% | 89.1% | 46.8% | 36.4% | 156.0% |
| 2000 | 49.8% | 13.4% | 66.6% | 44.1% | 72.6% | 44.5% | 51.2% | 150.6% |
| Average | 46.7% | 83.3% | 52.6% | 58.5% | 78.4% | 44.5% | 37.8% | 139.9% |

[a]From Standard and Poor's COMPUSTAT data annual tapes from 1980 to 2000.

## Table 13.4
### Dividend Yields for Unregulated and Regulated Firms: Only Dividend-Paying Firms[a]

| Year | Unregulated | Petroleum | Transportation | Tele-com | Utilities | Banking and financial services | Insurance | REITs |
|------|------------|-----------|----------------|----------|-----------|--------------------------------|-----------|-------|
| 1980 | 3.71% | 1.40% | 4.36% | 5.04% | 10.65% | 6.13% | 4.51% | 10.46% |
| 1981 | 4.00% | 2.76% | 4.91% | 5.26% | 10.95% | 5.97% | 4.71% | 9.74% |
| 1982 | 4.02% | 3.43% | 3.90% | 4.66% | 9.72% | 5.69% | 4.33% | 10.32% |
| 1983 | 2.76% | 2.75% | 3.25% | 4.79% | 9.81% | 4.64% | 3.69% | 8.04% |
| 1984 | 3.40% | 52.02% | 3.20% | 5.67% | 9.16% | 4.62% | 3.39% | 8.62% |
| 1985 | 2.80% | 4.20% | 2.75% | 4.89% | 7.82% | 3.65% | 2.46% | 23.25% |
| 1986 | 2.50% | 6.03% | 2.46% | 4.17% | 6.56% | 3.30% | 3.72% | 8.16% |
| 1987 | 3.24% | 6.64% | 3.08% | 4.63% | 7.62% | 4.31% | 2.96% | 11.65% |
| 1988 | 3.28% | 6.92% | 3.44% | 3.54% | 7.04% | 4.63% | 3.19% | 10.83% |
| 1989 | 3.93% | 3.22% | 10.57% | 2.79% | 6.19% | 4.24% | 2.63% | 12.56% |
| 1990 | 3.46% | 2.69% | 5.37% | 3.61% | 6.85% | 6.21% | 3.72% | 12.99% |
| 1991 | 3.27% | 3.83% | 3.36% | 3.26% | 5.85% | 3.73% | 2.79% | 10.18% |
| 1992 | 2.41% | 2.87% | 4.13% | 4.34% | 5.76% | 2.77% | 2.08% | 9.61% |
| 1993 | 2.30% | 2.98% | 3.16% | 2.27% | 5.34% | 2.26% | 1.94% | 6.49% |
| 1994 | 2.50% | 2.19% | 2.63% | 2.95% | 6.57% | 2.86% | 2.24% | 7.77% |
| 1995 | 2.38% | 2.99% | 3.63% | 2.64% | 5.69% | 2.39% | 1.98% | 8.25% |
| 1996 | 2.37% | 1.73% | 2.65% | 2.73% | 5.76% | 2.69% | 1.85% | 7.03% |
| 1997 | 2.09% | 2.06% | 2.19% | 2.39% | 4.66% | 1.76% | 1.60% | 6.12% |
| 1998 | 2.33% | 3.12% | 2.81% | 2.77% | 4.22% | 2.33% | 1.87% | 8.29% |
| 1999 | 2.80% | 2.36% | 3.15% | 2.09% | 5.14% | 3.23% | 2.97% | 14.89% |
| 2000 | 2.80% | 1.37% | 3.52% | 2.92% | 4.22% | 3.24% | 1.69% | 12.27% |
| | | | | | | | | |
| Average | 3.0% | 5.6% | 3.7% | 3.7% | 6.9% | 3.8% | 2.9% | 10.4% |

[a]From Standard and Poor's COMPUSTAT data annual tapes from 1980 to 2000.

costs of equity and presumably results in a higher valuation. Easterbrook (1984) noted that by raising the payout, a firm increases the likelihood that it will have to sell common stock to raise capital. This will subject the firm to increased capital market scrutiny by analysts, investment bankers, investors, and other capital suppliers. Thus, one potential benefit of the increased payout is reduced agency costs of equity resulting from the higher level of capital monitoring.

Moyer *et al.* (1989) suggested that electric utilities use dividends as a way of subjecting the regulatory body to market discipline. This is consistent with Smith's (1992) certification hypothesis. Moyer *et al.* (1992) found that security analysts' monitoring activities of firms are lower when the firm is a public utility and when the level of insiders is relatively high.

Collins *et al.* (1996) (CSW, subsequently) recognized the potential differences in dividend policy between regulated and unregulated firms and examined the agency cost and monitoring explanations for the relevance of dividends. They argued that insiders should play a reduced role in determining dividend policy for utilities and, to some extent, financial services firms because these industries have regulators who serve as the low-cost informants to the capital markets.

CSW developed an explanatory model whereby a firm's dividend payout ratio is related to its historical and projected revenue growth rate, the firm's beta coefficient, the natural log of the number of common stockholders, and intercept and slope dummy variables for utilities and financial services firms. The intercept dummy variables are simply two separate variables that take on the value of zero (0) or one (1) if the firm is a utility (financial services firm). A significant coefficient on the UTILITY or FINANCE variable suggests that the dividend payout ratio is statistically different than for nonutility or nonfinancial services firms.

CSW also used two slope dummy variables that consist of the product of the utility/financial services dummy (0, 1) multiplied by the value of insider holdings. For utilities, if insider holdings act as a *substitute* for regulatory monitoring, then the differences in dividend policy between unregulated firms and utilities should diminish as the level of insider holdings increases. If this were true, then the coefficient on the utility slope dummy variable should be negative and significant.

Alternatively, if utility insider holdings act as a *complement* to regulatory monitoring, the coefficient on the slope dummy should be positive and significant.

The results of the CSW analysis confirm that dividend payout ratios for utilities are statistically larger than for nonregulated firms, although the payout ratios for financial services firms are not. CSW also found that the coefficient on the variable designed to test whether insider holdings substitutes for or complements regulatory monitoring is negative and significant for utilities and not significant for financial services firms. Thus, their results suggest that the regulatory environment enhances, rather than reduces, the importance of insiders for utilities.

Hansen *et al.* (1994) (HKS, subsequently) argued that the "extraordinary" dividend policies of utilities cannot be well explained by signaling or clientele theories, and that it is also unlikely that utility dividend payouts are merely a residual distribution of earnings. HKS noted that utilities payout ratios historically have greatly exceeded those of industrial firms, although utilities are frequently among the largest sellers of common stock. These two phenomena, taken together, are inconsistent with a signaling rationale of utility dividends.[8]

Also, according to HKS, signaling is implausible for utilities because their investment opportunities are well understood, and it is unlikely they have more valuable "hidden" information than industrial firms. This assertion is highly questionable, especially in light of the 2001 energy crisis, and the Enron debacle of 2001–2002. In fact, we argue that there is no industry, not even the suppliers of energy, whose "investment opportunities are well understood," or anticipated with perfect certainty.

The clientele argument "whereby corporations provide payout ratios that correspond to investors' preferences for payouts" (Miller and Modigliani, 1961) also does not withstand close scrutiny. The tax liability associated with the receipt of dividends as ordinary income, plus the flotation costs associated with new issues (precipitated by large payouts), would have to be less than the net transactions cost of receiving the income as capital gains.

HKS and Chaplinsky and Seyhun (1990) suggested that there is no clear evidence that personal tax rates are sufficiently low to accommodate the clientele argument. Finally, the large dividend payouts associated with utilities are not likely to be understood as a residual, given the propensity of utilities to accompany these payouts with heavy financing. Several authors, in addition to HKS, support the idea that the level of dividends paid by utilities is influenced by the cost of monitoring of regulators.[9]

Miller (1986) remarked that "Public utility managements have found a policy of high dividends combined with frequent external equity financing to be a useful strategy for forcing their regulators to keep utility rates high enough to continue attracting new funds from investors [cited in Hansen *et al.* (1994), p. 17].

In contrast to Miller (1986), Smith (1986) argued that

---

[8]There are many other phenomena (e.g., constant dividend payout) just as inconsistent with the signaling proposition/principle. This inconsistency, however, never kept finance academics from hitching their research program to the signaling bandwagon.

[9]These quotes also appear in Hansen *et al.* (1994).

by paying high dividends, the regulated firm subjects both its regulatory body as well as itself to capital market discipline more frequently. Stockholders are less likely to receive lower-than-normal levels of compensation due to lower allowed product prices when the regulatory authority is more frequently and effectively monitored by capital markets (p. 10).

HKS focused on the potential for dividends to promote monitoring of the "stockholder–regulator" conflict. An implication of this monitoring rationale is that these firms (electric utilities in the case of HKS) have the incentive to return large dividends to investors in order to bring primary market monitoring to bear on subsequent expenditures for new investments. It is precisely this payment of large dividends, even in the face of known subsequent investment needs, that brings the capital market scrutiny to bear.

HKS argued that the utility industry is expected to have a higher dividend payout ratio than other industries. This is because the marginal benefit of dividends from utilities is greater than for nonregulated firms, reflecting the reduction in stockholder–regulator agency costs and the possibility that utilities may face lower flotation costs if some of these costs can be passed onto ratepayers. They develop two empirically testable hypotheses from this "story."

The first test compares the dividend payout for electric utilities with that of the Standard and Poor's (S&P) 400 industrials. The null hypothesis is that the dividend payout for utilities exceeds that of industrials. For 1981–1985, the mean payout for the utilities is 66.25%, whereas that of the S&P 400 industrials is 36.2%. During 1986–1990, these figures were 69.6 and 33.8%, respectively. These differences in mean payout between electric utilities and industrials are significant at the 99% confidence level. The null hypothesis of equal payments for the two types of firms for both periods is rejected at the 0.01 level of significance.

The second test relates the electric utilities' dividend payout to the level of the shareholder–manager conflict and the shareholder–regulator conflict. HKS suggested that the payout ratio should be negatively related to the cost of dividend-induced monitoring and the need for external financing associated with a high payout. The HKS model relates the dividend payout to the utilities' regulatory rank, a Herfindahl index of the firm's common stock ownership, the utilities' historical average flotation costs incurred in selling common stock, and the 5-year growth rate in total assets. HKS found that the utilities' payout ratio is significantly negatively related to all four predictor variables, and they concluded that these results are consistent with the monitoring hypothesis. Accordingly, the conclusion is that these utilities use dividend-induced equity financing to control equity agency costs that arise out of the stockholder–regulator and stockholder–manager conflicts.

Booth and Smith (1986) provided indirect evidence that the dividend policy for regulated firms differs, at least partially, because of the monitoring role that regulators play. Booth and Smith (1986) developed a theory on the role of the underwriter in certifying that the prices paid for capital in the new issue market, equity and debt, reflect potentially adverse inside information. They test whether underwriter compensation is related to the relative proportion of non-market to market risk, total firm risk, and the size of the capital issue. They find these relationships to be significant for industrial firms, but not for public utilities and banks. Their results are consistent with the fact that these industries are regulated in such a way that certification by underwriters is redundant because of the monitoring role played by regulators.

## 13.2 REAL ESTATE INVESTMENT TRUSTS

Real estate investment trusts (REITs) are perhaps the most striking example of the impact of regulation on dividend policy. Congress created REITs in 1960 to provide an extra incentive to investors in making investments in income-producing real estate. A REIT is a firm organized to own and usually operate income-producing real estate, such as apartments, shopping centers, or offices. There are approximately 300 REITs in the United States, with assets in excess of $300 billion. Approximately two-thirds of these REITS trade on the national stock exchanges.[10] REITs are frequently classified into equity REITs, mortgage REITs, and hybrid REITs.

A REIT is a firm that has elected to qualify under certain Internal Revenue Code provisions to become a pass-through entity that distributes substantially all of its earnings and capital gains to its shareholders. The REIT does not pay taxes on its earnings but distributes these earnings through dividends to its shareholders, who are taxed at their personal marginal income tax level. To qualify as a REIT for tax purposes, the enterprise must satisfy conditions relating to assets, income, and distribution. These conditions are listed in Table 13.5. Nevertheless, the cardinal proviso as far as dividend policy is concerned is the requirement that REITs distribute to shareholders at least 95% of taxable income.

## 13.3 SUMMARY

It is clear that the dividend policy for many regulated firms differs from their nonregulated counterparts. While many have struggled to provide rational explanations for the payment of dividends by nonregulated firms, the regulatory environment facing banks and other financial service firms, utilities, and REITs,

---

[10]From the National Association of Real Estate Investment Trusts (REIT). See www.nareit.com.

**Table 13.5**

**Requirements for Trusts to Qualify as a REIT for Tax Purposes**[a]

Asset requirements
   At least 75% of the value of the REITs assets must consist of real estate assets, cash, and government securities
   Not more than 5% of the value of the assets may consist of the securities of any one issuer if the securities are not includable under the 75% test
   A REIT may not hold more than 10% of the outstanding voting securities of any one issuer if those securities are not includable under the 75% test
Income requirements
   At least 95% of the entity's gross income must be derived from dividends, interest, rents, or gains from the sale of certain assets
   At least 75% of gross income must be derived from rents, interest on obligations secured by mortgages, gains from the sale of certain assets, or income attributable to investments in other REITs
   Not more than 30% of the entity's gross income can be derived from the sale or disposition of stock or securities held for less than 6 months or real property held for less than 4 years other than property involuntarily converted or foreclosed on
Distribution requirements
   Distribution to shareholders must equal or exceed the sum of 95% of REIT taxable income

[a]From Bruggeman, William, and Jeffrey Fisher. 1997. *Real Estate Finance and Investments*. 10th ed. Homewood, IL: Irwin Press.

in particular, mitigates, either wholly or in part, the classical financial economics model whereby the firm's dividend policy is a residual one, made only after the financing and investment decision. Bank regulators (e.g., the Federal Reserve, the FDIC, the Comptroller of the Currency, and state regulatory agencies) have an incentive to impact dividend policy so as to insulate depositors from bank failure, whereas utility regulators are concerned about ratepayers. Finally, in the case of REITs, the enabling legislation includes codes requiring payment of dividends at certain levels.

Over the two decades from 1980 through 2000, the average dividend payout (dividend yield) for utility firms has been approximately 75% (6.6%), whereas the average payout for unregulated firms has been 24% (1.6%). The numbers are even more dramatic for REITs, whose average dividend payout exceeded earnings per share. Other industries, with various levels of regulation, such as petroleum, transportation, telecommunications, and insurance, generally have historical levels of dividend payout that exceed those of nonregulated firms, although not by as large a margin as for utilities or REITs.

Most research on dividend policy of regulated firms has focused on the role of corporate monitoring as a rationale for utilities' dividends. For example, the payment of dividends (especially high levels of payout) increases the likelihood that these firms will have to sell common stock to raise capital. This subjects the firm to capital market scrutiny and has the potential of reducing agency costs of equity.

If differences in dividend policy between regulated and nonregulated firms relate to the regulatory status of these firms (as opposed to say the investment opportunity set facing them), then it might be expected that these historical differences in dividend policy will diminish as many of these industries are deregulated.

# REFERENCES

Asquith, Paul, and David W. Mullins, Jr. 1986. "Signalling with dividends, stock repurchases, and equity issues." *Financial Management* 15:27–44.

Black, Fisher. 1976. "The dividend puzzle." *Journal of Portfolio Management* 2:5–8.

Booth, J. R., and R. L. Smith. 1986. "Capital raising, underwriting, and the certification hypothesis." *Journal of Financial Economics* 15:261–281.

Bruggeman, William, and Jeffrey Fisher. 1997. *Real Estate Finance and Investments.* 10th edition. Homewood, IL: Irwin Press.

Chaplinsky, S., and N. Seyhun. 1990. "Dividends and taxes: evidence on tax reduction strategies." *Journal of Business* 63:239–260.

Collins, M. Cary, Atul Saxena, and James W. Wansley. 1996. "The role of insiders and dividend policy: a comparison of regulated and unregulated firms." *Journal of Financial and Strategic Decisions* 9:1–9.

Easterbrook, Frank H. 1984. "Two agency-cost explanations of dividends." *American Economic Review* 74:650–659.

Hansen, Robert S., Raman Kumar, and Dilip Shome. 1994. "Dividend policy and corporate monitoring: evidence from the regulated electric industry." *Financial Management* 23:16–22.

Miller, Merton H. 1986. "Behavior rationality in finance: the case of dividends." *Journal of Business* 59:S451–S468.

Miller, Merton H., and Franco Modigliani. 1961. "Dividend policy, growth, and the valuation of shares." *The Journal of Business* 34:411–433.

Miller, Merton H., and Kevin Rock. 1985. "Dividend policy under asymmetric information." *Journal of Finance* 40:1031–1051.

Moyer, R. C., R. Chatfield, and P. Sisneros. 1989. "Security analyst monitoring activity: agency costs and information demands." *Journal of Financial and Quantitative Analysis* 24:503–512.

Moyer, R. C., R. Rao, and N. Tripathy. 1992. "Dividend policy and regulatory risk: a test of the Smith hypothesis." *Journal of Economics and Business* 44:127–134.

National Association of Real Estate Investment Trusts (NAREIT). www.nareit.com.

Smith, Clifford W., Jr. 1986. "Investment banking and the capital acquisition process." *Journal of Financial Economics* 15:3–29.

Smith, Clifford W., Jr. 1992. "The investment opportunity set and corporate financing, dividends, and compensation." *Journal of Financial Economics* 32:263–292.

# CHAPTER 14

# What if We Do Not Pay Dividends?

On May 31, 2002, FedEx Corporation, the parent of Federal Express, declared a 5¢/share dividend, the first dividend in the firm's long history. A day before the announcement, FedEx was selling $53.79/share. Since then the price has been moving around $56 for the month of June 2002. The high for the previous 12 months was around $61 on March 5, 2002.

Bird-in-the-hand theorists would argue that the market anticipated this announcement of dividend as early as 1970, and the declaration of the dividend was in sync with the market's expectation that dividends will come, at one point or another, in the life of the firm. Promoters of other theories (e.g., signaling) would argue that the change in dividend policy is a signal to the market that FedEx's future is bright and shiny and that it can maintain or possibly increase dividend payouts in the future *ad infinitum*.

Nevertheless, some undoubtedly will argue that FedEx initiated the "constant" stream of payouts because it has nothing better to do with its funds (i.e., reinvestment in profitable projects) or perhaps FedEx is invoking the old/new remedy for depressed stock prices by joining the long line of other firms that prop up the market price of their shares with dividends, something that works not unlike candy to cheer up children.

Whatever the case might be, there are still a large number of firms in the exchanges that never pay a dividend. Obviously, this observation pertains to established firms with long histories of existence because new and upcoming firms do not pay dividends, as a matter of routine, until and unless they can support a dividend payment pattern for years to come. Financial officers of firms know well and an untold number of "event studies" showed statistically that the market "punishes" firms that either reduce quarterly dividends or skip payment altogether.

Academic research into nondividend paying firms is almost nonexistent. Forbes and Hatem (1998) addressed the phenomenon directly by studying the history of firms on the NYSE and AMEX that do not pay a dividend by share price and market value of equity for the two decades 1974–1993. Forbes and Hatem found that a dramatic change took place in the dividend policy of firms. Whereas at the beginning of their study period only 2 out of every 10 firms in their sample did not pay dividends, this number had nearly doubled by the early 1990s. That is, just about 40% of the firms did not pay dividends.

Examining the connection between share price and dividend amount, Forbes and Hatem found that although predominantly low-priced shares did not pay dividends during the 1970s and 1980s, this pattern changed at the end of the period studied. By the early 1990s, only 60% of the firms with less than the median share price did not pay dividends and this figure further declined to less than 53% by 1993.

The study also found an emerging pattern in equity market value. At the beginning of the period, nondividend-paying firms typically had low equity capitalization: "By 1993 only the very largest firms are distinguishable for their small share of firms not paying dividends" (Forbes and Hatem, 1998, p. 48). The study then concluded that although once only lower capitalized firms with low stock prices were predominantly nondividend payers, this behavior changed considerably toward the end of the 20th century.

The general results of the Forbes and Hatem study are also confirmed by the Fama and French study reported in *The Economist* (1999) article (and see later in Fama and French, 2001). Fama and French predicted the continuous disappearance of dividends.

What about firms that do not pay dividends, ever? Microsoft, Apple Computer, and FedEx (FedEx broke rank just as this book went to print) have never paid a dividend. In fact, Microsoft, with a cash hoard of $32 billion, is not taking the option of shoveling out cash to the shareholders. In a February 13, 2002 report, Duff Mcdonald of ipo.com writes that only 8% of high-technology firms pay dividends compared to 50% of nontechnology firms. In fact, Intel, Compaq Computer, and Computer Associates are the only large tech firms that began paying dividends in the last 20 years. There is a hint in the Mcdonald report that Intel might have changed its policy regarding not paying dividends because it wanted to appeal to those institutional investors that are required by law to invest in firms that pay regular dividends.

Another interesting side of the story is, of course, firms that pay dividends because they want to be included in "legal listings." Inclusion in legal listings requires a minimum number of years of consecutive dividend payments. The benefit of being a legally listed firm is, *ceteris paribus*, lower interest rates on these firms' publicly issued debt. We have no data, and we suspect no one else does, regarding the number and motivations of these firms and whether paying dividends for the sake of being included in legal listing is an economically rational decision.

As reported elsewhere in this book, the tendency of reducing or not paying dividends that emerged at the end of the previous century has begun to reverse. More firms are paying out more dividends than in the late 1990s, mainly for two reasons: (1) To bolster their stock price and (2) to get rid of excess cash. The first reason is also an important factor in the increase in volume and frequency of share repurchases. The second reason makes the study of the policy of nondividend firms that much more complicated.

The second reason is something that is closely related to expectations regarding the future of the economy in general and that of the firm (or industry) in particular. The bursting of the techno bubble in early 2000 and the ensuing recession has been, undoubtedly, a cardinal reason for the reversal of the behavior pattern many observed at the 20th century's *fin-de-siécle* and that which inspired Black (1990) in his now famous editorial to make the prediction: "I think dividends that remain taxable will gradually vanish" (p. 5). During the early 2000s, this prophecy, as many other predictions of financial "mavens," seems to be proven wrong.

Not paying dividends and yet commanding a positive price at the equity marketplace, however, is the bane of many cherished academic theories. The first to fall hard in the face of firms not paying dividends, yet trading at positive prices, are the bird-in-the-hand theories. Of course, "bird-in-the-handites" can always argue that one may never know how and why the market properly predicts the eventual payment of dividend in the future, which is the underlying cause of the positive price. We do not think that many will subscribe seriously to this explanation, however. There must be a limit to both naiveté and fanaticism.

Not too far behind in bankruptcy are the garden–variety "agency" stories, namely the free cash flow and a policy that would call for a 100% dividend payout. Both are intended to disgorge cash from the dastardly hands of management that otherwise would surely use it for unnecessary perquisites. Dividends are a simple, fast, and, most of all, positive way to accomplish the objective of taking cash away from spendthrift management. Although the fact that the firm does not pay dividends is no proof that management is not a shameful usurer of shareholders' trust, the fact that these shareholders do not demand dividends vociferously, and that the share is selling for a positive price, makes the agency scenarios less than probable.

That would leave the tax explanations, such as the high–low tax bracket of shareholders and the clientele effect, still standing. The problem with the tax stories is that an untold number of studies failed to show a clear empirical connection to either one of the two. Specifically, no study has examined the question of the firms' and the shareholders' tax status regarding those firms that never pay dividends. Surely, giants such as Microsoft, Apple, Cisco Systems, and Oracle are present in institutional as well as private investors' portfolios, not to mention hundreds of other stocks.

There is no question that in a world of both corporate and individual income taxes, paying dividends is a paradox that cannot be explained by the logic of the *homo economicus*. At least one must admit that such explanations could not find clear and decisive empirical verification. The only exception would be the case of liquidating dividends.

That most firms pay dividends can be explained only by factors that are inconsistent with the logic of this economic person. Although these rationales have been emphasized throughout the book, they are mentioned here again for the sake of recap.

- Protecting the share price
- Increasing the share price in order to make management stock options more valuable
- Pacifying shareholders who were educated on the value of dividends since time immemorial
- Not being able to reinvest in profitable projects
- The firm reaching its decline in its life cycle.

Murphy (2002) made the parallel between the conditions of the equity markets today and that of the periods of 1802–1860 and 1873–1933. During these two periods, bond yields were superior to returns on equity in the United States, and Murphy sees it as a reasonable assumption that the beginning of the 21st century will replicate this historical phenomenon. Murphy quotes an increasing (in size) chorus of financial economists who argue that this unwelcomed repetition of history might be the result of historically low dividends. If indeed the economy is slow to pick up, or if firms' expectations will be "doom and gloom" for some time to come, an across-the-board dividend increase might be expected.

If this prediction comes to pass, then the question of why firms pay dividends will be answered by the necessity of equity competing with bond returns. However, one must not forget Warren Buffet's aphorism, if history would be a decisive factor in the stock markets, then librarians would be the richest persons on earth.

We still maintain that the question to answer should be why all firms do not pay dividends. To answer this question in a meaningful way, academic research must leave the course of neoclassical economics and turn to a logic that is different from the reasoning of the *homo economicus*. This drastic departure from the beaten path of academic research in finance is not too soon to come. In the meantime, one should expect new and contradictory "discoveries" of dividend research using new data and more complex models of econometrics. And the show goes on *ad perpetuo*.

# REFERENCES

Black, Fischer. 1990. "Why firms pay dividends." *Financial Analysts Journal* 46:5.

*The Economist*. 1999. "Shares without the other bit." November 20:93.

Fama, Eugene F., and Kenneth R. French. 2001. "Disappearing dividends: changing firm characteristics or lower propensity to pay?" *Journal of Financial Economics* 60:3–43.

Forbes, Shawn M., and John Hatem. 1998. "NYSE & AMEX listed firms that pay non-dividends: a recent history." *Journal of Financial and Strategic Decisions* 11:47–51.

Murphy, Austin. 2002. "Stock investments may earn less than bonds in the 21st century." *Journal of Investing* 11:23–24.

# CHAPTER 15

# Other Methods of Distribution

## 15.1 STOCK DIVIDENDS AND STOCK SPLITS

### 15.1.1 PROLOGUE

In the May 1993 issue of *CFO*, James S. Altschul, the author of the featured piece "Cheap Tricks with Stock Dividends," asked the rhetorical question: "Why do stock dividends defy the laws of finance?" The implication is that academic financial theory has failed to explain satisfactorily the number of benefits that such noncash transactions believed to produce for both the issuer and the recipient.

Both stock dividends and stock splits[1] involve the distribution of additional shares of stock to the existing shareholders in proportion to their ownership. The accounting profession recommends treating stock distributions of greater than 20–25% as stock splits. Similarly, the New York Stock Exchange labels distributions of 25% or greater as stock splits. Lesser distributions would be defined as stock dividends. These divisions between splits and dividends are not strictly enforced and are frequently disregarded by firms. More importantly, the market seemingly ignores the distinction.

Although stock dividends/splits are just one piece of the much larger puzzle of dividends, financial economists have devoted considerable attention to

[1]Although the accounting treatment and definition of stock dividends is different from stock splits, most academic work does not distinguish between the two. In this chapter, unless otherwise is stated, the two terms are used interchangeably.

the subject. During the last four decades, several ad hoc theories have been posited to explain the rationale of stock dividends/splits, to be rejected and replaced by alternative explanations. The common underlying thread of these academic attempts to explain the practice is, with the exception of a study by Baker and Phillips (1993), a general lack of concern with the perceptions of both those who initiate stock dividends and those who receive them.

Two basic questions surround stock dividends/splits: (1) why does management want to declare a stock dividend and (2) why does the market react favorably, on average, to its announcement? A popular textbook states that stock splits and stock dividends are used to keep the firm's stock price in a desired trading range, with splits used for large price reductions and stock dividends used regularly ". . . to keep the stock price more or less constrained" (Brigham et al., 1994, p. 640). The same text also avers that the observed positive market reaction results from ". . . the fact that investors take stock splits/dividends as signals of higher future earnings and dividends. . . ." [In another textbook, Brigham and Daves (2002) also asserted that stock splits/dividends "provide management with a relatively low-cost way of signaling that the firm's prospects look good.] These two positions are not necessarily consistent with each other.

The usual answers to these two questions elicit the argument (analogous to Altschul's) that these distributions are more than what they seem. Academic explanations are either predictive or invoke a scenario of asymmetric information between managers and shareholders. In the former case, the argument is that additional shares foster a change in the distribution of ownership by lowering stock price or otherwise influencing liquidity. In the latter instance, distribution supposedly signals management's expectation of higher future earnings, cash flows, or cash dividends. However, there are other more esoteric explanations as well.

These arguments persist despite inconsistencies in the empirical evidence. For example, Dowen (1990) rejected the information hypothesis, whereas McNichols and Dravid (1990) supported it. Both studies consider analysts' forecasts and the size of the distribution. For splits and the liquidity hypothesis, Baker and Powell (1993) and numerous articles in the practitioner press found managers to believe that liquidity is increased by a split, whereas academicians generally observe decreased liquidity [Conroy, et al. (1990), among others]. Presumably, effects for stock dividends would be smaller than for splits because of the smaller increase in the number of shares.

Thus, these arguments are not unlike Rudyard Kipling's *Just So Stories*— explanations consistent with (*ex post*) facts, containing a moral, but still not factual. Putting it into more rigorous terms, these explanations, like many other exegeses in modern finance, are the product of *post hoc* rationalizations.

At least one analyst has an even darker view. Charles B. Carlson of *Dow Theory Forecasts* is mentioned by Lazo (1993) as arguing that in 1992, splits were motivated by executives wanting to exercise options under more favorable tax rates, and trying to exploit the market's favorable reaction to announcements of splits and stock dividends.

A more recent study by Banker *et al.* (1993) found the market reaction to announcements of stock dividends to be partially explained by previously disclosed accounting information. The authors assumed that stock dividends are declared as a signal of improved future prospects and asserted that the market's response is dependent on the declaring firm's prior financial condition.

Unasked (and, of course, unanswered) is how, if this is so, a stock dividend meets the nonambiguity criterion of signaling. Also uncertain is whether, as Banker *et al.* (1993) argued, the accounting information is complementary to information disclosed in the stock dividend announcement or, alternatively, the market distrusts accounting numbers and requires some other activity to verify their informational content. The circular logic here is that managers rely on the same accounting information that Banker *et al.* (1993) discredited in order to formulate their future expectations, which they supposedly signal in a manner they consider credible. Perhaps the whole idea of signaling, in this and some other context, should be left to thaumatology.[2]

Academic formulations of the stock dividend phenomenon, such as that of Banker *et al.* (1993), deduced managerial motives from analyses of the issuers' financial condition and shareholders' opinions from prediction errors of event studies. An exception to this practice is Baker and Phillips (1993). Baker and Phillips surveyed financial executives to identify managements' views of and motives for stock dividends. Regretfully, Baker and Phillips (1993) framed their questionnaire in terms of existing academic theories, potentially constraining and thus biasing the responses. For example, 78% of the respondents agreed that "Stock dividends convey favorable information . . ." and 23% identified "Signal[ing] optimistic managerial expectations . . ." as the primary motive for the stock dividend (not surprising, given that managers are required to disclose all "material information"). At the same time, however, only 26% agreed that "Stock dividends trigger reassessments of the firm's future cash flows" and 70% agreed with the statement that "Stock dividends are cosmetic changes. . . ." Consequently, it is difficult to agree with Baker and Phillip's conclusion that the signaling hypothesis is convincingly supported by their data.

The three-way lack of agreement among academic theory, academic empirical evidence, and opinions expressed in the practitioner press underscores the need for both rigor and understanding of perception of the initiators (i.e., managers) of stock dividends.

Although the academic literature on the subject is not infinite, it, nevertheless, is voluminous. In addition to papers by Elgers and Murray (1985), Ezzel and Rubiales (1975), Lakonishok and Lev (1987), and Millar and Fielitz (1973)

---

[2]The scientific study of miracles.

that are exploratory in nature, many works can be categorized along a fashion-able theory. Consistent with this theory-inspired taxonomy, the discussion that follows is aimed to provide an overview of what has been accomplished so far.

## 15.1.2 DISTRIBUTION–LIQUIDITY

One of the most common rationalizations of stock dividends, and the positive market reaction to stock dividend/stock split announcements in general (Grinblatt et al., 1984; Lamoureux and Poon, 1987), is the idea that more shares would induce more frequent trading on the stock and thus it would be dis-tributed more widely, meaning a more diffused ownership. Also, frequent trading is desirable, and not just because it makes stockbrokers happy, but also because then the market provides a more continuous trading pattern (which goes hand-in-glove with more frequent price quotes). The subject has also been studied, with varying results and conclusions, by Copeland (1979), Defeo and Jain (1991), Hausman et al. (1971), Murray (1985), and Peterson and Peterson (1992).

## 15.1.3 VOLATILITY OF RETURNS–BETA

Although not exactly the same factors, volatility and the stability of beta, a proxy and a synonym for systematic risk, intrigued the "miners" of market data from time immemorial. This line of inquiry into the mysteries of stock dividends got further boosting with the discovery of the event study method of analysis. In fact, one of the first such studies was about stock dividends by Fama et al. (1969). The queue of such studies, with inconclusive evidence (if for no other reason than the severe statistical problems associated with the empirical valida-tion of the stability of a regression coefficient–beta), is quite extensive: Bar-Yosef and Brown (1977), Brennan and Copeland (1988a), Dubofsky (1991), French and Dubovsky (1986), Klein and Peterson (1988), Ohlson and Penman (1985), Sheikh (1989), and Wiggins (1992).

## 15.1.4 BID–ASK SPREAD AND MARKET MICROSTRUCTURE

A more recent mode of investigation of the stock dividend/split phenom-enon is the application of some aspects of the blossoming literature of market microstructure and the bid–ask spread. Worth noting in this literature are the works of Branch (1985), Brennan and Copeland (1988b), Conroy et al. (1990), and Maloney and Mulherin (1992).

## 15.1.5 TARGET PRICE

Keeping the stock price within a range management perceives as optimal both for the purpose of liquidity and for making the ownership structure as diffuse as the stewards of the firm think to be optimal is another favorite explanation of the motives for stock dividends/splits. Furthermore, this hypothesis is substantiated by the few managerial surveys, such as Baker and Powell (1993). Academic work in this domain of research includes Finn (1974), Reilly and Gustavson (1985), and Strong (1983).

## 15.1.6 INFORMATION CONTENT AND SIGNALING

This line of research vis-à-vis dividends in general has been discussed in length in previous chapters of this monograph. As the notion of signaling spread like wildfire in the academic finance literature, it also found its way into the stock dividend/split scenario. The origins of the idea, however, go back to a much earlier era when the idea of signaling in the context of economics perhaps never occurred to Spence (1973).

Perhaps it is the work of Barker (1956) that started with the notion that stock dividends/splits increase the stock price initially in anticipation of increased cash dividends to commence, later. However, the whole idea of preference for a cash distribution that necessarily involves a value-dissipating tax effect was not explored until the advent of the notions of asymmetric information and signaling, which saw its birth at the dawn of agency theory of Jensen and Meckling (1976).

The intriguing aspect of this work, especially with respect to signaling, is the fact that stock dividends/splits fail some basic requirements of the signaling scenario. As stated earlier, signals must be unambiguous. They must also be costly. Although it is often argued that stock dividends/splits are administratively more costly than cash dividends, these costs are not at the same level as the tax costs incurred by the shareholder in the case of cash dividends. Accordingly, both conditions invalidate the necessary requirement of a signaling framework. The weak argument of signaling with respect to dividends in general and with respect to stock dividends even more is resoundingly repudiated in an editorial by Black (1990).

Academic work falling in this category are by Brennan and Hughes (1991), Charest (1978a,b), Dowen (1990), Liljeblom (1989), Nichols and McDonald (1983), Reilly and Drzyclmski (1981), and Strong (1983).

Still, there are additional "angles" of the stock dividend/split phenomenon. Among those are Szewczyk and Tsetsekos (1993) work on ownership effects, earning forecast revisions of Klein and Peterson (1989), and analysts following the firm of Brennan and Hughes (1991).

## 15.1.7 PERCEPTIONS

As stated earlier, the only published work in the literature that attempted to discern the motives and perceptions behind the decision of stock dividends/split is by Baker and Phillips (1993). As stated earlier, the Baker and Phillips survey of financial executives suffers from several shortcomings. To overcome some of these shortcomings and to attain a better understanding of the phenomenon, Frankfurter and Lane (1998) (FL, subsequently) also studied the perception of stock dividends of top financial executives of firms.

The purpose of the FL study is to survey financial managers of publicly traded firms that declared a stock dividend during 1986–1993 and are included in the Center for Research in Security Prices (CRSP, subsequently) database to determine their perception of the benefits (shortcomings) derived from stock dividends.

The means by which FL investigate the perception of these executives is a survey, consisting of 37 statements, with the possible response to each statement ranging from strong disagreement to strong agreement on a continuous scale. The middle of the scale represents a neutral response to the statement, and no response means that statement has no relevance to that firm/executive. The continuous range of responses is converted to a 17-point scale for analysis. The survey form, with instructions to the recipient, is in the Appendix of this chapter.

FL's concern is, exclusively, with stock dividends. However, their result can be perfectly germane to the case of stock splits as well. Nevertheless, the reader should be advised that their findings, strictly speaking, hold for stock dividends only. Also, FL do not deal with possible tax effects, mentioned previously in the literature (see Lazo, 1993). Both of these considerations are made in the interest of getting the highest possible response rate by keeping the survey form as short and least complicated as possible.

The survey statements are designed to minimize their influencing the *a priori* perceptions of those surveyed. The intention in preparing the survey is to provide important insight to the financial executive regarding the benefits, use, and appropriateness of stock dividends as a strategic financial instrument.

All 366 firms that paid at least one stock dividend between the years of 1986–1993 were selected from the CRSP files as the initial sample. The firms so selected showed a broad industry representation of the four-digit SIC codes. The 37-statement survey was sent with a personalized cover letter to the CFO/comptroller/vice president for finance of each firm, so identified from DISCLOSURE data. All firms not responding to this initial solicitation received a follow-up mailing. The two completed mailings resulted in a total of 127 valid responses, a 34.7% response rate. In light of similar prior studies, this response rate is considered excellent. Hereafter, these 127 responses are referred to as the *primary sample*.

Also identified from the CRSP files were all firms that *never* paid a stock dividend during the same time period. A *control sample* of 150 firms was selected from these at random to correspond roughly to the same industries as the initial sample. These firms received the same cover letter and survey. As in the case of the primary sample, one initial mailing and one follow-up mailing were implemented. A total of 38 valid responses were received, for a response rate of 25.3%.

### 15.1.7.1 The Primary Sample

A simple tabulation of the responses from the primary sample is shown in Table 15.1. Table 15.1 presents the statement number, the frequency (as a percentage of all responses to the statement) of responses expressing disagreement (scale values 1–8), neutrality (scale value 9), and agreement (10–17). Also, in columns 5–7, the ratio of agreement to disagreement responses, the median, and the mode for each statement are presented.[3]

#### *15.1.7.1.1 Disagreement*

Statements garnering the greatest frequency of disagreement indicate that the respondents believe their stockholders are interested in stock dividends, a rising stock price is not a prerequisite to paying a stock dividend, paying a stock dividend once is not an obligation for the firm to pay again in the future, and an increase in cash dividends is not the only indication of the firm's well-being.

If we also look at those statements with a low ratio of agreement to disagreement, we find that firms paying stock dividends generally do not believe such distributions are controversial or a bad omen when paid in lieu of cash. Their managers see a short-term and a permanent price response to the announcement, but not due to any "option" to sell shares. The respondents are not interested in having a large portion of their shares held by institutions and do not see cash dividends as a drain on the firms' resources.

#### *15.1.7.1.2 Neutrality*

The most frequent neutral responses seem to indicate that these executives are not concerned with accounting or regulatory aspects of stock dividends and that they are unsure whether stock dividends create small percentage increases in

---

[3]Statement 7 contains a typographical error and does not make sense as it appears in the survey. Naturally, this statement got one of the highest (second highest) neutral responses. Also, the number of responses to the statement was the lowest (some respondents indicating, quite correctly we may add, that they did not understand the statement). Although the error was an accident for which we must take full responsibility, responses to the statement are a reflection that the responses were not indiscriminate and that the survey was dealt with by knowledgeable persons. Of course, as is always the case in a survey, we cannot know for sure whether the addressee responded or someone else.

**Table 15.1**

**Simple Statistics of Raw Results: Primary Sample**

| Statement No. | Scale value | | | Ratio | Median | Mode |
|---|---|---|---|---|---|---|
| | 1–8 | 9 | 10–17 | | | |
| 1 | 19 | 8 | 73 | 3.84 | 13.50 | 13.00 |
| 2 | 30 | 17 | 53 | 1.77 | 11.00 | 13.00 |
| 3 | 19 | 30 | 51 | 2.68 | 10.00 | 9.00 |
| 4 | 19 | 28 | 53 | 2.79 | 11.00 | 9.00 |
| 5 | 53 | 21 | 26 | 0.49 | 7.00 | 9.00 |
| 6 | 18 | 17 | 65 | 3.61 | 12.00 | 13.00 |
| 7 | 33 | 41 | 26 | 0.79 | 9.00 | 9.00 |
| 8 | 19 | 13 | 68 | 3.58 | 13.00 | 13.00 |
| 9 | 71 | 9 | 20 | 0.28 | 5.00 | 5.00 |
| 10 | 52 | 24 | 24 | 0.46 | 8.00 | 9.00 |
| 11 | 26 | 13 | 61 | 2.35 | 12.00 | 13.00 |
| 12 | 19 | 32 | 49 | 2.58 | 9.00 | 9.00 |
| 13 | 22 | 27 | 51 | 2.32 | 10.00 | 9.00 |
| 14 | 50 | 13 | 37 | 0.74 | 8.50 | 9.00 |
| 15 | 24 | 15 | 61 | 2.54 | 13.00 | 17.00 |
| 16 | 56 | 11 | 33 | 0.59 | 7.00 | 5.00 |
| 17 | 51 | 17 | 32 | 0.63 | 8.00 | 9.00 |
| 18 | 20 | 14 | 66 | 3.30 | 13.00 | 13.00 |
| 19 | 20 | 23 | 57 | 2.85 | 11.00 | 9.00 |
| 20 | 12 | 10 | 78 | 6.50 | 13.00 | 15.00 |
| 21 | 73 | 13 | 14 | 0.19 | 5.00 | 5.00 |
| 22 | 26 | 23 | 51 | 1.96 | 10.00 | 9.00 |
| 23 | 40 | 38 | 22 | 0.55 | 9.00 | 9.00 |
| 24 | 38 | 15 | 47 | 1.24 | 9.00 | 13.00 |
| 25 | 13 | 8 | 79 | 6.08 | 13.00 | 13.00 |
| 26 | 48 | 13 | 39 | 0.81 | 9.00 | 1.00 |
| 27 | 44 | 31 | 25 | 0.57 | 9.00 | 9.00 |
| 28 | 64 | 6 | 30 | 0.47 | 5.00 | 5.00 |
| 29 | 56 | 13 | 31 | 0.55 | 7.00 | 5.00 |
| 30 | 32 | 30 | 38 | 1.19 | 9.00 | 9.00 |
| 31 | 9 | 7 | 84 | 9.33 | 13.00 | 13.00 |
| 32 | 33 | 43 | 24 | 0.73 | 9.00 | 9.00 |
| 33 | 34 | 34 | 32 | 0.94 | 9.00 | 9.00 |
| 34 | 63 | 14 | 23 | 0.37 | 6.00 | 5.00 |
| 35 | 8 | 16 | 76 | 9.50 | 13.00 | 13.00 |
| 36 | 88 | 2 | 10 | 0.11 | 1.00 | 1.00 |
| 37 | 28 | 26 | 46 | 1.64 | 9.00 | 9.00 |

cash dividends, bypass the investment banker, or provide free publicity. The last two responses are in stark contrast with conventional wisdom and/or popular explanations for the reason of stock dividends. It should be noted that for those statements (save investment banker fees and provide free publicity), more respondents disagree and agree, respectively, than are of a neutral opinion.

### 15.1.7.1.3 Agreement

The respondents tend to agree with statements that their stockholders do not trade the stock often, institutional investors are sophisticated as far as stock dividends are concerned, stockholders like to receive a stock dividend, and for financial managers, both increasing the trading frequency of the stock and obtaining a wide distribution of the stock are important objectives.

Turning to those statements with a high ratio of agreement to disagreement, it was found that many of these address attitudes toward cash dividends relative to stock. There is weak agreement that some stockholders, including institutions, prefer cash, whereas others prefer stock distributions. Nonetheless, the common perception is that stockholders expect cash dividends. Although stock dividends result in higher future cash distributions, they save cash now.

The remaining statements to which the majority agree focus on specific effects of a stock dividend. Stock dividends are perceived to increase the frequency of trading of the stock, keep the price in an optimal trading range, and signal that the firm is doing well, as evidenced by an increase in stock price when a stock dividend is announced. All these characteristics of the stock dividend are usually recognized.

### 15.1.7.1.4 Other Issues

Preliminary inspection of this simple tabulation indicates that responses were not haphazard, but rather well thought out, reflecting the heterogeneous nature of the population and the concomitant *divergence* in the perception of the use of stock dividends as a financial instrument. Perhaps this is the most important message we receive from the survey. The logical conclusion one can reach from this message is that it is not only difficult to formulate a unified theory, but it is not wise to try. Different firms with different objectives and different perceptions will use or not use stock dividends to support a strategy.

In order to better understand this last point, more complex statistical analyses of responses was performed. Applying techniques of factor analysis and hierarchical grouping, it was found that the responses of the primary sample align the statements into 13 common themes. This is reported as a fact without making the attempt to interpret and/or identify these factors, an endeavor, which, by nature, is subjective. Instead, these factors are used to group the respondents into several clusters of similar perceptions. Significant differences

**Table 15.2**

**Frequency of Stock Dividend Payments: Primary Sample**

Number of stock dividends paid

| 1–3 | 4–6 | 7–9 | 10 or more | Average |
|-----|-----|-----|------------|---------|
| 89  | 26  | 10  | 2          | 2.80    |

between these clusters[4] are observed, particularly with respect to only eight statements.[5]

For example, one difference among clusters is the extent to which they disagree with the statement that stock dividends are controversial. Surprisingly, given that these firms have all paid stock dividends, of the 11 clusters, 2 of the smaller clusters agree with that statement and 1 of those disagrees with the statement that stockholders like to receive regular stock dividends.

With the exception of that cluster and one expressing neutrality, all of the others agree that stockholders like to receive regular stock dividends, but the means range from weak agreement (mean of 10.4) to very strong agreement (mean of 17.0), and again differ significantly. Similarly for the other five statements, while there may be general agreement or disagreement, certain identifiable groups of the respondents hold stronger beliefs than the others. Thus, firms that have paid stock dividends are not homogeneous in their perceptions, but rather reveal a significant diversity.

This diversity is reflected in the extent of their use of stock dividends. Table 15.2 presents the frequency of stock dividend payments for the primary sample. Dividend frequency is (expectedly) positively correlated with the perception that stockholders like stock dividends, with the presence of a regular stock dividend program, and with the belief that interrupting a stock dividend program is not a good sign. Greater frequencies are also identified with the perception that stockholders trade the stock infrequently, whereas smaller frequencies are associated with the belief that stock dividends save cash. The frequency of the use of stock dividends differs significantly across the aforementioned clusters of respondents.

[4]That is, the mean response for at least one cluster is statistically significantly different from the means of the other clusters.

[5]Specifically, statements 1, 2, 8, 9, 12, 20, 27, and 31. Although they can be found in the Appendix, for the convenience of the reader, we group and repeat them here. *Stockholder preferences*: (1) Stockholders like to receive a regular stock dividend. (2) Some stockholders prefer a stock dividend instead of a cash dividend. (9) We do not believe our stockholders are interested in stock dividends. *Liquidity effects*: (8) Increasing the number of stockholders in our firm is one of our important objectives. (20) Increasing the liquidity of our firm's stock (frequency of trading) is important because it ultimately increase the share price. (31) Many of our stockholders do not trade at all whether the price is going up or down. *Image of stock dividends*: (12) A stock dividend gives us favorable free publicity. (27) Stock dividends are a controversial practice.

## 15.1.7.2 The Control Sample

The initial appearance of the responses from firms that did not pay a stock dividend in the period is that perceptions of these executives are similar to those for the primary sample, particularly for the statements receiving the greatest agreement. Table 15.3 summarizes the responses from the control sample.

As these firms did not pay a stock dividend, more frequent negative responses to some statements are to be expected. These firms do not have a regular stock dividend program, are not planning on paying one anytime soon, and do not see stock dividends as being more valuable than cash dividends. As with the primary sample, executives of the control sample do not believe that a rising stock price must precede a stock dividend[6] and that an initial stock dividend is not an obligation for future stock dividends.

In both samples the majority of respondents also disagree with statements that large institutional ownership is desirable, that stockholders are not interested in stock dividends, that there is no short-term price effect, and that only increases in cash dividends are a mark of success.

For the control sample, the most frequent neutral responses are for the notions that stock dividends keep the stock price in an optimal trading range, save investment banker fees, and increase the frequency of trading. These respondents are also neutral about whether institutional investors prefer cash to stock dividends. In a negative way, it seems that the major impetus for stock dividend-paying firms is justified by those who do not believe that stock dividends accomplish these ends.

The statements that elicit the greatest agreement in the control sample are the statements pronouncing that

- institutional investors understand stock dividends
- executives would like to increase the number of stockholders in their firms
- increasing the trading frequency of the stock is important
- stockholders do not trade the stock often.

These four statements are also among the six statements receiving the greatest frequency of agreement for the primary sample. The conclusion is that with respect to these issues, perceptions are homogeneous for the two samples.

But the homogeneity does not stop here. A majority of both samples also agree that stockholders expect cash dividends and prefer them to stock dividend, especially institutional investors, and that stock dividends save cash now, but result in larger cash payouts later.

There remain, still, notable differences, mostly along predictable lines in perceptions between the two samples. Almost two-thirds of the primary sample

---

[6]The statement, however, is at variance with what is observed, on average. Market data show that stock dividends/splits are observed for firms during periods of rising stock price.

**Table 15.3**

**Raw Results: Control Sample**

| Statement No. | Scale value | | | Ratio | Median | Mode |
|:---:|:---:|:---:|:---:|:---:|:---:|:---:|
| | 1–8 | 9 | 10–17 | | | |
| 1 | 34 | 5 | 61 | 1.77 | 12.50 | 15.00 |
| 2 | 42 | 13 | 45 | 1.06 | 9.00 | 13.00 |
| 3 | 14 | 19 | 68 | 5.00 | 13.00 | 15.00 |
| 4 | 16 | 32 | 51 | 3.17 | 11.00 | 9.00 |
| 5 | 58 | 21 | 21 | 0.36 | 5.50 | 5.00 |
| 6 | 24 | 32 | 43 | 1.78 | 9.00 | 9.00 |
| 7 | 15 | 50 | 35 | 2.40 | 9.00 | 9.00 |
| 8 | 11 | 8 | 82 | 7.75 | 13.00 | 13.00 |
| 9 | 53 | 8 | 40 | 0.75 | 6.50 | 5.00 |
| 10 | 61 | 13 | 26 | 0.43 | 6.00 | 9.00 |
| 11 | 29 | 13 | 58 | 2.00 | 12.00 | 13.00 |
| 12 | 29 | 26 | 45 | 1.55 | 9.00 | 9.00 |
| 13 | 24 | 40 | 37 | 1.55 | 9.00 | 9.00 |
| 14 | 42 | 8 | 50 | 1.18 | 9.50 | 5.00 |
| 15 | 29 | 11 | 61 | 2.09 | 12.00 | 13.00 |
| 16 | 51 | 24 | 24 | 0.47 | 8.00 | 9.00 |
| 17 | 42 | 16 | 42 | 1.00 | 9.00 | 5.00 |
| 18 | 32 | 8 | 61 | 1.92 | 13.00 | 13.00 |
| 19 | 40 | 18 | 42 | 1.07 | 9.00 | 9.00 |
| 20 | 13 | 13 | 74 | 5.60 | 13.00 | 13.00 |
| 21 | 76 | 11 | 13 | 0.17 | 5.00 | 5.00 |
| 22 | 27 | 27 | 46 | 1.70 | 9.00 | 9.00 |
| 23 | 53 | 33 | 14 | 0.26 | 5.50 | 9.00 |
| 24 | 37 | 11 | 53 | 1.43 | 10.50 | 13.00 |
| 25 | 8 | 8 | 84 | 10.33 | 13.00 | 13.00 |
| 26 | 81 | 13 | 6 | 0.08 | 1.50 | 1.00 |
| 27 | 42 | 25 | 33 | 0.80 | 9.00 | 9.00 |
| 28 | 61 | 16 | 24 | 0.39 | 5.50 | 5.00 |
| 29 | 42 | 13 | 45 | 1.06 | 9.00 | 13.00 |
| 30 | 47 | 16 | 37 | 0.78 | 9.00 | 9.00 |
| 31 | 18 | 8 | 74 | 4.00 | 13.00 | 13.00 |
| 32 | 40 | 32 | 29 | 0.73 | 9.00 | 9.00 |
| 33 | 53 | 24 | 24 | 0.45 | 5.00 | 9.00 |
| 34 | 50 | 8 | 42 | 0.84 | 8.50 | 13.00 |
| 35 | 13 | 11 | 76 | 5.80 | 13.00 | 13.00 |
| 36 | 47 | 3 | 50 | 1.06 | 11.00 | 17.00 |
| 37 | 63 | 23 | 14 | 0.23 | 4.00 | 1.00 |

is of the opinion that stock dividends increase liquidity. In contrast, less than one-half of the control sample shares that perception. Support for the optimal trading range and signaling explanations is found in the primary sample, but not in the control sample. Those that pay stock dividends believe that doing so increases the value of the firm; the majority of the control sample sees no such effect. Of course, admitting that stock dividends are value enhancing would be admitting that they do not perform their duties as agents satisfactorily.

Perhaps the most striking result of the study is the diversity of perception both within and between the two samples. Also, the fact there is no clear support for many of the administrative roles for stock dividends (provide free publicity, generate small percentage increases in cash dividends, etc.). Beauty, however, is in the eye of the beholder. Those executives who see benefits to stock dividends are already using them as a strategic tool. More importantly, the stronger those beliefs are, the more frequently stock dividends are issued.

The executives in general agree with the statements that imply there are benefits to increasing the liquidity of their stocks. The disagreement is whether stock dividends can accomplish this or not. Thus, the *perception* appears to be a motivating factor behind whether a firm pays a stock dividend or not.

Agreement in both sets of respondents is in the belief that stockholders expect cash dividends and that although their stockholders prefer cash dividends to stock dividends, they would be interested in stock dividends. There is also a great deal of agreement in *perception*, albeit differing *interpretations* of the usefulness of stock dividends.

General disagreement is given to statements that stock dividend announcements have no short-term effects on price, that a price run–up must precede a dividend, that irregular stock dividends are a negative sign, and that only cash dividends are a positive sign. Differences between the perceptions of the two samples on the price effects of stock dividends suggest that a belief in such effects is another motivating factor. Executives who presume stock dividends maintain an optimal trading range for the stock price, affect the value of the firm, and convey good news to the market are more likely to pay stock dividends than those who disagree or are uncertain about those effects.

### 15.1.7.3 Epilogue

The phenomenon of stock dividend/split has been a major topic of academic inquiry both as a subset of the larger issue of dividend policy and as an objective by itself. Throughout the history of what is now termed modern finance, hundreds of published and unpublished papers deal with the subject that is sometimes referred to as a tearing of a large piece of paper into several smaller pieces and the favorable reaction of the market to such an activity.

The evolution of the academic literature can be chronicled roughly along the lines of the maturation of fashionable paradigms that saw the light of publication as models to explain other phenomena. Consequently, a substantial segment of the more recent literature is more exploiting the round hole in vogue by forcing through it the square peg of the stock dividend/split problem than anything else. The most important lesson to learn from the few studies of motivation/perception is that different people understand different things about stock dividends/split. In many instances, respondents are split almost equally in both sides of the same statement. Also, a large percentage of the respondents show no concern about a notion/belief that is largely accepted as true in academe. The ultimate lesson is, therefore, to admit that no obscure theory can be applied to the economic agents "out there" and that we must learn much more about their motivations.

## 15.2 STOCK REPURCHASE

### 15.2.1 PROLOGUE

Theoretically, and from the point of view of the firm, the only difference between dividends and share repurchases is that the cash disbursement is not proportional to ownership. Other than that, the same shoveling out cash and partial liquidation of the firm occur as in the case of dividend payments.

From the point of view of the shareholder, however, share repurchases provide

- an option to sell some or all of the shares at a price that is usually higher than the going market price
- in most instances to be responsible for a capital gains tax, instead of an ordinary income tax, and
- perhaps most importantly, to have the option whether or not to receive a dividend, an option that a stockholder does not have in case of a regular, quarterly dividend.

The motives for a repurchase as opposed to a cash dividend, however, are quite different. This is so because of several institutional and tax considerations that make pure theory an incomplete answer. Before we go into details regarding stock repurchase, also called treasury stock, it should be noted that stock repurchase is not allowed in many countries because of the principle of a firm being precluded from doing business with itself. In some cases, stock repurchases can be a legal means to nefarious objectives.

## 15.2.2 ACCOUNTING CONSIDERATIONS

There are two methods to treat treasury stock (the firm's own stock kept in the "treasury"): the cost method and the par value method.

The transaction cannot be treated as an investment. Treating the transaction as an investment would be an open admission that the firm is doing business with itself, even though, *de facto*, this is what a repurchase for whatever reason amounts to. Thus, under either method the end result must be a *reduction* of both sides of the balance sheet.

Under the cost method, the cash account is reduced on the assets side of the balance sheet and an equivalent contraequity account is created on the liability side that reduces owners' equity by the same amount the assets side of the balance sheet has been reduced. This method is often used when the firm has no intention of permanently retiring the stock but rather accumulating it in the treasury for future use.

There are minute accounting details how to deal with the stock in the treasury when it is reissued and when its value is different than as it was recorded at the time of the repurchase. These minutiae, so typical of accountants, are perhaps important for a specific case, but nevertheless are only tangential to the discussion here. After all, this book is not an accounting text.

Under the par value method, the stock is treated as permanently retired (as in retiring the jersey number of a star basketball or football player, albeit for a much less laudatory occasion). The concept is the permanent severing of the relationship between the firm and its owner(s). This view of the stock repurchase makes sense only when and if a single or several shareholders are bought out, *en toto*, by the rest of the owners.

The accounting treatment is the reverse of the original issue of the stock. That is, the assets side of the balance sheet is reduced by the amount of the cash account's reduction (what is being paid for the repurchase), and the appropriate equity accounts (shares at par, paid in capital, and or other equity accounts) are reduced, proportionally as to reflect the impact of the repurchase on these accounts and to balance the two sides of the balance sheet. Of course, this is possible if, and only if, the shares repurchased can be identified uniformly as to make the correct adjustments to all these accounts.

Pertaining to both accounting methods discussed here is the principle that each stock class, if there are several classes of stock, must be adjusted appropriately.

## 15.2.3 TAX CONSIDERATIONS

The increased popularity during the last two decades of stock repurchase over paying dividends could be possibly and at least partially attributed to the double taxation of dividends. In most instances the IRS considers a stock repurchase a capital gain rather than ordinary income. Congressional conservatives are fighting a pitched battle for the elimination of the double taxation of dividends and for the reduction, or even the total elimination, of the capital gains tax (often under the disguise of helping small farmers, and not ultrarich shareholders). However, even when the capital gains tax and the marginal ordinary income tax rates are the same, the stockholder has an option of not taking the purchase offer, thereby eliminating the tax liability. With ordinary dividends, this option is forgone. Thus, the repurchase must have at least as much, and possibly, a higher value than regular, quarterly dividends.

Indeed, as Ross *et al.* (1998) claimed during the 1980s and much of the 1990s quite often, the addition of new equity to the stock markets was negative, largely because widespread repurchase of equity:

> In fact, net equity sales in the United States have frequently been negative in recent years. This has occurred because corporations have actually repurchased more stock than they have sold. Stock repurchasing has thus been a major financial activity, and it appears that it will continue to be one (p. 521).

Van Horne (1995, p. 332) acknowledged that the tax issue is not that simple, however. In certain instances, depending on ownership, the IRS will treat a repurchase as ordinary dividend:

> If the stockholder's percentage ownership of the company after the tender is greater than 0.80 of his ownership percentage prior to the tender, the repurchase can be treated as ordinary income by the Internal Revenue Service. This problem can be avoided if the company obtains an advanced ruling from the IRS that the repurchase of stock is not equivalent to a dividend (p. 332, footnote 16).

One must wonder, however, by what personal charm can the company convince the IRS that the repurchase is not a guise for ordinary dividends.

We are not taking sides here in the debate of double taxation of dividends. This is a very complex issue that has several sides to it. In many other countries, dividends are not double taxed. Nor is double taxation an act of nature that necessitates it in the United States. However, it must be noted that as long as dividends are taxed at the marginal tax rate as ordinary income of the recipient, even though they are paid out from after tax corporate earnings, both repurchase of shares and greenmail (see later) are a ruse for reducing the tax liability of the recipient.

## 15.2.4 MOTIVES OF STOCK REPURCHASE

There can be a wide variety of reasons why a firm would want to repurchase its own shares, if the law permits such a transaction. In many countries, repurchase is not permitted because it is construed as an attempt by the firm to manipulate the market price of the share. If one is, however, a religious believer of the efficient markets hypothesis (EMH) then, of course, such manipulation is not possible because the market sees through the ruse and will punish the manipulator. Therefore, one should not impose frictions, such as unnecessary rules, on the otherwise efficient functioning of the market. This is discussed a bit later.

Indeed, one of the first noticed incentives for share repurchase was *the support of the depressed price of the firm's stock*. If the firm buys back its shares, then fewer shares are outstanding and by the law of supply and demand, assuming no other factors present, the price of the share must go up. This is the reverse of what is called "trading on the equity" (meaning the dilution of future earning). There is one flaw, however, with this reasoning.

In order to buy back stock, the firm needs cash. Whether it has excess cash (funds it does not know what to do with), or it has to liquidate earning assets, or perhaps worse than both, it has to borrow in order to buy back its stock, the future earning potential is reduced. Although now fewer outstanding shares are competing for earning (or regular dividends), earning expectations and, conse-quently, what is available to common stock, are also reduced. What the last two decades showed us, however, was that stock repurchases became a significant factor in redirecting cash to the shareholder, and the initial market reaction was a more than proportional increase of the share price.

Another common reason for stock repurchase is a *windfall of cash* or, equivalently, *the dwindling of the firm's investment opportunities*. Naturally, a policy of paying higher dividends would do the job in such case as well because this is what is economically rational and consistent with the idea of partial liquidation. As we learned from several studies (cf. Lintner, 1956; Baker and Powell, 1999), manage-ment is reluctant to increase regular dividends when it believes that it cannot maintain such high dividends in the long term. Some repurchase explanations are quite upstanding about this. For instance, Georgia Pacific Corporation writes in its 1992 annual report (quoted in Van Horne, 1995, p. 330):

> Managing and reinvesting in our core business to add value for the shareholder is our prime responsibility. To the extent that we cannot identify satisfactory invest-ment opportunities, however, we are committed to returning cash to our sharehold-ers through dividends or share repurchases.

This is quite an honest description of what a share repurchase is about and also what avenues are open to the firm to return cash to the owners.

The report then goes on explaining why, because of fear of higher than desirable leverage, the company suspended a repurchase program in 1989. It is clear, therefore, that firms know exactly what repurchases are and what adverse effects might be associated with such transactions.

Closely related to the excess cash reason and the change in leverage argument is the excuse for buying back stock in order *to satisfy future needs for the exercise of employees' and executives' stock options* or for the *issuance of stock dividends*. Stock held in the treasury is a source for covering these needs if and when they arise.

The mechanics of treasury stock works like so. There are shares authorized, shares issued, and shares outstanding. Shares authorized are the number of shares the firm can issue without getting shareholders acquiescence for a larger number of stocks to be issued. Shares outstanding are the number of shares in public hands. Shares issued are the number of shares outstanding and the number of shares in the treasury. If the shares in the treasury are used to cover the exercise of stock options, the equity account is increasing, with other things remaining unchanged, leverage, i.e., financial risk is declining.

The problem with this argument is that the firm can always cover stock options from the shares authorized or, if the number of shares authorized and not outstanding is insufficient, it can always authorize, rather painlessly, new shares to be issued.

The repurchase is *a quick and convenient way to increase leverage* argument. By buying back shares, both sides of the balance sheet are reduced (see the accounting treatments, later), but on the right-hand side the reduction is in the owners' equity account. Therefore, the proportion of liabilities is increasing, relative to the before repurchase state, without going to a lender, or the bond markets.

The problem with this argument is that it increases financial risk (through increased leverage). At the same time, earning assets decrease or, alternatively, investment opportunities that would have been favorably leveraged by the return to equity (ROE, one of the key measures of the firm's profitability) cannot be taken. If one accepts the notion that the firm is trying to drift toward a target mix of operating and financial risk, then in order to keep expected earnings not less but possibly higher then before it must invest in ventures that would be consistent with this objective.

Although the tax subsidy on interest expense would be relatively higher, nevertheless, earnings are expected to decline, as well, if the firm liquidates assets. Accordingly, an increase of leverage through increased borrowing makes more sense than through repurchase of stock.

*The tax advantage of a repurchase for those stockholders who would tender their shares.* Even when the capital gains tax rate is equal to the marginal income tax rate of the shareholder, selling back the shares to the company would be preferred over selling the stock through a broker. Naturally, when the capital gains tax rate is lower or zero than the marginal tax rate of income, the benefits are even more pronounced. The problem with this consideration is that in the case of a widely held firm, the preferences of the shareholders are not usually known to management. A repurchase, however, may have adverse effect (see the discussion earlier) that may not just mitigate this motivation, but totally eliminate it.

*The struggle for corporate control.* Firms are often controlled by a group of stockholder that hold a relatively small fraction of the shares outstanding. It often happens that with, say, a mere 20% of the shares a group has a controlling interest. Accordingly, it can get the majority vote of the appointed directors, *de facto*, controlling almost everything the firm does. For this reason, many corporations have in their by-laws cumulative voting, meaning that minority groups can cast more than one vote for the same person.

The end result of this situation, and when the rest of the share holdings is sufficiently fragmented: not, a small number of shares can change controlling interest. If, under these circumstances, a minority group is successful in forcing a stock repurchase as a tender offer, and advising its group members not to tender their shares, it can gain control over the firm in a way that is not illegal, but nevertheless borders on the nefarious. This type of struggle for control is done, more often via greenmail (see later), rather than tender offer, but technically it is possible to do via a tender offer as well.

The firm may also use stock in the treasury for *acquisition* purposes. Whether the acquisition is a single asset, say, land, or another corporation, it does not matter if it is paid either partially or fully with stock. The stock payment can be newly issued stock for that purpose, stock held in the treasury, or a combination thereof. Because this is an investment transaction, there cannot be an immediate tax effect. That is, the value of the treasury stock can be anything the buying and selling parties agree on, regardless of any capital gain or loss that might have been incurred by the firm.

## 15.2.5 MODES OF STOCK REPURCHASE

We start with the three known forms of stock repurchase: tender offer, open market purchase, and Dutch auction.

In a tender offer repurchase, the firm's management advertises the intention of purchasing a given number of shares for a fixed price (which usually represent a premium over the going market price) for a fixed time period. Management usually reserves the right to halt the repurchase at its discretion.

The second form is purchasing shares directly in the open market or from a dealer who holds a large block of shares of the firm. The exact means to be selected would be determined by the size of the firm, the total cash it wishes to use for the repurchase, and market conditions. A typical announcement of a repurchase program, found on the internet, will look similar to that of Synopsys Corporation.

**Synopsys Inc. Announces New $500 Million Stock Repurchase Program**

MOUNTAIN VIEW, Calif., July 5, 2001—Synopsys, Inc. (Nasdaq: SNPS) today announced that its Board of Directors has authorized a new stock repurchase program under which Synopsys common stock with a market value up to $500 million may be acquired in the open market. Under the program, share purchases may be made at prevailing prices beginning immediately and ending October 31, 2002. The purchases will be funded from available working capital. The repurchased shares may be used for ongoing stock issuances such as for existing employee stock option and stock purchase plans and acquisitions.

Synopsys also announced that it had recently completed the purchase of Synopsys common stock with a market value of approximately $500 million under its previous stock repurchase program, authorized by its Board of the Directors in July 2000. Under the July 2000 program, Synopsys acquired a total of 11.7 million shares, at an average price of $42.72 per share. Thus far during its third fiscal quarter, Synopsys has acquired 2.0 million shares at an average price per share of $54.28, completing the July 2000 program.

An interesting variant is Cisco Systems' repurchase plan of $3 billion, announced on September 14, 2001, that will take hold over a 2-year period. The firm reserves the option in what form the repurchase will take place and declares:

The Cisco Systems Inc. (CSCO) board has authorized a $3 billion stock repurchase plan to take place over the next two years. The move was made *as a vote of confidence* [our italics] in financial markets, which halted trading Tuesday after terrorist attacks shattered New York's World Trade Center. The markets are expected to resume trading Monday, although the city's financial district remains largely shuttered (from www.idg.net/spc_693804_190_9-10025.html).

In whose book is shoveling out all that cash considered "a vote of confidence" is not entirely clear to us. It seems that one tries to squeeze out as much publicity from what one is doing as possible. At the end of October, 2001, Cisco Systems was selling around $17 a share and the 52-week range was $11.04–$57.62.

In a Dutch auction, the tender offer is, again, for a specified number of shares, over a specified time period, but shareholders submit their bid for selling the number of shares they will tender and the tender price. In a Dutch auction, the firm usually specifies a bracket for prices it will accept (minimum, maximum).

## 15.2.6 WHAT ACADEMIA HAS TO SAY ABOUT STOCK REPURCHASE

Academia lines up on both sides of the issue and in between. In a press release, at the internet website www.admin.uiuc.edu/NB/99.12/stocktip.html, titled "Firms Gain Value When They Don't Repurchase Stock, Study Shows," one finds the following text:

CHAMPAIGN, Ill. It has become almost a truism on Wall Street that stock repurchases by a company increase the value of the firm. From Intel Corp. to Walt Disney, so many companies have bought back shares of their own stock in the last 15 years that "a major realignment of corporate financial policy" has taken place in America, says James A. Gentry, a finance professor at the University of Illinois.

In 1996 alone, corporate stock buy backs hit a record $176 billion compared with under $2 billion for the entire decade of the 1960s. Management repurchasing of stock through tender offers or on the open market is taken by investors as a positive sign that the firm is posed for future growth or that the stock is undervalued. Hence, an upward bounce of the share price invariably takes place after a repurchase announcement.

But do companies that buy back stock actually experience higher long-run growth than companies not pursuing a repurchase strategy? In the first comprehensive study of this question, Gentry and John P. Evans, a finance professor at the Curtin University of Technology in Australia, studied 369 companies that announced 398 repurchase programs from 1978 through 1993.

Financial and market data were collected for each company for two years prior to the announcement. The minimum period of study following repurchase was two years, while the maximum period was 17 years. The large majority of the companies were listed on the New York Stock Exchange.

Gentry and Evans found that "firms create more value with a strategy of not repurchasing their shares." Non-repurchasing firms had a 20.8 percent mean growth rate, while repurchasing companies had a mean rate of 16.5 percent. The difference in growth rates was not apparent, however, until about three years after the repurchase program.

Corporate size had a major impact on the growth rates. In companies with more than $2 billion in annual sales, repurchase programs tended to have a small, though still significant, effect on growth rates, but in companies with less than $300 million in revenues, stock repurchases had a significant retarding effect on long-term growth.

Gentry and Evans concluded that working capital was the most important indicator of long-term growth, and companies who repurchased shares had a lower proportion of cash going to working capital.

"It appears that the strategy employed by the non-repurchasing companies of investing a higher percentage of total outflows into working capital and capital investment was instrumental in their outperforming companies that repurchased shares," the researchers concluded in a working paper issued last month by the U. of I. College of Commerce and Business Administration.

In stark contrast to the Gentry and Evans position is that of Peterson's (1994). In her textbook, titled *Financial Management and Analysis*, she has to say this about stock repurchase.

Still another reason for stock repurchase is that it could tilt the debt-equity ratio so as to increase the value of the firm. By buying back stock—thereby reducing equity—the firm's assets are financed to a greater degree by debt. Does this seem wrong? It's not (p. 531).

Then, Peterson goes on with a numerical example in which she shows how through retirement of stock, both sides of the balance sheet are reduced, and the leverage increased through the reduction of the equity held in the treasury, and the unchanged debt. Peterson continues:

> If financing of the firm with more debt is good—the benefits from deducting interest on debt outweigh the cost of increasing the risk of bankruptcy [how on earth can one measure this, our comment]—repurchasing stock may increase the value of the firm.

What Peterson conveniently forgets to mention, however, is where did the cash come from in the first place? If the firm had to liquidate an earning asset, then the increase of financial risk, resulting from the increased leverage, is coupled now with a lower anticipated cash flow. So, how come that the knee-jerk reaction of the market is favorable to repurchase announcements? In all fairness, Peterson admits it that it is not so easy to explain why the market reaction is favorable because so many other things are going on, simultaneously. But, "By piecing bits of evidence together, however, we see that it is likely investors view the announcement of a repurchase as good news—a signal of good things to come" (Peterson, 1994, p. 533).

Peterson, however, is not clear at all what bits of evidence one must piece together in order to see why investors view (just a synonym for seeing, sort of a double vision) the repurchase transaction as good news. In the *Tales of Hoffmann*, an opera by Jacques Offenbach (based on the original play by Jules Barbier and Michel Carré), the protagonist is madly in love with Spalanzani's (an inventor) pretty daughter, Olympia. Hoffmann, according to one of the three tales, has to wear special eyeglasses (while he is dancing himself almost to death with Olympia and a collection of other automatons) in order to see his lover properly. Everything goes according to plan until Coppélius, who manufactured Olympia's eyes (a subcontractor, one may say), appears and smashes the android (what Olympia, in today's sci-fi vernacular would have been called) to smithereens because Spalanzani cheated him out of his dues.

In the Peterson tale, the investor has to wear special glasses in order to see the good in repurchase because the market views it in this way, and the market, as we all know, cannot be wrong. It is so unfortunate then that Gentry–Evans–Coppélius appear now and then and we see things as they really ought to be. However, several generations of MBA and undergraduate business students are taught that the market knows best, and if there is a positive price reaction to a repurchase, which more than the proportionate retirement of shares is, we do not know what the market knows, and we have to find Spalanzani's eyeglasses.

## 15.2.7 SIGNALING REDUX

The signaling literature regarding dividends was discussed in detail in Chapter 9 and again at the beginning of this chapter. It seems that one just cannot get away from it, because it gave academia a scientific explanation to what otherwise could not be explained. Because we are getting to the end of our story about dividends, perhaps it would be useful to examine, one more time, this literature and explanation in the light of the dividend puzzle.

In June 2000, a fascinating debate got its start about teaching and research of economics. A group of French students published a manifesto on the Web demanding a reexamination of the teaching of economics in institutes of higher education. Specifically, the French students protested

- Economics' "uncontrolled use" and treatment of mathematics as "an end in itself," and the resulting "autistic science,"
- The repressive domination of neoclassical theory and derivative approaches in the curriculum, and
- The dogmatic teaching style, which leaves no place for critical and reflective thought.[7]

The students' manifesto demanded that the economics curriculum be changed with regard to:

- Engagement with empirical and concrete economic realities,
- Prioritizing science over scientism, and
- A pluralism of approaches adapted to the complexity of economic objects and to the uncertainty surrounding most of the big economics questions.

They also demanded that their professors ". . . initiate reforms to rescue economics from its autistic and socially irresponsible state."[8]

The "French revolution," after receiving national attention in the daily print media in France, spilled over to the economics department of Cambridge University, and by mid-August of 2001 to North America, and practically to all the Western world. Based on the French initiative that was called *Le Movement Autisme Économie*, the worldwide movement is calling itself "post-autistic economics," PAE for short. It has its own website (www.pae.org) and a quarterly publication, titled *PAECON Newsletter*.

This is not the place to go into great detail of the imbroglio the French students started. Let us just say that it is the first time that the debate about the

---

[7] http://www. From paecon.net.
[8] http://www. From paecon.net.

domineering economic methodology has been public and at length. What is important, however, and perfectly germane to the present topic, is what is at the heart of this debate, concerning economics, and by straight transference, financial economics as well.

The best summary of the philosophical/methodological facets of the issue are spelled out by Tony Lawson (2001) in an article, titled "Back to Reality," excerpts of which appeared in the March 27, 2001, issue of *Le Monde*. Lawson contended that the debate between the French students and the proponents of neoclassicism is about which research methodology is more appropriate to economics. Whereas the students argue for pluralism (i.e., research methodologies from the other social sciences), modern economics is restricted chiefly to mathematical modeling.

The response to the students' claim is that economics needs to be scientific and that without mathematics it would not be scientific. If one accepts this framing, then, according to Lawson, the responses to the students' arguments seem inadequate. It is so because Lawson questions both contentions hidden in the responses to the students, namely that economics needs to be "scientific" and mathematics makes something scientific that *sans* mathematics would not be scientific.

Those who make the claim justifying the use of mathematics argue that event regularities not only give reason for mathematical modeling, but also beg for it. Lawson (2001) then quoted Maurice Allais (1992) (1988 Nobel laureate in economics) as an apropos (even French) authority formulating this claim:

> The essential condition of any science is the existence of regularities which can be analysed and forecast. This is the case in celestial mechanics. But it is also true of many economic phenomena. Indeed, their thorough analysis displays the existence of regularities which are just as striking as those found in the physical sciences. This is why economics is a science, and why this science rests on the same general principles and methods of physics (p. 25).

Lawson contends, rather convincingly, that event regularities in the social sciences are hard to come by and that econometricians find correlations nonexistent as soon as they find one as significant (are markets efficient?). More important, even in the natural sciences, event regularities—with the exception of celestial mechanics—are restricted to controlled experiments. Now, the question is: What is the role of science? Is it to reproduce events in a laboratory or to find the prevailing mechanics that create the events?

Here is one place, as good as any, to reflect a bit on event studies. If one accepts Lawson's arguments, then one must reject *en toto* the event study method of analysis and, as a consequence, the event study literature as a whole. In event studies, an artificial, nonrealistic model is assumed to be the mechanics explaining the event and the event itself is the proof or disproof that the event is the result of this artificiality. This is not to mention the fact that there is not a single finance event study that is a true laboratory experiment.

As Lawson (2001) made clear:

> Gravitational forces may give rise to event regularity in an experimental vacuum, but gravitational forces continue to act on autumn leaves wherever the latter may fly, and help us to send rockets to the moon. It is an understanding of the mechanism not the production of an event regularity that is the essential goal here.

Lawson's argument, in a nutshell, is the basic difference between positivism and realism. Correlating surface observations is one thing, but the role of science is to find the mechanisms below the surface reality, even when observable correlations, for one reason or another, are not to be (immediately) present. Interestingly, neoclassical economics stuck with Friedmanian positivism (*de facto*, instrumentalism) instead of the more progressive approach of realism—it is axiomatic instead of being realistic. We can only speculate that the reason must be the sociology of academia, a topic too complex and more controversial than we would dare to approach here.

Mathematics does not make economics a science, and economics can be scientific without mathematics. In certain instances, mathematics may help (it is not hard for us to imagine where in finance, for instance), and it is for the common good, but mathematics by no means is a *sine qua non*. In fact, Lawson sees a quite limited use of mathematics in the social realms, especially when one considers national, ethnic, and cultural differences.

Let us go back to *Herr* Hoffman and carry the "Tales of Hoffmann" metaphor a bit further. If all what has been said so far was not enough in the case of stock repurchase, it becomes clearer than ever that signaling is tantamount to Spalanzani's eyeglasses. This is the attempt of academia to explain market efficiency with a tale because otherwise the market would be an android, an unacceptable proposition to those who are committed deeply and religiously to the "let the market alone" creed, and often personify the market. That is why the market behaves, the market rewards (the righteous), and the market punishes (the unjust).[9]

All empirical signaling studies are event studies. Moreover, the paradox in using such a method of analysis (although many textbooks and untold number of published papers refer to them as methodology) in the case of stock repurchase is more obvious than anywhere else. The overwhelming cases of repurchases occur to remedy, partial or otherwise, a situation that is not good and, for all practical purposes, leaves the firm with less rather than with more. In case of

---

[9]We cannot pass up the opportunity to reproduce here a little verse from Lord Bowen's *Sounds of Time*:

> The rain it raineth on the just
> And also on the unjust fella:
> But chiefly on the just, because
> The unjust steals the just's umbrella

supporting the stock price, if it is successful, it is clearly an attempt to "fool mother nature." This is so because the market "sees through" (another personification, if we ever knew one) the machinations of those who try to manipulate it and punishes the wicked severely. Then, how can a repurchase be a signal of good things to come? And if this is a signal, then the market cannot be efficient—a severe case of circular logic.

As we already know, the idea of signaling is to convey information to the market that otherwise the market would have missed (although the market is omnipotent and the avatar of God). It is the "we know something you don't know" state of affairs that management is trying to remedy in a way that is, necessarily, not costless, but rather cost effective.[10] If the market reaction is favorable, meaning the price of the stock goes up, then it is a good thing that is being signaled. If the market reaction is negative, then the signal is a herald of future doom.

What follows is not meant to be a thorough coverage of the event study research of stock repurchases. It is rather a selective summary of this type of work and what conclusions it managed to come up with. This we do because (1) we do not believe that you can conclusively prove anything with statistical work and (2) of our little faith in event studies.

Dann (1981) and Vermealen (1981) found evidence for signaling in significant price increases that occurred around the announcement dates of tender offer stock repurchases. Effects occurred around "several days" of the announcement. But should not the market adjust, instantaneously, if one is offering a higher price, subject to certain conditions, than the going market price?

Bilingsley *et al.* (1989) examined share repurchases by bank holding companies. They found that the market does not react significantly to share repurchase announcements. However, they reported that repurchase announcements are associated with an increase in the idiosyncratic risk of bank holding company stocks.

Hertzel and Jain (1991) contended that repurchase tender offer announcements convey favorable information about the level and riskiness of future earnings in that the analysts revise their forecasts of earnings per share upward following repurchase announcements. These price reactions are positively correlated with revisions in short-term forecasts, but are not correlated with revisions in long-term forecasts. Thus, the information is primarily transitory in nature. If there are fewer shares outstanding, but earnings are not expected to decline, at least proportionally with the contra dilution the repurchase amounts to, why would analysts think otherwise?

Comment and Jarrell (1991) found that Dutch auction repurchases are a less credible signal than tender offer repurchases (one wonders why is this not obvious).

---

[10]Cost effective in the sense that it is less expensive than other means, say direct advertising, would be, more credible, or there would not be another alternative, at the first place.

Sinha (1991) suggested a model in which takeover target firms' managers borrow funds to repurchase stock. This, according to the author, *voluntarily* forces management to reduce perquisite consumption and increases investment in the firm. (Why should one be forced to reduce consumption of perquisites, and voluntarily for that matter, when one is fighting for one's existence? Would people in a lifeboat pour out drinking water just to convince the occupants that this resource must be rationed?) The resulting value increase makes the firm a less attractive target.

According to the Sinha model, the optimal level of share repurchases is the result of a trade-off between the benefit of a reduced probability of takeover and the cost of an increased probability of bankruptcy (and we were under the impression that this trade-off idea had been abandoned, long before, because one simply cannot obtain the probabilities of either or both. Silly us!) The merit of this "model" is in the explanation of the leverage transaction being independent of the extent of shareholding by target management. One must not forget that this explanation, which amounts to an excessive increase of leverage coincidental to shoveling cash out of the firm, was posited during an era when debt and leverage were the good thing to do. It is not any more!

Ikenberry *et al.* (1995) examined long-term performance following open market share repurchase announcements for the period 1980–1990. They reported that the average abnormal 4-year buy-and-hold return measured after the initial announcement is 12.1%. For "value" stocks, the repurchase of shares is more likely to be because of undervaluation. For these stocks the average abnormal return is 45.3%. For repurchases announced by "glamour" stocks, where undervaluation is less likely to be an important motive, no positive drift in abnormal returns is observed. The authors therefore concluded that, at least with respect to value stocks, the market errs in its initial response and appears to ignore much of the information conveyed through repurchase announcements.

Persons (1997) presented an asymmetric information model of share repurchases when shareholders have heterogeneous reservation values. Consistent with empirical evidence, managers in the model repurchase shares at a premium above the postrepurchase share value—transferring wealth from shareholders who do not tender to those who do—in order to signal that the firm is undervalued. Such dilutive repurchases would not occur under the classical assumption of perfectly elastic share supply; they depend critically on shareholder heterogeneity.

Persons also argued that repurchases are more efficient signals than other strategies, such as dividends and "burning money." (Whatever that means, although it sounds as an erroneous reference to potlatch) (See Frankfurter and Lane, 1991.)

Finally, Stephens and Weisbach (1998) studied the three forms of repurchases from 1981 to 1990. They commented that unlike Dutch auction repurchases and tender offers, open market repurchase programs do not precommit firms to acquire a specified number of shares. In a sample of 450 programs, firms, on average, acquire 74 to 82% of the shares announced as repurchase targets within 3 years of the repurchase announcement. Stephens and Weisbach (1998) found that share repurchases are related negatively to prior stock price performance, suggesting that firms increase their purchasing depending on its degree of perceived(?) undervaluation. In addition they contend that, consistent with liquidity arguments, repurchases are related positively to levels of cash flows.

As the reader might have concurred from our parenthetical and openly snide remarks, we are not firm believers of these studies and what they prove or disprove. Several of them reflect the opinions of the times, both in terms of academic research thrusts and what the investors in the markets happened to be believe at the moment. We do believe, however, in elementary economic rationality, and none of these studies changed our beliefs as expressed here and in the other chapters of this book.

## 15.3 GREENMAIL

The word is a play on the word blackmail because the color green is a synecdoche of money. Greenmail is a convenient way to funnel large sums of cash from the firm to the hands of a selected few. For instance, in the case of a hostile takeover, the target firm can offer a premium price to selected shareholders of the "raider," whereby it can accomplish two things:

- Rid itself, fast, of idle cash that might have been one of the reasons for the takeover at the first place.
- Acquire interest in the raider as to change the raider's determination to go ahead with a hostile takeover.

Whatever the case might be, greenmail is also a variant of repurchase, albeit the premium might be much higher than in the case of the latter. The fact remains that either scarce resources are converted to cash and funneled out of the firm or the worse-case scenario, the firm borrows in order to complete the transaction. The end result, in either case, is the increase of financial risk (leverage) and, at the same time, the reduction of expected earning potential because either earning assets are liquidated or investment opportunities are not taken. It seems a contradiction in economic logic, and it is.

## REFERENCES

Allais, Maurice. 1992. "The economic science of today and global disequilibrium." In *Global Disequilibrium in the World Economy*, edited by Baldassarri M. Basingstoke. New York: Macmillan.

Altschul, James S. 1993. "Cheap tricks with stock dividends." *CFO: The Magazine for Senior Financial Executives* 9 (May):65–68.

Baker, H. Kent, and Patricia L. Gallagher. 1980. "Management's view of stock splits." *Financial Management* 9:73–77.

Baker, H. Kent, and Aaron L. Phillips. 1993. "Why companies issue stock dividends." *Financial Practice and Education* 3:29–37.

Baker, H. Kent, and Gary E. Powell. 1993. "Further evidence on managerial motives for stock splits." *Quarterly Journal of Business and Economics* 32:20–31.

Baker, H. Kent, and Gary E. Powell. 1999. "How corporate managers view dividend policy." *Quarterly Journal of Economics and Business* 38:17–35.

Banker, Rajiv D., Somnath Das, and Srikant M. Datar. 1993. "Complementarity of prior accounting information: the case of stock dividend announcements." *Accounting Review* 68:28–47.

Barker, Austin C. 1956. "Effective stock splits." *Harvard Business Review* 34:101–106.

Bar-Yosef, S., and Brown, L. D. 1977. "A reexamination of stock splits using moving betas." *Journal of Finance* 32:1069–1080.

Billingsley, Randall S., Donald R. Fraser, and G. Rodney Thompson. 1989. "Shareholder wealth and stock repurchases by bank holding companies." *Quarterly Journal of Business and Economics* 28:3–25.

Black, Fischer. 1990. "Why firms pay dividends." *The Financial Analysts Journal* 46:5.

Branch, Ben. 1985. "Low priced stocks: discrimination in the brokerage industry." *American Association of Individual Investors* 7:9–11.

Brennan, Michael J., and Thomas E. Copeland. 1988a. "Beta changes around stock splits: a note." *Journal of Finance* 43:1009–1014.

Brennan, Michael J., and Thomas E. Copeland. 1988b. "Stock splits, stock prices, and transaction costs." *Journal of Financial Economics* 22:83–102.

Brennan, Michael J., and Patricia J. Hughes. 1991. "Stock prices and the supply of information." *Journal of Finance* 46:1665–1691.

Brigham, Eugene F., and Philip R. Daves. 2002. *Intermediate Financial Management.* 7th ed. Mason, OH: South-Western.

Brigham, Eugene F., Louis C. Gapinski, and Philip R. Daves. 1994. *Financial management: theory and practice.* 7th ed. Fort Worth, TX: Dryden Press.

Charest, G. 1978a. "Split information, stock returns and market efficiency—I." *Journal of Financial Economics* 6:265–296.

Charest, G. 1978b. "Split information, stock returns and market efficiency—II." *Journal of Financial Economics* 6:297.

Comment, Robert, and Gregg A. Jarrell. 1991. "The relative signalling power of Dutch auction and fixed price self-tender offers and open market share repurchases." *Journal of Finance* 46:1243–1271.

Conroy, Robert M., Robert S. Harris, and Bruce A. Benet. 1990. "The effects of stock splits on bid-ask spreads." *Journal of Finance* 45:1285–1295.

Copeland, Thomas E. 1979. "Liquidity changes following stock splits." *Journal of Finance* 34:115–142.

Dann, Larry Y. 1981. "Common stock repurchases: an analysis of returns to bondholders and stockholders." *Journal of Financial Economics* 9:113–138.

Defeo, V. J., and Jain, P. C. 1991. "Stock splits: price per share and trading volume." *Advances in Quantitative Analysis of Finance and Accounting* 1b:1–22.

Dowen, Richard J. 1990. "The stock split and dividend effect: information or price pressure?" *Applied Economics* 22:927–932.

Dubofsky, David A. 1991. "Volatility increases subsequent to NYSE and AMEX stock splits." *Journal of Finance* 46:421–432.

Elgers, Pieter T., and Dennis Murray. 1985. "Financial characteristics related to managements' stock split and stock dividend decisions." *Journal of Business Finance and Accounting* 12:543–552.

Ezzell, John R., and Carlos Rubiales. 1975. "An empirical analysis of the determinants of stock splits." *Financial Review* 10:21–30.

Fama, Eugene F., Lawrence Fisher, Michael C. Jensen, and Richard Roll. 1969. "The adjustment of stock prices to new information." *International Economic Reviews* 10:1–21.

Finn, F. J. 1974. "Stock splits: prior and subsequent price relationships." *Journal of Business Finance and Accounting* 1:93–108

Frankfurter, George M., and William R. Lane. 1992. "The rationality of dividends." *International Review of Financial Analysis* 1:115–129.

Frankfurter, George M., and William R. Lane. 1998. "The perception of stock dividends," *Journal of Investing* 7:32–40.

French, Dan W., and David A. Dubofsky. 1986. "Stock splits and implied stock price volatility." *Journal of Portfolio Management* 12:55–59.

Grinblatt, Mark S., Ronald W. Masulis, and Sheridan Titman. 1984. "The valuation effects of stock splits and stock dividends." *Journal of Financial Economics* 13:461–490.

Hausman, W. H., West, R. C., and Largay, J. A. 1971. "Stock splits, price changes, and trading profits: a synthesis." *Journal of Business* 44:69–77.

Hertzel, Michael, and Prem C. Jain. 1991. "Earnings and risk changes around stock repurchase tender offers." *Journal of Accounting and Economics* 14:253–274

Ikenberry, David, Joseph Lakonishok, and Theo Vermealen. 1995. "Market underreaction to open market share repurchases." *Journal of Financial Economics* 39:181–208.

Jensen, Michael C., and William H. Meckling. 1976. "Theory of the firm: managerial behavior, agency costs and ownership structure." *Journal of Financial Economics* 3:305–360.

Klein, Linda S., and David R. Peterson. 1988. "Investor expectations of volatility increases around large stock splits as implied in call option premia." *Journal of Financial Research* 11:71–80.

Klein, Linda S., and David R. Peterson. 1989. "Earnings forecast revisions associated with stock split announcements." *Journal of Financial Research* 12:319–328.

Lakonishok, Josef, and Baruch Lev. 1987. "Stock splits and stock dividends: why, who, and when." *Journal of Finance* 42:913–932.

Lamoureux Christopher, G., and Percy Poon. 1987. "The market reaction to stock splits." *Journal of Finance* 42:1347–1370.

Lawson, Tony. 2001. "Back to reality." *PAECON Newsletter* 6.

Lazo, Shirley A. 1993. "Speaking of dividends." *Barron's* 73:53.

Liljeblom, Eva. 1989. "The informational impact of announcements of stock dividends and stock splits." *Journal of Business Finance and Accounting* 16:681–698.

Lintner, John. 1956. "The distribution of incomes of corporations among dividends, retained earnings and taxes." *American Economic Review* 46:153–185.

Maloney, M. T., and Mulherin, J. H. 1992. "The effect of splitting on the ex: a microstructure reconciliation." 21:44–59.

McNichols, Maureen, and Ajay Dravid. 1990. "Stock dividends, stock splits, and signaling." *Journal of Finance* 45:857–880.

Millar, J. A., and Bruce D. Fielitz. 1973. "Stock-split and stock-dividend decisions." *Financial Management* 2:35–46.

Murray, Dennis. 1985. "Further evidence on the liquidity effects of stock splits and stock dividends." *Journal of Financial Research* 8:59–68.

Nichols, William D., and Bill McDonald. 1983. "Stock splits and market anomalies." *Financial Review* 18:237–256.

Ohlson, James A., and Stephen H. Penman. 1985. "Volatility increases subsequent to stock splits: an empirical aberration." *Journal of Financial Economics* 14:251–266.

Persons, John C. 1997. "Heterogeneous shareholders and signaling with share repurchases." *Journal of Corporate Finance: Contracting, Governance and Organization* 3:221–249.

Peterson, David R., and Pamela P. Peterson. 1992. "A further understanding of stock distributions: the case of reverse stock splits." *Journal of Financial Research* 15:189–206.

Peterson, Pamela P. 1994. *Financial Management and Analysis*. New York: McGraw-Hill.

Reilly, Frank K., and Eugene F. Drzyclmski. 1981. "Short-run profits from stock splits." *Financial Management* 10:64–74.

Reilly, Frank K., and Sandra G. Gustavson. 1985. "Investing in options on stocks announcing splits." *Financial Review* 20:121–142.

Ross, Stephen A., Randolph W. Westerfield, and Bradford D. Jordan. 1998. *Fundamentals of Corporate Finance*. 4th Ed. Homewood, IL: Irwin.

Sheikh, Aamir M. 1989. "Stock splits, volatility increases, and implied volatilities." *Journal of Finance* 44:1361–1372.

Sinha, Sidhart. 1991. "Share repurchase as a takeover defense." *Journal of Financial and Quantitative Analysis* 26:233–244.

Spence, Michael. 1973. "Job market signaling." *The Quarterly Journal of Economics* 87:355–374.

Stephens, Clifford P., and Michael S. Weisbach. 1998. "Actual share reacquisitions in open-market repurchase programs." *Journal of Finance* 53:313–333.

Strong, Robert A. 1983. "Do share price and stock splits matter?" *Journal of Portfolio Management* 10:58–64.

Szewczyk, Samuel H., and George P. Tsetsekos. 1993. "The effect of managerial ownership on stock split-induced abnormal returns." *Financial Review* 28:351–370.

Van Horne, James C. 1995. *Financial Management and Policy*. 10th ed. Englewood Cliffs, NJ: Prentice Hall.

Vermealen, Theo. 1981. "Common stock repurchases and market signalling." *Journal of Financial Economics* 9:139–183.

Wiggins, James B. 1992. "Beta changes around stock splits revisited." *Journal of Financial and Quantitative Analysis* 27:631.

# Appendix A

# Stock Dividend Survey

Please indicate the extent to which you agree or disagree with each of the following statements by placing an "X" on the scale provided. The scale should be treated as a continuous range from "strongly disagree" to "strongly agree." If you have no opinion about a statement, or if that statement does not pertain to your situation, leave that scale blank. Placing an "X" in the middle, on "Neutral," indicates that your opinion is balanced, neither agreeing nor disagreeing with the statement.

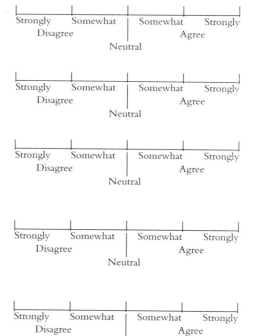

1. Stockholders like to receive a regular dividend.

   Strongly Disagree — Somewhat — Neutral — Somewhat — Strongly Agree

2. Some stockholders prefer a stock dividend instead of a cash dividend.

   Strongly Disagree — Somewhat — Neutral — Somewhat — Strongly Agree

3. The stockholders of my firm prefer a cash dividend instead of a stock dividend.

   Strongly Disagree — Somewhat — Neutral — Somewhat — Strongly Agree

4. Institutional investors always prefer a cash dividend instead of a stock dividend.

   Strongly Disagree — Somewhat — Neutral — Somewhat — Strongly Agree

5. Our firm would like to see a large portion of its shares owned by institutions.

   Strongly Disagree — Somewhat — Neutral — Somewhat — Strongly Agree

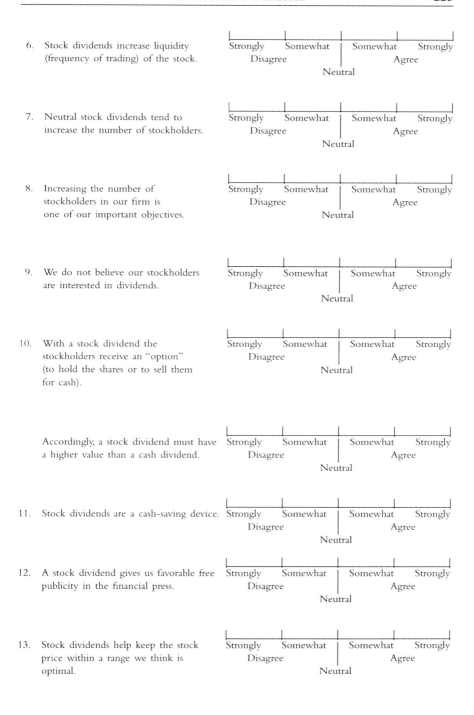

6.  Stock dividends increase liquidity
    (frequency of trading) of the stock.

    Strongly    Somewhat    |    Somewhat    Strongly
    Disagree                 |              Agree
                        Neutral

7.  Neutral stock dividends tend to
    increase the number of stockholders.

    Strongly    Somewhat    |    Somewhat    Strongly
    Disagree                 |              Agree
                        Neutral

8.  Increasing the number of
    stockholders in our firm is
    one of our important objectives.

    Strongly    Somewhat    |    Somewhat    Strongly
    Disagree                 |              Agree
                        Neutral

9.  We do not believe our stockholders
    are interested in dividends.

    Strongly    Somewhat    |    Somewhat    Strongly
    Disagree                 |              Agree
                        Neutral

10. With a stock dividend the
    stockholders receive an "option"
    (to hold the shares or to sell them
    for cash).

    Strongly    Somewhat    |    Somewhat    Strongly
    Disagree                 |              Agree
                        Neutral

    Accordingly, a stock dividend must have
    a higher value than a cash dividend.

    Strongly    Somewhat    |    Somewhat    Strongly
    Disagree                 |              Agree
                        Neutral

11. Stock dividends are a cash-saving device.

    Strongly    Somewhat    |    Somewhat    Strongly
    Disagree                 |              Agree
                        Neutral

12. A stock dividend gives us favorable free
    publicity in the financial press.

    Strongly    Somewhat    |    Somewhat    Strongly
    Disagree                 |              Agree
                        Neutral

13. Stock dividends help keep the stock
    price within a range we think is
    optimal.

    Strongly    Somewhat    |    Somewhat    Strongly
    Disagree                 |              Agree
                        Neutral

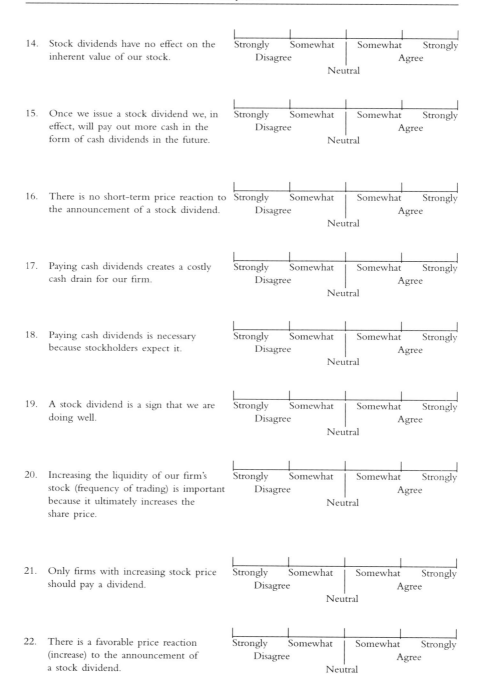

14. Stock dividends have no effect on the inherent value of our stock.

Strongly Disagree — Somewhat — | Neutral — Somewhat Agree — Strongly

15. Once we issue a stock dividend we, in effect, will pay out more cash in the form of cash dividends in the future.

Strongly Disagree — Somewhat — | Neutral — Somewhat Agree — Strongly

16. There is no short-term price reaction to the announcement of a stock dividend.

Strongly Disagree — Somewhat — | Neutral — Somewhat Agree — Strongly

17. Paying cash dividends creates a costly cash drain for our firm.

Strongly Disagree — Somewhat — | Neutral — Somewhat Agree — Strongly

18. Paying cash dividends is necessary because stockholders expect it.

Strongly Disagree — Somewhat — | Neutral — Somewhat Agree — Strongly

19. A stock dividend is a sign that we are doing well.

Strongly Disagree — Somewhat — | Neutral — Somewhat Agree — Strongly

20. Increasing the liquidity of our firm's stock (frequency of trading) is important because it ultimately increases the share price.

Strongly Disagree — Somewhat — | Neutral — Somewhat Agree — Strongly

21. Only firms with increasing stock price should pay a dividend.

Strongly Disagree — Somewhat — | Neutral — Somewhat Agree — Strongly

22. There is a favorable price reaction (increase) to the announcement of a stock dividend.

Strongly Disagree — Somewhat — | Neutral — Somewhat Agree — Strongly

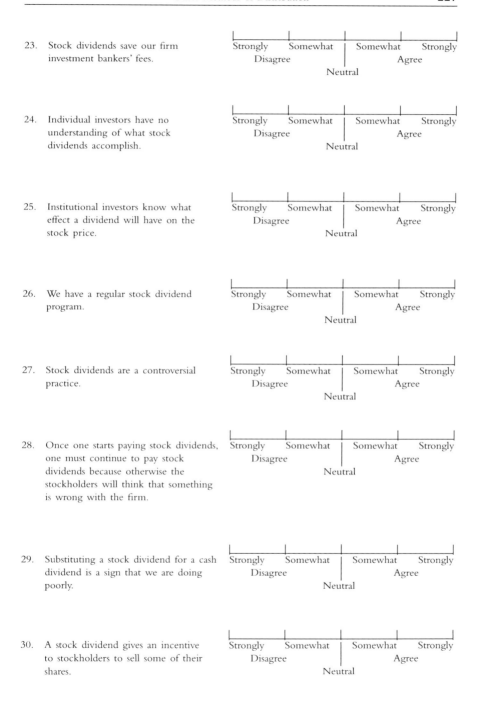

23. Stock dividends save our firm investment bankers' fees.

Strongly Disagree — Somewhat Disagree — Neutral — Somewhat Agree — Strongly Agree

24. Individual investors have no understanding of what stock dividends accomplish.

Strongly Disagree — Somewhat Disagree — Neutral — Somewhat Agree — Strongly Agree

25. Institutional investors know what effect a dividend will have on the stock price.

Strongly Disagree — Somewhat Disagree — Neutral — Somewhat Agree — Strongly Agree

26. We have a regular stock dividend program.

Strongly Disagree — Somewhat Disagree — Neutral — Somewhat Agree — Strongly Agree

27. Stock dividends are a controversial practice.

Strongly Disagree — Somewhat Disagree — Neutral — Somewhat Agree — Strongly Agree

28. Once one starts paying stock dividends, one must continue to pay stock dividends because otherwise the stockholders will think that something is wrong with the firm.

Strongly Disagree — Somewhat Disagree — Neutral — Somewhat Agree — Strongly Agree

29. Substituting a stock dividend for a cash dividend is a sign that we are doing poorly.

Strongly Disagree — Somewhat Disagree — Neutral — Somewhat Agree — Strongly Agree

30. A stock dividend gives an incentive to stockholders to sell some of their shares.

Strongly Disagree — Somewhat Disagree — Neutral — Somewhat Agree — Strongly Agree

31. Many of our stockholders do not trade the stock at all whether the price is going up or down.

Strongly Disagree — Somewhat — Neutral — Somewhat Agree — Strongly Agree

32. Stock dividends are important because they allow us to convert retained earnings into permanent equity capital.

Strongly Disagree — Somewhat — Neutral — Somewhat Agree — Strongly Agree

33. Stock dividends are important because they make it possible to create small percentage increases in our cash dividends.

Strongly Disagree — Somewhat — Neutral — Somewhat Agree — Strongly Agree

34. Only an increase in cash dividends is a sign that we are doing well.

Strongly Disagree — Somewhat — Neutral — Somewhat Agree — Strongly Agree

35. Increasing the liquidity of our firm's stock (frequency of trading) is important because it ultimately reduces the bid–ask spread.

Strongly Disagree — Somewhat — Neutral — Somewhat Agree — Strongly Agree

36. We have never paid a stock dividend.

Strongly Disagree — Somewhat — Neutral — Somewhat Agree — Strongly Agree

37. We are thinking about paying a stock dividend in the near future.

Strongly Disagree — Somewhat — Neutral — Somewhat Agree — Strongly Agree

# CHAPTER 16

## Conclusions: Future Research and Thinking

*The trouble of people is not that they don't know, but that they know so much that ain't so. Henry Whealer Shaw* Josh Billing's Encyclopedia of Wisdom

In the October 25, 2001, issue of the *Wall Street Journal*, a column by Henny Sender, titled "Dividends Appear Appetizing, but May Give Thin Sustenance" (*Heard on the Street* section) bemoaned the sad state of affairs of the equity markets. The opening question of Ms. Sender, a staff writer, is "How does a company lure investors into its shares at a time when potential buyers are risk averse?" The answer of Miss Henny is that historically it was done (the luring) with dividends and a great many stocks (read firms) are doing just that, because they "look quite appealing."

If the unfortunate metaphor of the title was not enough, the question itself and all that follows is just a royal mess of understanding basic economic issues. The misinterpretation of financial economics concepts that are lurking behind the "appetizing" (read slovenly) language of the street, Wall Street, that is, by a staff writer of the official house organ of the investment community "out there," is not short of dreadful.

It would be worthwhile to take a closer look at the meaning of the opening salvo of the piece because it may possibly help understand the depth of the chasm that separates preconceived notions in the investment community and what economic rationality is really about. This is perhaps even necessary for the sake of pitching the central tenet of the concluding chapter of this book. The precept that in order to comprehend the dividend phenomenon and practice, we need a better understanding of what investors and their professional advisers think about dividends and how they should be educated to overcome mistaken beliefs.

What time is it, exactly, "when many potential buyers are risk averse?" Or better yet, what time is it when potential buyers of equity, that is, are *not* risk averse? The whole theory of modern finance in general and the notion of market efficiency in particular are based on the axiom of investor's risk aversion. Although there might be "out there" gamblers who get their satisfaction from risk and are possibly indifferent to return,[1] they are not the ones who move the markets and certainly not the ones we consider to be professional investors.

What is the exact meaning of ". . . a company luring investors into buying their shares?" For crying out loud the piece is about dividends, or better yet, dividend expectations, which necessarily means a firm that is not just traded publicly, but that is already established. Otherwise, for one, firms do not commence paying dividends right after they leave the starting gate, and for another, one needs some degree of experience to form one's expectations. If none of these two conditions hold, then dividends are irrelevant for the investor (see the so-called Internet bubble) and they cannot lure investors into "shares."

After throwing the reader into confusion at the outset, we are treated to an array of conflicting "signals." For instance, how dividend yields have increased, and that ". . . 100 companies in the Standard & Poor's 500-stock index are now offering dividends with yields that are more generous than the current return on money-market funds." So, there is a tendency "to shovel out cash the front door," as Miller and Scholes (1978) observed. However, they also observed that, concurrently, the "shovelers" borrowed back the money, in access of what was shoveled through the back door.

This is not happening now, however, according to Ms. Sender, because, as she quotes one Mr. Richard Bernstein, a strategist at Merrill Lynch & Co., "we are in a recession." But there are also firms that cut dividends, and even drastically (making the money managers of hedge funds who shorted in time such stocks very happy). Apparently, when one is cash starved, not reckless, and hopes for a better future after all, retaining cash is an obvious way to go.

And lest not forget the elusive nature of dividend yields. The numerator is expected dividends, a subjective figure, based on past experience, and the probability of that past experience is a good predictor of the future. The denominator is the current stock price that is observable as the ticker tape moves on. It may be changing several times a day, and definitely quite a few times over a quarter for which dividends are expected to be declared.

In essence, dividend yields are that much today, quite different tomorrow. In a recession when most stock prices are depressed, the yield can look reassuring one moment and totally lousy the next. Also, there is this little problem of taxes, which may be avoided in a case of a tax-exempt bond, for which both price and yield are more stable, constituting a less risky investment instrument.

We learn further that Mr. Bernstein worked up a list of 100 firms "whose dividends are more secure" (more secure than what?) yielding, at the moment, 5% and up. Guess what firms top the list? You guessed it right: public utilities. Now, there is no serendipity in Mr. Bernstein's discovery because for the better

---

[1] It is hard to imagine that there might be even gamblers who would be return averse.

part of their existence, public utilities were always high dividend paying firms. In fact, they fell in that category of common stock, which has been called "income stocks." But even if dividends are secure, prices are not, so yields can change for income stocks as well. This is so even if cash flows of public utilities are more or less stable, regardless of what is happening in the economy otherwise.

What does this new "discovery" of dividends mean, however? It means, first and foremost, that investors, even professional ones have little or no understanding of dividends. It also means that some of the academic hypotheses developed as models that fit universally are a less than correct description of the dividend phenomenon.

For instance, if during hard times the firm increases its dividend payout is it a "signal" of good things to come? That is, insiders know about the future something others cannot observe, and therefore by shoveling out cash, a limited resource, they are advertising the good fortunes of the firm to come? Or the sudden increase of outflow of cash is a liquidation of earning assets (or equivalently not investing), which necessarily reduces future earning potential? If the latter, then it should be a bad signal, and the market should react accordingly. However, it does not. So what is wrong here, the theory or what our believes are considering "market efficiency?" One or the other, or perhaps both?

What about firms that cut dividends drastically? Is it a signal that we should stay away from stocks like that or is it a sign of prudent management, with long-term survival as the prime objective in mind? As Ms. Sender's story unfolds, Dana, an auto parts maker, reduced quarterly dividends drastically, from 31¢ a share to a meager 1¢ a share.

Dana, according to Ms. Sender, was "just about the most generous around" when it came to dividends. Was it good to be "the most generous" before and is it bad now, when the firm uses its cheapest source of funds, those that are generated internally, in order to survive? If you subscribe to the post-Keynesian theory of the firm, perhaps it was bad before and good now (see Gordon, 1994). If the market "punishes" Dana by pulverizing its stock price, much to the joy of short sellers, is the market really "efficient?"

As discussed in this book, there are some preconceived notions among financial decision makers, one of which is to maintain dividends and increase dividends only if the firm can continue paying the higher dividend for years to come. But is it rational, even if we never questioned the *a priori* rationality of the love of dividends? Is it not more rational to presume that shareholders will reward a prudent response to the ever-changing economic conditions rather than sticking to a strategy that may bring about tragic consequences?

Our belief is that both investors and financial decision makers must be educated in order to understand the true economic meaning of the dividend phenomenon and that academic models thus far were less than supportive of this education process. If we in this book made a contribution toward the better understanding of dividends, and dividend policy, the untold number of trees that were required to print this book were not cut down for naught.

# REFERENCES

Gordon, Myron J. 1994. *Finance, Investment and Macroeconomics: The Neoclassical and a Post-Keynesian Solution.* Hants, UK: Edward Elgar Publishing Company.

Miller, Merton H., and Scholes, Myron S. 1978. "Dividends and taxes." *Journal of Financial Economics* 6:333–364.

Sender, Henny. 2001. "Dividends appear appetizing, but may give thin sustenance." *Wall Street Journal* Heard on the Street.

# INDEX

Page numbers followed by t indicate tables.